Children of the Camp

CHILDREN OF THE CAMP

*The Lives of Somali Youth Raised in
Kakuma Refugee Camp, Kenya*

Catherine-Lune Grayson

berghahn
NEW YORK • OXFORD
www.berghahnbooks.com

First published in 2017 by
Berghahn Books
www.berghahnbooks.com

Library of Congress Cataloging-in-Publication Data
A C.I.P. cataloging record is available from the Library of Congress

British Library Cataloguing in Publication Data
A catalogue record for this book is available from the British Library

ISBN 978-1-78533-631-7 (hardback)
ISBN 978-1-80073-179-0 (paperback)
ISBN 978-1-78533-632-4 (ebook)

To the children of Kakuma

CONTENTS

FIGURES

Acknowledgments

Many people have made this book possible. Throughout my research, Deirdre Meintel's support and responsiveness have been incredibly precious. I am thankful to my former colleague Maria Vargas Simojoki, who read my first draft and never failed to ask insightful and critical questions, while also making very sensitive observations about Somalis, Somalia and humanitarianism. Thanks as well to Randa Farah for her careful reading and her very valuable comments. The many and challenging discussions that I have had with displaced people and aid workers over the years have also greatly stimulated my reflection.

I wish to thank my father, who has paid patient attention to every single comma and, earlier on, made me realize that the history of my own family was probably not foreign to my interest in the experience of exile. Displacement does ring a fairly intimate bell. Sometimes in Kakuma, speaking with youth about the past of their family, I wondered why their stories were so fragmentary, until they would return the questions to me and I would realize how little I knew about my own family's path into exile.

All my appreciation goes to Hubert, who has not only been a wonderful and encouraging interlocutor, but has also cared for Simone so I could write. I am also immensely indebted to FilmAid, which provided me a lively home there. Wholehearted thanks to Dawn, Craig and Gwyneth for always receiving me so generously in their cozy Nairobi home. I would also like to express my gratitude to Vanier Canada for funding this research.

Above all, thank you to the residents of Kakuma who turned the camp into a hospitable place. Day after day, you welcomed me warmly into your homes. You offered me so many meals and conversations. I am incredibly grateful to all those who shared their time, thoughts and amazing stories with me, helped me navigate the camp and invited me into their lives. As you are not named in this book, I will not do so here.

ABBREVIATIONS

AMISOM	African Union Mission in Somalia
BBC	British Broadcasting Corporation
DRA	Department of Refugee Affairs
EU	European Union
ICU	Islamic Courts Union
ID	Identity document
IOM	International Organization for Migration
JRS	Jesuit Refugee Services
KSh	Kenyan shilling
LWF	Lutheran World Federation
NGO	Nongovernmental organization
RCK	Refugee Consortium of Kenya
SNM	Somali National Movement
SPLA	Sudan People's Liberation Army
SYL	Somali Youth League
TFG	Transitional Federal Government
UN	United Nations
UNHCR	United Nations High Commissioner for Refugees
USY	Union of Somali Youth
WUSC	World University Service of Canada

On January 1, 2013, US$1 was worth 84.5 Kenyan shillings. Unless otherwise specified, this is the exchange rate used in this book.

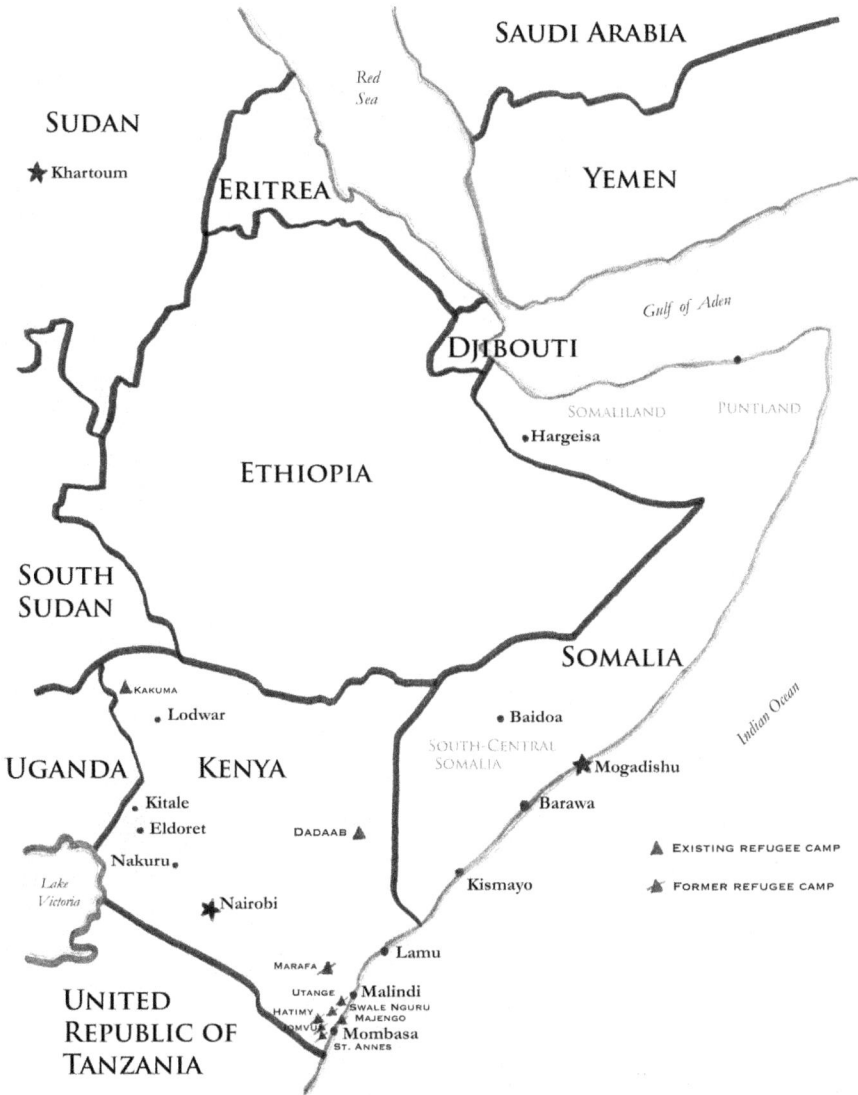

The Horn of Africa and Kenyan refugee camps.
Map adapted by the author from Map No 4188 (Horn of Africa) of the UN
Department of Field Support and from Montclos 1999a: 29

Key:
- Graveyard
- Food Distribution Centre
- Field Post

Kakuma refugee camp.
Map adapted by the author from Layout Map of Kakuma Refugee Camp, prepared by the UNHCR and National Council of Churches of Kenya, February 2012

INTRODUCTION

❧⊙•⊙☙

The year was 2010, and I was spending time in Dagahaley, one of the Dadaab refugee camps in northeastern Kenya, to conduct some research for Médecins sans frontières. That is how I came to meet one of the organization's medical assistants, a twenty-year-old Somali[1] who started talking about the recent birth of his first child. He said it had reinforced his desire to find a way out of the camp, a place that felt like an open-air jail. He did not want his son to be like him, someone who knows only life in the camp. He explained that he was born in Dagahaley and had never even been to the town of Dadaab, just a few kilometers away. Some days later, the program manager of a nongovernmental organization (NGO) mentioned that at least 10,000 children had been born in the camp to parents who were also born there.

I gradually came to realize that a whole generation of exiled Somalis had been born and raised in the Dadaab camps, and that they were now young adults. I should have become aware of this long before, given that the camps had existed for more than twenty years and that I had been working in such settings for many years. Nevertheless, this was the first time I had grasped this fact of their lives. I started reflecting on their experience. Few nations have been so massively displaced for so long. Palestinians, Afghans and the Sahrawi come to mind. I was used to hearing refugees talking about how things were back home before they fled. But these young people, unlike their parents, had no recollections of Somalia, no other experience to compare their current conditions with. Yet, their community had certainly told them many stories about their homeland. So I wondered how they imagined the land of their parents, how they experienced the camp and how they imagined their future, given all the constraints imposed by camp life and exile.

My questioning quickly became intertwined with interrogations about how and why camps have become such a usual response to mass displacement, given their unsuitability. Very strong criticisms of camps as a long-term solution have been leveled not only by academics but also by the United Nations agency specifically mandated to protect and assist refugees, the United Nations High Commissioner for Refugees (UNHCR). It has been repeatedly noted that camps are far from being ideal places for the development and fulfillment of individuals. As early as 2004, the UNHCR stated that:

> If it is true that camps save lives in the emergency phase, it is also true that, as the years go by, they progressively waste these same lives. A refugee may be able to receive assistance, but is prevented from enjoying those rights—for example, to freedom of movement, employment, and in some cases, education—that would enable him or her to become a productive member of a society. (UNHCR 2004: 3)

I found convincing perspectives on what has turned the camp into such a usual response pertaining to containment and the ordering of "undesirable" populations in the writings of Arendt (1968 [1951]), Hyndman (2000), Malkki (1995a) and Nyers (2006). But I noticed that although displacement situations continue to occur and persist, so that more and more young people living in camps are likely to have grown up in them or to have been born there, their experience has hardly been studied and no one has focused on Somali youth. This is what motivated the present study. I conducted it in Kakuma, another Kenyan camp where thousands of Somali youth have spent most of their lives, rather than in Dadaab, because it offered a safer research environment.

While I had spent significant periods of time in Dadaab as an aid worker, I had only been to Kakuma once before, living there for six months, from October 2012 to April 2013. Located in northwestern Kenya, one hundred kilometers from the border with South Sudan and one thousand kilometers from Nairobi, Kenya's capital, Kakuma looks like some faraway city. Established in 1992, it does not match the widespread image of a camp as a temporary place where people sleep in tents, waiting for the guns to go quiet before returning home. Shelters are made of branches, mud and metal sheets, and schools, clinics and markets are part of the landscape. It may look like a city, but it is an odd one, as its inhabitants are not allowed to move freely, work or settle where they choose.

This ethnography is about the experience of young Somalis, aged sixteen to twenty-six who have spent most or all of their lives in Kenyan camps and who now live in Kakuma. Some were born in Kenya; others arrived in the early 1990s as small children. Their parents fled along with millions of people when the Somali State collapsed in 1991. They thought their displacement would be brief. More than two decades later, they are still in exile. The babies they were carrying when they crossed into Kenya are now adults. Most first lived in several camps located near the coastal city of Mombasa. Between 1997 and 1998, when these camps closed, they were transferred to Kakuma. A few had also lived in Dadaab or in a Kenyan city before arriving in Kakuma. These young people often claim that growing up there might not have been ideal, but it was better than being in Somalia. Unlike many children who remained behind, their lives have been relatively free of violence and they were able to study, even though the quality of their education was unsatisfactory. Once they grow older, the camp becomes a space of frustration and limitations, a place to leave. Indeed, although a fair number of refugees[2] have been living in Kakuma for up to two decades, it is still seen as a transitory place.

In this introduction, I approach Kakuma by examining how global policies intended to confine particular populations have made the opening of camps the usual response to mass displacement. I then present my methodology and discuss the rationale of my research. Subsequent chapters are organized in chronological order. They look at youth's perspectives on their past, their present and their future, and include sections devoted to themes that weigh heavily in their experience. Chapter 2 considers young people's accounts of the collapse of Somalia and their families' past, which seem to help them cope with the present and justify their aspirations for the future. Chapter 3 recounts their arrival in Kakuma in the late 1990s and examines how the early days of the camp have been turned into a foundational story that has contributed to the emergence of a sense of community. The following three chapters focus on young people's lives in the camp. I first reflect on what it means to grow up in such a setting, then examine how this has affected their cultural identity, and finally discuss the camp's connectedness to other spaces and places. In Chapters 7 and 8, I study two related notions: (mis)trust and representation. Chapter 9 looks to the future. Although youth's ambitions vary, most believe that in order to achieve their dreams, they must be resettled in the United States. This chapter is followed by a short note on life after the camp, based on interviews with people who used to live in Kenyan camps but no longer do. The conclusion sums up the findings of this book, focusing on points of tension in the camp experience. Each chapter pursues its own line of questioning and its own particular logic, but several themes also run through this book. These include the tension between victimhood and agency, the role of narratives in structuring people's experience, the camp's connection to the wider world and the importance of mobility in a rather immobile setting. Throughout this study, I aim to look at both the large and small-scale reality of the camp to understand how the refugee experience is shaped by (and shapes in return) the social, political, economic and historical dynamics in which it is embedded.

Contextualizing the Camp: From the Right
to Seek Asylum to the Right to Stay Home

Figures compiled by the UNHCR invariably show that the vast—and ever-growing—majority of refugees live in developing countries (86 percent in 2015, compared to 73 percent in 2006), most often in a country neighboring their country of origin (UNHCR 2007a: 6; 2016a: 2). Taking into account refugees in an irregular situation and those not registered with the authorities of the country of asylum or with the UNHCR, the proportion of refugees in poor countries[3] is even greater (Malkki 1995a: 503). The share of the refugee population received by rich countries is therefore minimal. Two main factors play a role in explaining these numbers. First, while in the period following the end of the Second World War, refugees were predominantly European, most large-scale displacements in the last few decades have occurred in regions of the world far from the West (Sassen 1999: xiiv). Also, since the end of the Cold War, rich countries have enacted increasingly stringent policies on asylum and migration to "protect" themselves from refugee populations, which are seen as threatening (Bauman 1998a: 76; Hyndman 2000: 2–3). The "War on Terror" rhetoric that spread after the September 11, 2001 attacks particularly stigmatizes Muslim communities, which constitute a large proportion of the current refugee population, including Somalis (Zetter 2007: 185).[4] Asylum, theoretically granted to people whose lives are in danger,[5] has become perceived as an irregular path to immigration and therefore as something that should be contained (Zimmerman 2009: 74). Consequently, the refugee phenomenon is treated as a problem to be solved, by means that include the use of migration policies unsuited to the protection needs of refugees, but appropriate to limiting influxes (Feller 2006: 536; Nyers 2006: 5). Hence, if the West does not have problems of refugees on its borders, this "is clearly not a simple accident of geography or history" (Malkki 1995a: 503). In a context of increased mobility and deterritorialization of information, ideas, people, goods and services, while borders are more and more meaningless for a part of humanity, poor populations are increasingly forced into immobility, locked in a territory, inexorably local. It has thus become commonplace to highlight the tension between the hypermobility of the privileged and the confinement of undesirable populations (e.g., Appadurai 1996; Bauman 1998a; Hyndman 2000).

While it remains easier to seek asylum in a poor country, even there, hospitality no longer rules. In order to seek asylum, an individual must cross an international border. Since 1990, relatively poor countries faced with a mass influx of people have closed their borders over a dozen times (Long 2010: 24), violating the principle of *non-refoulement*.[6] Another way to prevent people from fleeing to another country, which resorts to a similar containment logic without violating international law, is the promotion of regional solutions and "preventive protection" policies. These are at the basis of humanitarian and development programs aimed at providing protection and assistance to people within their country of origin. States and international organizations have come to see this as a substitute rather than a complement to refugee protection. Although the UNHCR has described this approach in rather positive terms,[7] preventive protection can be depicted as a threat to asylum (Dubernet 2006). This development has impelled Hyndman (2000: 21) to write that the international refugee regime has evolved from protecting the right to asylum to championing the right to stay home.

In spite of these restrictions, many refugees manage to cross the border of a neighboring country—generally a poor one, since these remain more open and accessible than their rich counterparts. This is due to traditionally generous asylum policies, the willingness of states to comply with their international commitments, the proximity of conflict-affected countries, and the difficulty of controlling long and porous borders with limited resources (Harrell-Bond 1986: 15; Long 2010). However, refugees' rights are not fully respected, since significant restrictions to their freedom of movement or work are often imposed by states, which tend to delegate their responsibility toward refugees to international organizations (Verdirame and Harrell-Bond 2005).

Presented as the best emergency (and, theoretically, temporary) solution to governments of poor countries increasingly reluctant to accommodate large groups of refugees, the opening of camps has become the norm in mass-influx situations since the 1980s (Fresia 2007: 102–3; Harrell-Bond 1986: 8–9). While the camp is designed to meet the emergency needs of arriving refugees, it remains in place well beyond that period as lasting solutions remain out of sight. Refugees are commonly treated as "temporary guests" (Kibreab 1999: 399) with curtailed rights, perceived as an excessive burden and a threat to stability and the social cohesion of states (Crisp 2003: 3–4; Loescher et al. 2008: 4; Maltou 1999: 136). Camps were not always the expected response to mass influxes: the term does not even appear in the 1951 Convention Relating to the Status of Refugees.[8] Historically, the local integration of refugees was the predominant solution (although often de facto) (Fresia 2007: 102; Jacobsen 2001: 2–3). Even today, despite steps taken to encourage or force refugees in Africa and Asia to live in camps, it is estimated that at least half of them have settled on their own (without assistance and often without being registered) in the community (UNHCR 2014a: 6). Yet, the vast majority of those who receive support live in camps that have become "almost synonymous with the refugee experience" (Harrell-Bond 2000: 1). In a growing number of countries, camps keeping refugees at "the margins of society" are not only the recommended solution, but an imposed one (Kagwanja and Juma 2008: 221). Such confinement is sometimes prescribed by law and sometimes enforced by the implementation of measures that make life outside the camps particularly difficult, such as the restriction of humanitarian assistance to camps, or tedious refugee status determination procedures for those outside (HRW 2009a: 43–50; Moret, Baglioni and Efionayi-Mäder 2006: 62). Although these provisions do not prevent refugees from settling outside camps, they have the effect of forcing them into illegality, making them vulnerable to abuse and the violation of their rights.

This predilection for camps has been explained by the complexity of assisting and protecting dispersed populations, concerns for the safety of refugees and the host community, and the desire to maximize the visibility of refugees in order to mobilize donors (Fresia 2007: 102; Harrell-Bond 1986: 8–9). Humanitarian assistance and protection policies are also closely associated with the will to contain noncitizens in a controlled space (Chimni 2000: 251–52; 2002; Hyndman 2000: 24). Camps were originally conceived as places that would allow refugees to live in decent and secure conditions, while contributing to the development of areas otherwise sparsely populated and underdeveloped (Harrell-Bond 2000: 3). However, they have become a key device in the exercise of arbitrary power to manage large-scale displacement (Malkki 1995a: 498).

Approaching the Experience of Somali Youth: Conceptual and Methodological Considerations

The complexity of the refugee experience has often been overlooked in portrayals that have depicted the displaced in turn as passive victims oppressed by humanitarian agencies or, conversely, as strategists with unsuspected resources and adaptability (Fresia 2007: 101, 105–8; Horst 2006a: 11–18). Many recent studies have, however, tried to capture both the constraints experienced by refugees and their agency. While camps can be envisioned as spaces of exception that fall outside of state sovereignty, where the humanitarian government composed of NGOs and government agencies, and coordinated and funded by the UNHCR, exercises power over bare life (e.g., Agamben 1998: 167-80; Agier 2008: 298–303; Fassin and Pandolfi 2010: 15–16), they cannot be reduced to places where all exits are hermetically sealed and where the disciplinary mechanism is so precise that refugees are crushed, reduced to their biological functions. First, social organizations are rarely perfectly ordered and controlled (Davis 1992: 159). Then, although the camp is unconducive to emancipation and development, this does not mean that refugees are totally deprived of their imagination and are unable to get around the control and power of the institution, at least partially, and regain or retain an identity and political subjectivity. Forced migration cannot be summed up as belonging to a new legal category, but must instead be considered in terms of experience and a process of rapid social transformation (Malkki 1995a: 496). Arendt (1968 [1951]: 286–87) reflects that a common experience stems from the passage to the status of refugee and therefore to that of noncitizen, i.e., to that of exclusion from the world of men. But beyond this "ban," it is reasonable to assume that there is no typical refugee or ideal-type experience, given that the experience of each individual is unique. Refugee camps become social and political environments in which people are born, marry and die, places of production of locality where new practices are developed (Appadurai 1996: 192).

Hence, camps can be construed as places of confinement where freedom is restricted and where individuals are treated as victims, but also as spaces of (re)invention and (re)definition, connected to the world. Refugees therefore navigate between the state of victim and that of subject, between control and (sometimes creative) avoidance strategies. In that respect, I find Vigh's concept of "social navigation" (2006: 13–15) profoundly valuable, as it allows one to take into account not only people's agency, but also the fact that social forces are at play, and thus people are neither perfectly free agents nor merely powerless victims. Vigh (2006: 32) underlines that the circumstances and limitations of the terrain being navigated influence people's possibilities and their understanding of their possibilities, which, in turn, affects their social navigation. Although refugees living in the same setting may experience similar restrictions, these might not affect people's navigation in the same way, as people's paths are unique, influenced by their history, their gender and their capacities (Clark-Kazak 2011: 6; Essed, Frerks and Schrijvers 2004: 2; Grabska 2010: 481).

Adjusting the Lens

When I started meeting with young Somalis in Kakuma, I noticed that they only began to define and consider themselves as youth in their late teens—and people in their thirties often still spoke of themselves as youth. While in Western contexts, definitions of youth are usually relatively narrow and age-based, in other parts of the world, including Africa, youthhood tends to be related to a stage of life rather than a particular age range (Sommers 2001: 3). It is understood as the passage between childhood and adulthood, a period in which one goes from dependence to independence, when fundamental decisions are made and new roles and responsibilities are taken on (Lloyd, Behrman, Stromquist and Cohen 2006: 1). In environments where young people have to assume "adult" responsibilities, the divide between childhood and adulthood is easily blurred.[9] In Kakuma, I came to realize that most of those who were still busy with school, especially primary school, were not yet openly engaged in a reflection about their future or, if they were, would not readily share their thoughts on the subject. Refugees typically complete their basic education at a later age than students who start at the standard age and have never had to interrupt their studies. Someone in his or her late teens might still be in primary school. Often the emergence of a reflexive stance seemed linked to the approach of the end of schooling. This generally happened later for boys than for girls. Indeed, while many boys have a relatively long passage from "childhood" to "adulthood," many girls leave school and take on adult responsibilities at an early age and without much transitional time, owing to marriage and motherhood. For boys, coming of age is complicated by their lack of financial means to pay a dowry and create a home for the family. In fact, the camp appears to obscure categories and life paths. While an eighteen-year-old working for an NGO for a small monetary incentive might be the main source of income for his family, he may nonetheless remain unable to marry in the absence of a proper job. Such constraints may not be particular to the camp. Honwana and De Boeck (2005: 9) stress that "a growing number of children and youth in contemporary Africa are excluded from education, health-care, salaried jobs, and even access to an adult status, given their financial incapacity to construct a house, formally marry and raise children."

In the end, I focused on people who, in addition to having lived in Kenyan camps from an early age, defined and perceived themselves as youth. Nearly all were in their late teens or early twenties, from sixteen to twenty-six. In March 2013, the UNHCR statistics showed that about 2,600 Somali youth of that age had arrived in Kakuma before the age of ten. The number of those actually living in the camp was most likely significantly lower, as people leaving the camp by their own means to settle elsewhere in Kenya, return to Somalia or move to another country are unlikely to report their departure.[10] Most of the people I met had spent time in the coastal camps before being transferred to Kakuma. A few already had children and were no longer living with their parents. Most still had limited responsibilities and were at a turning point, trying to make the right decisions for their future and hoping to become independent from their families and take on adult roles. Within their families, they were no longer treated like children, but were not seen as fully adult. People who had grown up in the camp who had different experiences and were at different stages of their life were thus considered together in my research, as they shared the feeling of belonging to the social category of youth and not yet seeing themselves as full adults.

Inspired by Throop's understanding of personal experience as structured by the sensory experience of the present in its raw state and its reflective and narrative retrospective analysis, I considered that grasping the experience of youth entailed combining retrospective assessments by young people themselves with a systematic observation of daily life that "focuses upon capturing the often pre-reflective, real-time unfolding of social action" (Throop 2003: 235). I worked through a combination of participant observation, teaching journalism and photography, and in-depth interviews with refugees and other relevant individuals, with the aim of engaging with people's immediate experience and their reflections about it.

Watching Life as it Happens

I spent a lot of time simply being present in the camp, carrying out participant observation in a number of public areas. From the start, I knew I could neither observe nor participate in the life of refugees in an uninterrupted manner, as living in the camp was not an option. Camps tend not to be a setting in which a researcher can easily live for extended periods of time. In this case, the Department of Refugee Affairs (DRA) forbade visits to the camp after dark for security reasons (although I believe I could have safely spent nights in a family compound). I could have opted to stay in one of the private guesthouses in the nearby town, but chose instead to "embed" with a relatively small American NGO, FilmAid,[11] and to live in the NGO compound with hundreds of aid workers hired by various organizations that are present in the camp. Jansen (2011) decided not to stay with an NGO or the UNHCR when doing his Ph.D. research in Kakuma to emphasize his separation from the humanitarian system. I concur that to prevent confusion between the roles of researcher and aid worker, a researcher should try not to live or be supported by an aid organization (although being "embedded" with FilmAid did allow me to witness how humanitarian staff engaged with refugee staff and refugees in general, which I found valuable). However, as a woman, I did not feel comfortable with staying on my own in a guesthouse.

Being a white woman in her mid thirties and a former aid worker meant that I was perceived as wealthy and possibly able to influence aid organizations, notably on resettlement matters. This led to my receiving a number of requests for assistance. In a few instances, I was asked if I could plead on someone's behalf to Canadian officials or give significant sums of money. Refugee camps are a setting where people receive assistance and are used to visitors coming to assess their needs. Consequently, when I first met with groups of refugees, I was often asked what I was going to provide and I had to clarify that although I was hosted by FilmAid, I was not there on behalf of an aid organization or a donor, but as a student doing independent research. I think that working with youth for a sustained period of time and in an open and transparent manner helped erode the view that I was working for and in the interests of an NGO or that I was involved in the distribution of humanitarian assistance—to the extent that when I met with older people who would ask what I could do for them, youth often responded on my behalf that I was not working with an NGO, but was "just a student" conducting research and teaching voluntarily. However, refugees did know that I had good access to NGOs and the UNHCR (and had worked for the UNHCR and NGOs for several years) and I did sometimes help refugees to meet with aid workers. This probably accentuated the impression that I held more power or influence than they did as refugees, but I felt that it would be morally wrong not to provide this very limited support.

It is commonly thought that giving assistance or rendering services will alter the research process and thus the findings. According to that view, giving might exacerbate the power imbalance between the researcher and the researched, and lead people to participate in a project they would not otherwise have been interested in. But as Lammers (2007: 76) points out, one might instead wonder why anyone would engage in a meaningful, trustworthy and respectful relationship with a researcher if no giving-receiving relationship is established. This also wrongly assumes that informants are passive subjects and researchers are powerful agents. But power is not only a matter of wealth and status, but also of qualities such as physical power, intellectual skills, leadership and creativity (Lammers 2007: 74). On all of these dimensions, researchers are not experts—quite the opposite. I feel an affinity with Hecht (1998: 9), who says that while he never "came to terms with the inequality between [himself] and the Brazilian street children" he was spending time with, he came to realize that he was the one depending on the children and not the other way round. In all cases, the very presence of a researcher influences social interactions and cultural configurations, and has some impact on the construction of accounts and representations (Turner 2000: 51, 59).

I went to the camp every day, except on a few occasions. I spent time in the public markets and visited the main hospital, some schools and training centers, one of the field posts and a food distribution center. I regularly visited people whom I had come to know in their place of work, recreation or at home and sometimes accompanied youth while they took part in various activities, such as literacy classes they were organizing, film screenings, training sessions and food collection. If I was going to nearby areas, I usually walked, as that allowed me to meet people in an informal way. After a few months, I inevitably ran into people I knew whenever I was walking. Otherwise, I moved around by taxi-bicycle or *bodaboda* (a taxi-motorcycle), or was dropped off by the FilmAid car.

When I first arrived in the camp, I encountered a number of people to whom I explained what I was interested in and asked if they knew anyone I should meet. I used several entry points in making contacts. I first spoke with refugees I had become acquainted with during my previous trip, as well as those working for FilmAid and other NGOs. I gradually met some youth who had spent most of their lives in the camp, who in turn introduced me to other young people they had grown up with and to people they saw as influential in their community. I also came to know several young people through the classes I was giving, and they introduced me to more people, many of them out of school. At a later stage, youth leaders and community leaders introduced me to yet more young people. Quite soon I was being referred to people I had already met, and thus I realized in the early stages of my research that most of those who had grown up in the camp and still lived there were part of a relatively small group of persons who usually knew one another. Over time, I ended up developing relatively close relationships with a number of young people who introduced me to various aspects of their lives. While it would be incorrect to say that I thoroughly selected key informants, I did strive to ensure that I was spending time with young women and men with diverse backgrounds and social characteristics, notably in terms of age, clan affiliation or occupation.

I paid attention to interactions and social dynamics among youth, as well as with other members of the community, teachers, humanitarian workers and representatives of the authorities. I considered how people filled their days and observed the social, financial and domestic responsibilities that youth were assuming. This relatively unstructured time in the camp allowed me to be a witness of daily life, of life as it happens. People often shared small pieces of information that they did not necessarily see as worth mentioning in an interview, such as their daily chores or feelings of boredom, whom they liked spending time with and where, or where they would go for dating. In the course of informal interactions, inconsistencies in people's stories sometimes became clear, either through their actions or as they altered (or contradicted) stories they had previously told me.

I integrated photo-taking into my participant observation, as I worked on a series of portraits. I offered to snap and print family portraits for people with whom I had developed fairly close relationships. I also took individual portraits of my photography students. My intention was to see how distant people's desired representation would be from the typical imagery of refugees. This allowed me to verify the obvious: that people would not present themselves as victims, but would want to look the best they could.

Participatory Research Methods: Teaching Photography and Journalism

In addition to participant observation, I wanted to experiment with participatory approaches. This was partly because I was not comfortable with asking for time, insights and trust without giving something in return. This appeared even more important in a context where refugees regularly express their fatigue vis-à-vis the constant surveys, censuses and studies undertaken by aid organizations and researchers (Cooper 2005: 468). Of course, reciprocity could have simply consisted in being genuinely attentive and interested. I also found this a compelling way to establish sustained relationships and believed that refugees were in a privileged position to identify matters of interest and give meaning to findings, as underlined by Horst (2001: 14). The involvement of youth took different forms. Many accompanied and assisted my reflection by informally discussing with me the topic of my research and how to approach it. Some also helped me identify people to meet with. When I interviewed older people in the community to whom I had been introduced by a youth, either because they were his or her parents or someone he or she deemed worthy of attention, the youth would sometimes accompany me, but not always. This depended on the matters to be discussed and the views of the youth and the interviewee. When they came along, I included them in the interview, asking if they wanted to make comments or ask questions. Once it was over, we usually reflected together on what had been said. I shared my impressions and conclusions with many, asking for their input. During the writing of this book, I have also shared completed chapters with a number of them. In fact, I wrote this in English, rather than in French, my mother tongue, so that Somalis would be able to read it and comment on it. Those who did send feedback had usually paid very close attention to parts that felt close to them and often commented on how reading their stories told by someone else had been moving.

Then I gave an unplanned journalism class, in addition to a planned three-month photography and writing class. After arriving in Kakuma, I was asked by FilmAid to develop a curriculum for a journalism course and to start the class while they were recruiting a teacher. (As a journalism graduate, I worked as a journalist for the Canadian public radio broadcaster, Radio-Canada, before becoming a humanitarian worker.) I agreed, in part because FilmAid was giving me precious support, but also because I thought that teaching journalism would contribute to my understanding of the camp. For a month and a half, I gave biweekly classes to fourteen students, aged nineteen to twenty-nine, from Somalia, South Sudan, Sudan, the Democratic Republic of Congo, Ethiopia and Uganda. Half of them had spent most of their lives in the camp; of these, four were Somalis. I regularly asked students to come up with ideas for articles, which gave me valuable insight into their interests and concerns, and what they felt were important stories to tell about Kakuma. They commonly suggested topics related to security, coexistence between various nationalities, the situation of women, the unsatisfactory provision of water and food or access to medical care, camp politics and corruption, and problems related to humanitarian governance. When it came to researching and writing articles, students voiced concerns for their security and feared they might lose resettlement opportunities if they were to write anything critical about the UNHCR or the authorities. Interestingly, they often stressed that they were comfortable discussing those subjects in class because I was white. While I felt that being white created a barrier and that it could prevent people from talking in depth about their survival strategies or certain topics deemed sensitive or alter people's perception of my influence on aid organizations, I also realized that in some instances, people were able to articulate fears and uneasiness because I was seen as too distant from their reality to constitute a threat. This brings to mind the Indian anthropologist Palriwala who, reflecting on her work in the Netherlands, writes that her outsiderness was an advantage because "many informants felt confident that what they had told me would not filter back into their lives" (2005: 166).

Previous experiences in the Dadaab camps and several other settlements of displaced Somalis in both Somalia and Yemen had convinced me that teaching community-based photography can help establish a lasting dialogue with people who might otherwise be difficult to engage with (Grayson 2007, 2009). In addition, the photographs themselves sometimes facilitate discussion and exploration by revealing scenes of everyday life that are rarely seen by an external observer. For this reason, I used photography teaching, combined with nonfiction writing, as a research tool (see Ewald (2001) on teaching photography and writing to children). I held classes from January to the end of March 2013 with eight boys and eight girls in the secondary school, aged between fifteen and twenty-one. Nine were South Sudanese, six were Somali and one was Ethiopian. Five of the Somalis were born in the Mombasa camps and one South Sudanese was born in Kakuma. The others arrived in Kakuma before they were five. In the beginning, students attended a short theoretical and practical training session. We also agreed on themes to explore. They included family, home, self-representation, daily life, dreams for the future and negative aspects of the camp. The next page presents an example of their work. The photograph shows eighteen-year-old Luula's room, while she describes her dream home. Like all names in the book, Luula's is a pseudonym. Most interviewees were comfortable with using their real names, but given the links between people in the camp, I felt it would be impossible to protect only the anonymity of some individuals. Details that would have made possible to identify certain people were also omitted, even though these might have given additional depth to the study.

In general, classes proved an interesting way to steadily engage with a group of youth, witness their interactions and dynamics (in particular between boys and girls, between people of the same and different nationalities and with teachers), and to participate in discussions with them. Seeing them on a regular basis meant that they ended up telling me about various details of their

MY DREAM HOME

I Want my dream home to be very beautiful I want
I want my dream home to have a big bad room and I want my
dream room to be a decorated one.

I want my home to have atleas 5 rooms a big seating
room. Sinning table. I want my dream house to look very beautiful
that when People saw The appericiot it

And also want it to have a Place where my
children can Play and enjoy where my guest's can fill
satisfied That is how I want my dream house to be.

Figure 0.1 Photograph by Luula. Courtesy of Luula

lives and their hopes for the future. The photographs and their accompany-ing texts, just like the articles written by the journalism students, helped me understand their reality and prompted more discussions.

Giving Meaning to Observations through Interviews

Interviews appeared a necessary complement to observation, as the sense of actions is not given and decipherable in itself. I thus conducted over a hun-dred in-depth interviews, mostly with youth, but also with parents, camp leaders and other adults, as well as employees of organizations working in the camps and local authorities. Seeking to attenuate the asymmetry between researcher and subject, I tried as much as possible to stay away from directed questionnaires and instead to define with the interviewees themselves matters they were interested in exploring, as suggested by Bourdieu (1993: 905–6). Nonetheless, there were a number of themes that I tended to broach system-atically. For example, I talked with youth about their life in the camp, their hopes for the future, and their perception of Somalia and of their compatriots who were raised there. With parents, I often spoke of cultural transmission and raising their children in a refugee camp. I chose not to ask about peo-ple's reasons for fleeing Somalia because of the sensitivity of the subject. This did not prevent many from talking about their families' paths into exile, but they were the ones bringing it up. In most cases, I also had numerous infor-mal interactions with the people I interviewed. Finally, I carried out semi-structured formal interviews with government representatives and NGO and UNHCR workers.

I had planned to work with a translator while I was taking Somali classes. In the end, the youth who were of interest to me all spoke English, as it is the language of education in Kenya. I therefore conducted most interviews in English. As a result, I decided to learn Swahili rather than Somali, because it is the other shared language in the camp, along with English. Looking back, I think this was a mistake: learning Somali would have helped me establish more intimate connections with youth, engage directly with non-English-speaking adults and gain a better understanding of Somalis in general. My basic knowledge of Swahili did allow me to notice how frequently Somalis incorporated Swahili words into their own language, to remark that it was the language used in the camp between "old-timers" of different nationalities and to understand some of the interactions between youth of various ori-gins. The only times I needed a translator were when meeting with parents and older people, or with newcomers to the camp. In such cases, youth with whom I had been spending time helped me, which also allowed me to see how they reacted to certain stories and comments. This sometimes led to memorable moments. In one instance, Mahdi, a twenty-one-year-old who arrived in Kakuma when he was a few months old, accompanied me for an interview with a fifty-one-year-old Somali lawyer, Osman. In the end, the lawyer needed no translation, but Mahdi stayed. Osman started talking about the language changes that had occurred during his education in Somalia:

> In primary school, I learned in Arabic. At that time, the Somali language was not written. We would either attend Italian or Arabic schools. I remember that before entering the class, we used to stand and sing in honour of the flag in Arabic.

He stood up and proceeded to sing in Arabic:

> After studying in Arabic for three years, there was the military revolution [led by Siyad Barre in late 1969] and our Somali language was scripted [in 1972].[12]

He stood again and started singing the same song, this time in Somali:

> It means: "We are very happy for this flag that looks like the sky. We have to welcome and respect. We should never forget that we gained it through the shedding of war."

Mahdi was sitting there looking mesmerized. After the interview, he explained that he had never heard that song, that he would not be able to sing the Somali national anthem and that witnessing the discussion had been fascinating, as he was discovering new facts about his own country. Similarly, young people attending interviews with their parents sometimes remarked that they had learned new facets of their family history.

Why This Book?

To some extent, this study is the fruit of years of humanitarian work with refugees in Africa, mostly in the Great Lakes Region and the Horn of Africa, years spent wishing that the response to refugee movements were more adequate and wondering about the obvious discrepancy between theory and practice. When I embarked upon this ethnographic research, I wanted to explore holistically the impact of containment policies, which have turned the camp into a long-term response, on a specific group of people: refugee youth who have spent most or all of their lives in a camp. My aim was to loosely examine three interrelated spaces in time and the way they are perceived, understood and described by refugee youth: the lived present, the imagined past and the projected future. Underlying this undertaking was the belief that regardless of the considerable limitations they face, refugees are the ones defining their lives and giving meaning to their own situation and circumstances. I therefore intended to engage with the experience of refugees in a way that recognizes the agency of these social actors. I also sought to resituate their individual trajectories in a broader context that extends beyond the humanitarian system and encompasses transnational networks.

Refugee-related research has commonly focused on young children and adults, neglecting youth as a distinct social group. This could be because those younger than eighteen are often subsumed under the broad international legal category of children, while young people over eighteen are counted as adults (Clark-Kazak 2011: 7–8). While several relatively recent studies have been dedicated to the subject, they have mostly been from a psychological or psychiatric perspective, typically studying trauma and post-traumatic stress disorder (e.g., Farwell 2001; Goodman 2004; Halcón et al. 2004; Murray, Cohen, Ellis and Mannarino 2008). The camp experience has rarely been studied from the viewpoint of refugee youth who spent most of their lives in such closed settings. The anthropologist Dawn Chatty is a noteworthy exception, as she carried out or oversaw studies focusing on Palestinian youth, and then on Sahrawi and Afghan youth who grew up in exile (Chatty 2010a, 2010b; Chatty and Hundt 2005). These studies have shown that while the main concerns of youth living in various locations are similar, relating to life experience and agency, and to educational constraints and aspirations, the particular historical, political and economic contexts have significantly colored their experiences, just as their gender has done.

As will become evident throughout this book, these observations are equally significant when studying the experience of Somali youth who grew up in the Kakuma refugee camp. Their experience is gendered and influenced by their living environment. Their identity and sense of belonging are complex. Immense value is vested in education. And youth nurture great ambitions and show a remarkable resilience and optimism. Although there are resemblances between the situation of Somalis and Afghan, Palestinian or Sahrawi refugees—they all are in protracted displacement and are predominantly Muslims—there are also contextual, historical and sociocultural differences. For example, not all of the refugees involved in the aforementioned studies reside in camps, nor do they have the same legal status, which has an impact on people (un)settledness. As opposed to Afghans, Sahrawis and Palestinians, Somali refugees in Kenya have been and still are part of a sizeable resettlement program to the United States, which influences their camp experience and their ambitions for the future. In contrast to what I observed concerning the Somalis, the involvement of Palestinian and Sahrawi refugees in national liberation struggles affects their views on resettlement, local integration and return, and turns camps into spaces of collective mobilization (Farah 2009). In some locations, refugees have the right to work, settle outside of camps or move freely, which is not the case for Somalis in Kakuma.

The Camp as a Site of Tensions

My research shows that although camps, from the perspective of Somali youth, are not a good response to lasting displacement, they also believe that being in Kakuma has saved their lives. It has allowed them to grow up in a safer environment than they would have in Somalia. Until they completed their education, children and teenagers were busy with school, and had little time to wonder about their future and the "normality" of the camp. Frustration, fueled by connection to and awareness of the rest of the world, grows when education opportunities are exhausted and chances for leaving through resettlement remain vague, while at the same time many of their friends have been resettled in the United States. Although youth are better able than their parents to navigate the humanitarian system and Kenya itself, they still manage to gain only limited financial autonomy, making it hard to honor certain traditions and social responsibilities. While this might contribute to a renegotiation of traditions, it also catalyzes young people's will to leave the camp and "find a life."

Furthermore, growing up coincides with a greater awareness of the representation attached to being a refugee. Even though youth do not see themselves as lesser human beings, they believe they are perceived as people of little value, with limited or no rights, who cannot be trusted. Such feelings reinforce their determination to leave Kakuma. Despite the fact that refugees have been living there since the early 1990s, the camp remains a *lieu de passage*: no one plans to spend their lives there, although youth who grew up in the camp often say that "Kakuma is home." While satisfactory ways out are few, refugees do move, make plans and build their lives beyond the humanitarian system. Resettlement is the exit solution that is usually hoped for, but the process is lengthy, so youth often look for other temporary avenues. Those rejected for resettlement sometimes remain in the camp with growing levels of resentment, while others move by their own means and irregularly to Kenyan cities or to another country. Some might return to Somalia.

The camp experience appears to be traversed by tensions between seemingly opposite notions—such as mobility and immobility, isolation and connection, locality and globality, victimization and the affirmation of the subject, control and circumvention, fixed space and space of reinvention, citizenship and refugeeness—and conflicting temporalities. At first glance, Kakuma feels disconnected, largely because, like many other camps, it is established in a remote and sparsely populated border area with barren land. But this impression quickly gains layers of complexity: while distant, the camp is also in intense interaction with the wider world, an interaction that shapes the experience of refugees. Refugees cultivate relationships with people who have remained in their country of origin and others who have moved elsewhere. They are also in contact with merchants and aid workers from across Kenya and around the world. The media expose them to what is happening elsewhere, and policy decisions taken around the globe affect their daily lives. The camp may be geographically isolated, but it is also a connected place that is in constant motion. Mobility is actually the only way to accept and make sense of the camp's reality. Seen from this perspective, the camp becomes an endless passage in a difficult location, on an (imagined) trajectory that takes refugees from Somalia to the West. This value placed on movement can be linked to the Somali tradition of resilient nomadism and mobility. It is only by seeing it against this background that the camp becomes tolerable. To some extent, the camp can be regarded as a place of confinement that paradoxically induces movement.

Seemingly contradictory temporalities also coexist within the camp. People wait endlessly for a hypothetical resettlement, which gives the impression that time has stopped. Social time—which would normally command refugees to get married, settle down, have children or find a job—is chaotic, because accumulating sufficient resources to establish oneself is hard. The feeling of living in suspended time makes it difficult to plan for the future, but as biological time passes, some marry and establish families. Many camp dwellers speak of the tension between the primacy of waiting, chronic uncertainty and the passage of time that means that they are getting older (see Griffiths 2014). A temporal tension is also perceptible in the transitory yet permanent nature of the camp. Although refugees have been living there for decades, imbuing it with a feeling of permanency, people's experience reflects the fact that the camp is designed for temporary rather than permanent settlement. In such a setting, subtle identity and cultural changes occur. The younger generation is questioning tribalism and young women are increasingly open in criticizing their social role. This creates tensions between generations and between genders. The camp becomes a site of social, political and historical (trans) formation. Perceived as such, exile, even in a camp, can be considered productive and emancipating, as long as the camp is used properly and remains impermanent.

Such observations highlight the fact that the camp cannot be regarded only as a space of immobility and constraints, but must be approached as an ambiguous place, traversed and shaped by tensions. These tensions constitute the fabric of this ethnography.

Notes

1. In this book, I use "Somali" to refer to the nationality and not to the ethnic group, unless otherwise specified. This therefore includes Somalis who do not belong to one of the main Somali lineages, but to minority groups such as the Bantu or the Bajuni.
2. In this book I use the term "refugee" to refer to people who, in most cases, live in Kakuma refugee camp and, in all cases, define themselves as such. In reality, they might not all fit into the legal category of "refugee." The Convention Relating to the Status of Refugees defines a refugee as any person who, "for reasons of race, religion, nationality, membership of a particular social group or political opinion, is outside the country of his nationality and is unable or, owing to such fear, is unwilling to avail himself of the protection of that country." The 1969 Convention Governing the Specific Aspects of Refugee Problems in Africa of the Organization of the African Unity proposes a broader definition, a refugee also being someone who has been compelled to leave his place of habitual residence to seek refuge outside his country of origin or nationality "owing to external aggression, occupation, foreign domination or events seriously disturbing public order in either part or the whole of his country of origin or nationality."
3. I speak about poor/rich countries, despite the vagueness and relativity of these terms, as I find this more accurate than the South/North designation, which does not refer to the northern and southern hemispheres, but rather to a shifting and questionable divide between developed and developing countries.
4. In 2015, Syrians, Afghans and Syrians, who are predominantly Muslims, were the three most important groups of refugees and constituted more than half of the 21.3 million refugees falling under the UNHCR's mandate (UNHCR 2016a: 3). The United Nations Relief and Works Agency for Palestine Refugees in the Near East is responsible for the protection and assistance of some 5.2 million Palestinians.
5. In principle, the reception and protection of refugees and asylum seekers are not dependent on the generosity of states, but are governed by international instruments. While the right to leave one's country and to seek asylum in another one, set out in Articles 13 and 14 of the Universal Declaration of Human Rights, is not accompanied by the right of entry into a territory, the principle of *non-refoulement*, which requires states to allow refugees and asylum seekers onto their territory and prohibits the return of a refugee to a territory "where his life or freedom would be threatened," is enshrined in the 1951 Refugee Convention (Article 33) and is considered a rule of customary international law (UNHCR's introduction to the 1951 Refugee Convention: 4). It is therefore binding on all states.
6. Although the labeling of border closure as *refoulement* has been the object of significant divergence since the adoption of the 1951 Refugee Convention, such closure is now considered an act of *refoulement* (Long 2010: 62–63; UNHCR Excom 1981: Conclusion 22, II.A).
7. "Whereas the older paradigm can be described as reactive, exile-oriented and refugee-specific, the one which has started to emerge over the past few years can be characterised as proactive, homeland-oriented and holistic" (UNHCR 1995: Emerging trends and strategies).
8. The Convention Relating to the Status of Refugees is hereafter referred to as the 1951 Refugee Convention.
9. For a stimulating overview of the social studies of childhood and youth, see Benwell and Hopkins (2015: 4–14).

10. Statistics in refugee camps are far from perfectly accurate, but can be used as an indicator. Population data is normally updated and verified through periodical re-registration. This operation is also referred to as a "verification." The last verification of demographic data before I began my fieldwork took place from October 2010 to April 2011. Between these periodic verifications, changes occur within the population and might not be communicated. Refugees have limited interest in reporting deaths, as it means that their family size will be reduced, which affects the size of their food ration. In addition, registration figures do not take into account the mobility of refugees and include a number of local residents who register as refugees to receive some assistance.

11. FilmAid produces and distributes film and media to deliver information and entertainment to communities in crisis and trains community members in video production (www.filmaid.org). Its head office is in the United States and it runs operations in five countries. In 2012, fewer than ten Kenyan staff and many more refugee workers made up the FilmAid team in Kakuma.

12. In 1972, the military junta introduced a Latin script as the official orthography of the Somali language. It was accompanied by an edict making Somali the only official language. To diffuse the new orthography quickly, literacy campaigns were organized throughout the country (Abdullahi 2001: 73; Lewis 1993: 150).

Chapter 1

THE PAST IS A FOREIGN COUNTRY

৵৩·৬৯৽

> We are being told that our family has been killed there. But
> to talk of history, we don't know. When I imagine Somalia,
> I feel like crying. I think if I go there, people will kill me.
> —Amadi, eighteen years old

For over two decades, Somalia has been plunged into a maelstrom of violence that has driven hundreds of thousands of people from their homes. This is long enough for children who fled when they were toddlers or were born in exile to become adults. Having never seen their country of origin or, if they have, having little or no recollection of it, it is through family and community narratives, stories shared by newcomers to the camp and media reports that they have come to imagine Somalia and the circumstances in which their parents fled.

How would people who have never visited their country of origin and their family home imagine them? Which elements would they see as meaningful in depicting such an imaginary land? What about the events that led to their parents' departure and establishment in a refugee camp? Would such memories be central and nurtured or of minor importance; would they be private or collective; would the stories of parents and children be comparable? Would there necessarily be one standardized and more or less static "mythico-history" (Malkki 1995b) or would interaction with refugees of other origins and connection with the country of origin and the world through transnational flows of remittances and information have prevented such a static creation? What would individuals and communities choose to remember or to forget?

In Kakuma, the family stories that I most commonly heard from Somali youth (after being warned that they had very limited knowledge of the history of Somalia) recounted that before the war, when Siyad Barre was in power, life was fine. The land was lush, fruit and vegetables abounded, and milk, meat and fish were readily available. Their parents earned their living decently. Then the war, sparked by tribalism, started and things fell apart. Members of their families were killed, while others fled. They ended up in Kenya, first living in one of the coastal camps. The camp was burned down, they moved to another one, then to another one, until there were no options left, other than relocating to Kakuma or returning to Somalia. Their parents opted for Kakuma, as the violence was raging in Somalia then as it is now. They are fortunate their parents left: had they stayed in Somalia, it is unlikely that they would be alive to tell their story.

This chapter is about life before Kakuma and how youth narrate the history that has transformed their lives and those of their families. To reflect on this, I first present an overview of forced displacement in Somalia and the arrival of refugees in Kenya. I make a detour to the Mombasa camps, on the Kenyan coast, as this is where most of the youth lived when they first arrived in Kenya. I then focus on these young people's narrations of their personal history and show that while young people's accounts are individualized, they also share certain characteristics and have to be placed into the broader sociopolitical context. The history of the collapse of Somalia is important because it led to the flight of parents of youngsters who then grew up in Kenya. It also matters because it has nourished the imagination of young people growing up in exile, has helped them cope with their present in making them appreciate Kenya's relative safety and has often made their return to Somalia inconceivable.

A Short History of the Somali Exodus

> We came with few belongings. We left our homes thinking
> we would be back soon. We left the whole family album
> there. I only have a few ID photos of my father. That is
> how hasty it was. We were relocating to Afmadow for
> a few days. Twenty years later, we are still not back.
> —Absame, twenty-seven years old

The longlasting violence and political instability that have characterized Somalia since the collapse of the centralized government in 1991, compounded by recurring droughts and floods, have substantially destroyed infrastructure and livelihoods and have forced up to a quarter of the population to flee (Farah, Muchie and Gundel 2007: xi; Menkhaus 2008: 4, 8), turning Somalia into "a country in exile" (Farah 1998: 715).[1] No part of the country has been spared. The majority of displaced people have stayed in Somalia. Most of those who became refugees have remained in eastern Africa. Although movement has been ongoing since the late 1990s, three key periods of displacement can be roughly distinguished (Lindley 2011a). The first significant one, from 1988 to 1992, was provoked by the collapse of the state and the ensuing clan war, an extreme situation aggravated by a drought. Parents of youth who grew up in Kakuma fled during this period. When movement resumed in 2006, with the ousting of the Islamic Courts Union (ICU) and the subsequent unremitting violence, hundreds of thousands of people joined the previously displaced or were forced to move again. In 2011 and 2012, a severe drought exacerbated by governance failures resulted in a famine that, again, caused massive displacement.

The civil war that began in 1988 led to the fall of Siyad Barre's authoritarian regime in 1991. It first affected northwestern Somalia, where in response to Barre's repression, the Somali National Movement (SNM) was seeking an independent state corresponding to the colonial borders of British Somaliland. In May 1988, the SNM seized the cities of Hargeisa and Burao (Ambroso 2002: 5–6). Barre's infantry counterattacked with extreme force, leveling the two cities. Violence killed more than 50,000 people. Hundreds of thousands fled within the country. Up to 650,000 people sought asylum in the Somali regions of neighboring Ethiopia and Djibouti (Bradbury and Healy 2010: 10; Gundel 2002: 257). The conflict escalated during the next two years and spread to the capital, Mogadishu, where, from December 1990 onward, Barre's regime fought armed factions organized along clan lines, resulting in enormous destruction (Kleist 2004: 7). Within two months, the government was overthrown. The SNM gained command of the north and the self-proclaimed independent Somaliland progressively stabilized. In Mogadishu and most of southern Somalia, rebel groups failed to agree on the formation of a government (Lindley 2010: 6).

The Somali State had collapsed and a long period of clan-based warfare for control of rural and urban resources had begun (Bradbury and Healy 2010: 10; Lindley 2011a: 7). Fighting centered on Mogadishu and the interriverine agricultural area between the Jubba and Shabelle rivers, critically disrupting food supplies. Basic services and central security forces had disappeared, replaced by several clan militias. The violence and insecurity were such that most humanitarian agencies pulled out of the country. At the height of the civil war, in 1992, a major drought hit south-central Somalia (Ahmed and Herbold Green 1999: 120). The main victims of the violence and the drought were the traditionally marginalized riverine and interriverine agro-pastoral communities and coastal minority groups who were caught in the middle of the fighting (HRW 1993).[2] By the fall of 1992, it was estimated that violence and famine had killed up to 300,000 in the previous year (Bradbury and Healy 2010: 10; Canadian Forces 1997: vol. 1). Some 3.5 million people fled, including up to half of Mogadishu's 1.25 million inhabitants who moved to camps on the fringes of the city, or south to the Jubba regions, or, in the case of government soldiers and members of the president's clan, the Marehan, west to the Gedo region (Africa Watch and Physicians for Human Rights 1992; IRB 1991; Menkhaus 2005: 11). An estimated one million became refugees. A more affluent minority headed for the West, but most went to neighboring countries, including some three hundred thousand to Kenya (Bradbury and Healy 2010: 10; Gundel 2002: 264–65). For many, the only escape route open was the ocean. Within weeks, thousands of Somalis were arriving in Mombasa by boat (Verdirame and Harrell-Bond 2005: 5).

The dramatic humanitarian situation prompted an international response, but large-scale peacekeeping operations from 1992 to 1995 failed to re-establish stability and security. A US-led multinational military force, UNITAF, was launched in December 1992, known as "Operation Restore Hope." This was replaced by UNOSOM II in May 1993. On the ground, acts of great brutality committed by American, Italian, Belgian and Canadian troops fostered resentment among the Somali population, which strongly impacted on their support for the mission (de Waal 2007; Razack 2004: 37, 51). In the West, the popularity of a military intervention in Somalia dropped drastically as peacekeeping operations floundered and the dead bodies of eighteen American soldiers were paraded through Mogadishu by anti-United Nations (UN) protesters. By 1995, the international community had largely withdrawn from Somalia, leaving the country divided and without a government (Bradbury and Healy 2010: 11).[3]

From the mid 1990s to 2005, there was a period of relative stability. Most of those who had fled to Ethiopia and Djibouti from the northern part of the country repatriated.[4] However, the situation in the south-central region never became stable enough to prompt such substantial returns from Kenya (Hyndman and Nylund 1998: 27).

In late 2006, widespread violence resumed when the ICU, which had expanded its control over most of southern Somalia, was ousted by the Transitional Federal Government (TFG), backed by the Ethiopian army and later by an African Union peacekeeping mission, AMISOM. The ICU's hardline militia wing, al-Shabab, mounted a violent opposition against the TFG, Ethiopian and AMISOM forces, using new forms of urban violence. This marked a shift in the nature of the Somali crisis: the conflict was no longer described as clan-based, but as ideological (Bradbury and Healy 2010: 10). In the following years, the TFG failed to defeat or negotiate effectively with al-Shabab. The violence led to a massive humanitarian crisis and forced some 700,000 people to flee Mogadishu (Lindley 2011a: 9; Menkhaus 2010: S332). More than 170,000 refugees arrived in Kenya between 2007 and 2010 (UNHCRa). Most of the Somali refugees who have arrived in Kakuma over the last few years were part of this movement.

While insecurity was already causing displacement and seriously limiting humanitarian access, a severe drought hit southern Somalia from July 2011 to mid 2012. In the absence of a functioning government able to respond to the crisis and of sufficient humanitarian assistance, large numbers of agro-pastoralists and farming families who lost their livelihoods moved away. Some 290,000 Somalis crossed to neighboring countries. More than half of them arrived in Kenya and settled in one of the Dadaab camps (UNHCR 2011b: 89, 95). This movement was extremely visible in the media, but did not lead to significant numbers of new arrivals in Kakuma.

Around the same time, in October 2011, Kenya sent hundreds of troops to Somalia after a spate of kidnappings within its borders, citing the threat posed by al-Shabab to regional stability. A month later, shortly after the TFG requested help from the international community and neighboring countries to secure Somalia, Ethiopian forces also crossed the Somali border to combat al-Shabab (BBC, 2011c). The participation of Kenyan forces (which were still militarily engaged there under African Union command at the time of my research) was primarily intended to stabilize the border region and, possibly, help create a safe zone inside Somalia, both to stem the arrival of new refugees and to pave the way for the return of others (Lindley 2011a: 29–30).[5] It was feared that such an operation would lead to involuntary returns and thus fail to respect recognized standards. A new Somali President, Hassan Sheikh Mohamud, was elected in October 2012, ending an eight-year transitional government. Even though the situation improved somewhat in 2012, stability and safety remained uncertain, and although al-Shabab suffered several defeats in 2012, losing control of a number of key towns, it continued to carry out attacks throughout my stay in Kakuma (HRW 2013a).

The Somali conflict has often been reduced to a tribal feud exploited by warlords. Yet, in considering Somalia's recent past, it is evident that external meddling has played a significant role in shaping and exacerbating divisions and violence (Menkhaus 2009: 223; Samatar 1997: 687). Hence, the progressive collapse of Somalia must be understood in the light of internal factors as well as external ones, notably the colonial legacy of the British and Italians, as well as the lasting results of international aid and the Cold War, and the influence of Western politics.[6]

Routes into Exile

Fleeing is a chaotic process. People rarely have a clear idea of their final destination and have little time to plan their trip. The distinction between transnational migration and refugee movements is fundamental in that respect: although in both cases leaving is a choice, for refugees, options are often limited and the notice is very short, restricting the preparations for departure and leading to more risk-taking (Grabska 2010: 482; Meintel 1990: 61). Twenty-two-year-old Nuradin's detailed narrative of his family's path into exile offers a good illustration:

> We were living in Mogadishu. My father was an inspector in the presidential police. He was protecting the president. My mother was a housewife. When the war started, the president left for Bardere [a district of Gedo region, traditional home-base of the Marehan, Siyad Barre's clan]. My father went along. Me, my brother and our mother stayed in Mogadishu until the war broke very hard. We were the people who were targeted because we were of the same ethnic group as the president. My mom decided to take us to Bardere, but two weeks later, the war started there too, so the president went to Kenya and people started running. We had to leave. My father was not with us, only my mother and my aunt. We walked for eighteen days and nights without any food, just drinking the water we could find, begging for milk to cattle people … At some point, my father left everything and decided to look for us. He was told that people were moving that way. So he started walking behind us with an uncle who was very young. [A] militia got them and killed my uncle. My father escaped and finally, he reached us. We entered Kenya through Calqalow [in the Gedo region]. There was a white guy. My mom says he was a priest or working for the Red Cross. He was providing food, but it was not quite okay. I became very sick. The black of my eyes went up. I was taken to the hospital. I was about to die, but my time was not there.
>
> We were few families. The white man said if we wanted to go into Kenya, he would take us. Some decided to go back into Somalia. The man put us into a lorry and took us to Utange. There was a camp there. We settled and started living there. But after two years, a fire broke out and we were taken to Marafa for a year and a half. Then another fire broke out and we were taken to Benadir [or Swale Nguru].[7] In October 1996, there was another fire. We were told we had to go to Kakuma.

After staying in Kakuma for five years, Nuradin's family moved to Nairobi. His mother sold the gold jewelry she had received as a dowry to pay for the family's expenses. Two years later, there was a new registration in Kakuma and the family headed back to the camp so as not to lose their ration card. They did not return to Nairobi afterward.

Such a story seems emblematic of forced displacement dynamics. The majority of people fleeing their usual place of residence because of clashes in the streets of their city will take refuge in another part of the city or its suburbs, in areas somewhat removed from the violence. Some will travel to another region of the country, which is what Nuradin's family did when the war started in

Mogadishu. They moved to the Gedo region, which had been mostly spared from violence and was their clan's traditional area, making it a place where they would be protected. Like most people fleeing, they were hosted by relatives. However, a significant minority do stay with other displaced persons in informal settlements and sometimes receive humanitarian assistance. The significance of clan grew during the Somali conflict and flight followed clan patterns: people fled in the direction of the traditional locations of their families and clans, both within Somalia and across the border to Kenya (Horst 2006a: 47).

Most people fleeing do not leave their country of origin. Perhaps a third of them cross an international border, thus becoming refugees. Among those leaving their homeland, most settle in the border region of the host country, an area that often shares characteristics with the locality of origin, so as to monitor developments in their country and return when conditions allow. Most refugees are housed by the host community, are never registered and receive no international assistance. Smaller but significant numbers settle in camps set up by the government of the host country, UNHCR and humanitarian organizations, usually in underdeveloped areas, far from urban centers and close to the borders of the country of origin (Jacobsen 2005: 1, 6–7, 92).

Contrary to the popular image likening refugee flows to human tides, most refugees travel alone or in small groups. Their journeys are often unplanned, as highlighted by Ayan: "I asked my mom why they decided to come to Kenya. She said: 'We didn't decide. We were there, some cars came and we were told to get in. We were brought to Kenya and we went to camp Barawa [or Hatimy].' It was 1992. My mom was pregnant with me. That is where I was born." However, it is rare for refugees to flee in just any direction: they follow familiar routes and try, as much as possible, to go and join relatives who have already left (Gomes 2001: 301). These journeys frequently happen in successive steps, dictated by the situation in people's area of residence and place of refuge (Jacobsen 2005: 5). For example, Nuradin's family moved again because the situation degenerated in Gedo. Kenya was nearby. A number of refugees make several trips within their own country before crossing an international border. They may live in a camp and later move to an urban area in the hope of finding work or travel further to a third country (Jacobsen 2005: 7; Zimmerman 2009: 75).

Welcome to Kenya

We lived in Sako. I don't know in which district it is, but it is somewhere between Bardere and Buale, in Jubbaland. My father was a businessman. After the war broke out in 1990, all his cattle were looted. He said: "I no longer want

> to live in this country." We left in 1991. I was too young
> to remember. We were among the first to be welcomed
> as refugees in Liboi. We were there for six months and
> my younger sister died. We buried her there and then
> we went to Dagahaley refugee camp [Dadaab].
>
> —Yasin, twenty-eight years old

In the fall of 1989, when the Somali State was on the verge of collapsing, a few thousand Somalis crossed into northeastern Kenya and settled near the current site of the Dadaab refugee camps. Within weeks, the government of Kenya demanded their return to Somalia. Several were beaten and forced back to their country. Others dispersed inside Kenya (IRB 1991; Kagwanja and Juma 2008: 219). The unsympathetic reception did not stop people from coming. Starting in 1991, when the fighting was concentrated in Mogadishu and the interriverine area relatively close to Kenya, tens of thousands poured into the country. Those who came by land mostly crossed through the border town of Liboi. Some from coastal areas such as Kismayo and Mogadishu, sometimes described as "Africa's first boat people" (Verdirame 1998: 12), sailed crowded boats into Kenya, a four-day sea journey (Farah 2000: 31). In early 1992, the fighting spread to Gedo and the region's residents and those who had moved there for safety fled again to other parts of the country or crossed into northeastern Kenya. Most of them stayed near the Somali border. Significant numbers also settled in urban centers and on the coast, in the vicinity of the port cities of Mombasa and Malindi (Abdullahi 1993: 2; Lindley 2007a: 2). A number of richer people fled to Nairobi (Farah 2000: vi). By mid 1992, more than 300,000 Somalis had entered Kenya and another thousand were arriving every day (UNHCR 1994: 6), an exodus described by Abdullahi (1993: 2) in harrowing terms: "For the last two years frail and sickly Somalis have been pouring into neighboring countries many having walked for weeks, destitute on the verge of collapse, many drowned when their small boats capsized or died from thirst and hunger."

Policy Matters

Until Somalis began to arrive in large numbers, Kenya had "operated a policy of benign neglect," allowing refugees to settle in urban areas and find a livelihood (Verdirame and Harrell-Bond 2005: 31). The arrival of hundreds of thousands of people prompted significant policy changes (Kagwanja and Juma 2008: 220).[8] Newcomers were customarily helped by their local host, but were greeted with hostility by the population in general and by the government, which described them as a security threat (Abdullahi 1993: 4; Kagwanja and Juma 2008: 219).

The first Somali refugees arriving in Kenya in 1989 were mostly from clans opposed to the Barre regime. They were given food, shelter and medical assistance, but were denied access to the Kenyan Red Cross, UNHCR and other humanitarian organizations (IRB 1991). After their arrival, the Presidents of Kenya and Somalia met. In spite of Kenya's international obligations, Daniel Arap Moi agreed to return the refugees to Somalia. In the following years, the Kenyan military and police sealed the border and the coast several times. Concerns about the presence of Somalis were heightened by the relatively warm relations between Moi and Barre, but also by the perception that such a presence would threaten the ethnic balance and revive historical animosities (Kagwanja and Juma 2008: 220, 223; Montclos 1999a: 3). Indeed, Kenya has had a difficult relationship with its Somali neighbors and its Somali-Kenyan population since its transition to independence, when the country was struggling to consolidate its territory and maintain colonial borders. During the so-called "*Shifta* War"[9] of 1963–68, some ethnic Somalis in the Northern Frontier District (which became the North Eastern Province and, in 2013, the counties of Garissa, Wajir and Mandera) fought a secessionist war with the goal of uniting their homeland to Greater Somalia (Hyndman 2000: 44–47; Kagwanja and Juma 2008: 223). The paramilitary General Service Unit of the Kenyan Army forced civilians into "protected villages" (later described as concentration camps) and used harsh military tactics to maintain order (Odengo 2011: 2–3; Whittaker 2008: 1–2, 13–14). Subsequent decades were characterized by continued crackdowns, sporadic border violence and civilian deaths, culminating in the Wagalla Massacre in Wajir in 1984, where up to five thousand civilian casualties were covered up (Ongeri and Obure 2004; Whittaker 2008: 17). The propagandist rhetoric emanating from the conflict framed ethnic Somalis as infiltrators and economic scapegoats responsible for a plethora of social and environmental ills (Abdullahi 1993: 8–9).

Despite deterrence measures, Somalis arrived in Kenya in large numbers after the fall of Barre's regime. In the end, the Moi government was forced to tolerate Somali refugees, partly because the country was a signatory to international and regional conventions on the rights of refugees, but also because it had no real means of physically preventing the influx and it was under pressure from donors (Crisp 1999: 17; Milner 2009: 107). The country's refugee population shot from 16,000 in March 1991 to over 425,000 at the end of 1992 (Kagwanja and Juma 2008: 220). Somalis still faced antipathy when arriving in Kenya. Some who fled by sea were turned away before reaching the coast; others were detained on board their vessels and prevented from disembarking. This practice led to many deaths, as boats capsized or ran short of essential supplies. Once on Kenyan soil, some were harassed by the police, required to move into camps or forcibly returned to Somalia, a practice explicitly prohibited under international law (Abdullahi 1993: 20–21; HRW 1992).

During this period, the government abdicated its power to the UNHCR, first allowing the agency to undertake refugee status determination, then agreeing to or prescribing the encampment of refugees, an option the government had rejected for many years.[10] In 1992 and 1993, UNHCR spent forty million dollars on setting up refugee camps and border sites in Kenya (Hyndman and Nylund 1998: 24). The first camps for Somali refugees were established in northeastern Kenya and around Mombasa, Kenya's second largest city. Kakuma refugee camp was also opened during that period to host refugees from southern Sudan (Verdirame and Harrell-Bond 2005: 31–33). In the early 1990s, there were more than fifteen camps in the country; these were later consolidated into the Dadaab and Kakuma camps (IRB 1999; Montclos 1999b: 29). Between August 1992 and July 1997, the Kenyan authorities rounded up urban refugees a number of times for removal to camps (Hyndman 2000: 51), where humanitarian and security conditions were described as a "public scandal" by Human Rights Watch (HRW 1993).

Almost immediately after securing re-election in December 1992, Moi began calling for the quick return of refugees to Somalia (Hyndman and Nylund 1998: 24). In response to the pressure and a request by the Secretary General of the UN, the UNHCR initiated a Cross-Border Operation in southern Somalia. The aim was to curtail the influx of refugees into Kenya and to encourage voluntary repatriation through the creation of a cross-border "preventive zone" extending approximately three hundred kilometers into Somalia, and a number of quick-impact projects and small-return assistance (Chimni 1993: 447; Hyndman and Nylund 1998: 26; Kirkby et al. 1997: 182–3). By June 1993, some 30,000 refugees had returned to Somalia, 12,000 of them with the UNHCR's support (Hyndman and Nylund 1998: 27). It has been repeatedly noted that many of those who repatriated during that period did so because of the insecurity and deteriorating conditions in the camps, and not because conditions were conducive in Somalia (Waldron and Hasci 1994: 13–15). In 2000, the registered Somali refugee population had declined to some 137,400 and later stabilized at 150,000 (UNHCRa). However, a significant proportion of the departing refugees did not return to Somalia, but continued onwards to Kenyan cities or third countries (Kleist 2004: 9).

Before the influx of Somalis, the Moi administration had drafted a refugee bill that was shelved for over a decade. It was adopted and passed into law in 2006, becoming Kenya's first domestic legal instrument to deal with refugees. Through this law, the government took over the key functions of reception and registration (Kagwanja and Juma 2008: 220, 225). While Kenya never officially designated the camps as the site where refugees ought to stay,[11] the country has implemented a de facto encampment policy since the early 1990s, denying refugees freedom of movement and the right to earn a livelihood—rights included in the 1951 Refugee Convention (arts 17 and 26) (HRW 2009a: 43). The policy has "rested on two pillars: abdication of responsibility to humanitarian agencies, particularly UNHCR, and pushing refugees to the margins of society, away from the main economic activities in farmlands and urban areas" (Kagwanja and Juma 2008: 221). Several measures have been taken to ensure that refugees remain in camps: freedom of movement is restricted through the withholding of proper documentation,[12] the provision of humanitarian aid is generally limited to the camps[13] and the refugee status determination process in Nairobi is cumbersome (HRW 2009a: 43–47).

Kenya has justified its restrictive approach by stating that the scale of the influx initially overwhelmed the country's refugee procedure and that such a large population could only live in camps. The country claims that this policy has to be continued due to security concerns and insufficient burden sharing. While these factors are not insignificant, Milner (2009: 90, 107) remarks that Kenya's asylum policies have also been influenced by historical, domestic and international factors, the vulnerability of Moi's regime and the suspension of international aid to the country.

The Mombasa Camps

We left Somalia in 1992 because of the civil war … We went on a boat. It took around three days to get to a place called Kiunga, a port between Kenya and Somalia. We stayed there for about three weeks. Then we were relocated to Marafa camp, close to Mombasa. I don't remember how long we were in Marafa. After that, we moved to Jomvu, in 1993. We faced a lot of challenges: shortage of food, water, insecurity. There was no school. We went to the *madrassa*.[14] After five years, we relocated again, this time to Kakuma refugee camp. When we arrived here, we faced the same problems again.
—Ibrahim, twenty-four years old

Ibrahim's family was among many families who arrived on the Kenyan coast in the early 1990s. Some newcomers self-settled, mainly on the outskirts of Mombasa. Others moved (or were moved, sometimes by force) into one of the formal or informal camps that had been established in the area (Kagwanja and Juma 2008: 224; Verdirame 1998: 12): Utange, Marafa, Swale Nguru or Benadir, Kwa Jomvu, St. Anne's School or Jelliahda, Hatimy and Majengo (Montclos 1999a: 3, 5; UNHCR n.d.: 1). In 1995, some 75,000 to 92,000 registered refugees were living in the coastal area (Hyndman 2000: 158; Verdirame 1998: 12). The biggest camps, Utange and Marafa, hosted approximate populations of 19,000 and 27,000 refugees respectively (UNHCR n.d.: 1, 3).

These are the camps where most of the refugees who arrived in Kakuma in the late 1990s first lived. For some of those who grew up in camps, this is where their memories start. It is also the birthplace of a number of them. In the accounts of older youth, these camps are often idealized. Even though daily life was not trouble-free, it seemed easier and less constrained than in Kakuma. The proximity to urban areas facilitated relative economic integration and many initially felt more accepted than in Kakuma. Thirty-one-year-old Abdikadir is a Bajuni from Kismayo. He was eleven when his family came to Kenya in 1993. They were met by the UNHCR, the Red Cross and the government:

> They took us to a camp called Jomvu refugee camp in Mombasa. It was located on the top of a hill. From there, you could see the whole town surrounding you and the ocean. That camp was first run by some Islamic agencies. Later on, it was transferred to UNHCR. Sometimes other agencies would come and provide the refugees with something. Life there was much better than in Kakuma. You were living in the city, everything was cheap: the fish, the vegetables, the fruit. Everything you wanted was available … Many Bajuni immediately integrated in Kenya because they had family and close relatives. Bajuni Kenyans have been here for a long time. They are in Lamu, Malindi, all the way to Mombasa. You felt at home. In Jomvu, we didn't feel we were refugees. We did everything that other people did. We were not segregated.

Most of the Somalis arriving in northern Kenya and later settling in Dadaab were of a Darod subclan (Horst 2006a: 47). The population arriving on the coast had a different profile: some were Darod, but many came from coastal minority groups. The main groups were the Benadiri, the Barawa and the Bajuni,[15] at least until fairly significant numbers of refugees started moving by their own means from the Dadaab camps to the coastal ones. There were also a number of Somali Bantus,[16] as well as Ethiopians and Nubi from Sudan (Hyndman 2000: 153; Montclos 1999a: 6, 21).

In Mombasa, many refugees managed to open informal businesses from which to earn their living. In the absence of taxation (as the refugees' businesses were not legal), the camps became attractive economic centers (Verdirame 1998: 12, 33). Even though refugees complained about the lack of education and food, the fact that up to 40,000 people chose to move under their own steam from Dadaab to the coastal camps in 1993 points to the conclusion that life was easier there than in the Dadaab and Kakuma camps (Hyndman 2000: 153). According to a UNHCR staff member in Mombasa cited by Hyndman (2000: 153), the move was also motivated by refugees' perception that resettlement opportunities were greater on the coast.[17]

On the Road Again

In 1994, the government of Kenya asked the UNHCR to close all camps except Dadaab and Kakuma, so that there would no longer be refugees "anywhere in Nairobi or Mombasa" (Parliament of Kenya 1995: 832). Refugees were accused of causing insecurity, harming the Mombasa tourist industry and cutting into the profits of well-established businesses by establishing informal ones (Verdirame 1998: 12). Irritated because refugees would build homes outside the camp boundaries when the camps were full, the host community began burning down houses (Hyndman 2000: 154). The depiction of refugees by the former Minister for Home Affairs and National Heritage to the National Assembly in 1996 is unsympathetic: "They are stateless people, they do not know their destination and they tend to be destructive. That is why we had to close Utange and Marafa Refugee Camps because they were very close to our towns like Mombasa and Malindi, which have tourist hotels because they were a security threat to our hotel industry" (Parliament of Kenya 1996: 485–86).

The camps closed progressively from 1995 to 1999, with forcible evictions by the Kenyan police.[18] More than 11,000 refugees were resettled to third countries (IRB 1999; Montclos 1999a: 5; Montclos and Kagwanja 2000: 220). Those who were not resettled had to choose between repatriation to Somalia or relocation to Dadaab or Kakuma. Such relocation meant that refugees would have little opportunity to support themselves and would have to depend on humanitarian assistance (Verdirame and Harrell-Bond 2005: 33). Most rejected both options. Indeed, neither alternative was satisfactory, as underlined by Abdikadir, quoted earlier. He was fifteen or sixteen when the camps closed:

> The only other existing camps were Kakuma, where there were mostly Sudanese, and Dadaab, where Somalis were living. But in Dadaab there was insecurity. Dadaab is like Somalia and as a minority clan, you cannot survive there. You are being targeted, threatened, killed. Many refugees had gone to Dadaab a long time ago and had many problems. So going back to Dadaab was not an option. And Kakuma, no one knew what it was. When they closed Jomvu [where Abdikadir was living] in 1998, many went back to Somalia, but the Hawiye were there on the coast in Somalia and people could not even reach home.

By 1999, refugees were theoretically no longer living on the coast. Many just "vanished" into the cities of Mombasa and Malindi, and in Eastleigh, the traditionally Somali neighborhood of Nairobi (Montclos and Kagwanja 2000: 220).

The History of an Unknown Place:
Guns, Clans and Other Limited Memories

> We come from Baidoa [in southwestern Somalia]. I know
> nothing about Baidoa, but I watched it on the television
> and I was shown some pictures. Our house is too big.
> Sometimes I imagine staying in this place. My parents say
> that Baidoa was the best city, because the war was not
> reaching. But when it reached in 1995, it killed my sister
> and my uncle, my grandmother and my grandfather. They
> were living in the same city, but in a different house than us.
> That is when we migrated from there. Three of my brothers
> were left behind. I still don't know where they are.
> —Zaynab, eighteen years old

If I had written the history of Somalia and forced displacement based on
the narratives of young people, it would have been shorter and focused on
their families' flight, on tribalism and violence—a violence crystallized in a
few events that led to the departure of their parents and in relatively recent
incidents attributed to al-Shabab. I would have stressed that the country was
perfectly decent before the collapse of Siyad Barre's regime and mentioned
the lack of mourning for some long-gone idyllic past, maybe because the
wished-for ending is not repatriation, but resettlement in the West. Their
family narratives would have fit into a broader historical one. I would also
have spent more time describing the conditions of minority groups, and emphasized the displacement of the early 1990s and the violence of the latter
part of the decade from 2000 to 2010. I would probably not have mentioned
the recent drought. In short, the history I would have written would have
been in broad strokes, enriched with a few significant anecdotes, and more
focused on the very recent past and present. It would have been told by describing a family's path into exile.

A Few Observations on Narratives

Over a decade ago, I accompanied my father on a visit to the hometown of
his Jewish-Hungarian family, Timisoara, formerly in Hungarian Transylvania,
now Romania. He had never been there, as he was born in 1940, two years
after the family's arrival in the United Kingdom. He looked for streets and
parks that he felt he knew intimately, having heard so much about them,
even though he had never seen them. There was a particular park where his
mother used to walk with his older sister. We found a place he thought had
been the family home, but he was not sure. It was set on a square that had

lost its splendor. Even though these are places he did not know, he had vivid "memories" of them.

In Kakuma, listening to youth's autobiographical narratives, I encountered something very similar: while their narratives would be very fragmentary, there would be parts about places and events that they would talk of as if they had been there, even if that was not the case. Nuradin described very precisely how bored his young mother was, looking after the goats in a far-off area of Somalia. Zaynab talked in detail of the house where her family lived in Baidoa. They were speaking of a world they had never known, but which had acquired a material reality through stories of events that happened before their birth, while remaining deeply connected to their present. Hirsch (2012) uses the term "postmemory" to describe this "indirect form of recollection," "the relationship that the 'generation after' bears to the personal, collective, and cultural trauma of those who came before—to experiences they 'remember' only by means of the stories, images, and behaviors among which they grew up. But these experiences were transmitted to them so deeply and effectively as to seem to constitute memories in their own right." Postmemory's connection to the past is thus "mediated not by recall but by imaginative investment, projection, and creation." Hirsch, whose parents were Holocaust survivors, says that certain stories that her parents had told her "were more vibrant and more vivid in [her] memories than moments [she] recalled from [her] own childhood."[19]

Young people's autobiographical narratives about the period that precedes their arrival in Kakuma are remarkably similar and match those of the older generation. They mostly focus on stories shared by their parents that have become the family's narrative thread, in which the individual stories of the family members are embedded and knitted together, becoming intelligible. Their narratives are made up of historical memories they have learned of that serve as a background to their lives, but that they have usually not directly lived.[20] Stories give coherence and continuity to one's life and "shape our selves and the world in which we live," writes Fivush (2007: 46). In this sense, autobiographical narratives go beyond individuals. They are "about the historical time and place within which lives are lived and interpreted" (2007: 52). They are fluid and social, subject to constant remolding through people's interactions and sharing (Candau 2005: 73).

For a number of writers (e.g., Barthes (1966); Mink (1970)), a narrative is a fiction, a representation, or a way of giving coherence to an otherwise messy reality. From this perspective, there is discontinuity between reality and narratives. On the other hand, Carr (1986: 16) argues that narratives are "extensions and configurations" of everyday life, and in that sense there is continuity between reality and narratives. Ricoeur (1991: 188), through the notion of the narrative identity of a person or a historical community that is the "sought-after site of this fusion between narrative and fiction," proposes an apt in-between position in which narratives are neither pure fiction nor continuity. As in fiction, narratives are given a form, events are selected and many are forgotten.

When young people recount the flight of their families, they are telling a story they have shared many times before, in particular to newcomers to the camp and aid workers. It is a well-rehearsed account in which coherence is key, as it is a crucial feature in asylum and resettlement interviews. This is visible in the remarkable consistency of the events chosen and narrated by various members of the same family, and underlines that the context in which a story is told, its tellers and the audience are significant (Carr 1986: 5). There were instances where other members of the community would tell me a different version of the family's past, often related to painful events, such as the departure of a parent from the camp. A number of youths described how their father walked away and never came back. Later I would hear from their friends that the father in question had been resettled with another of his wives.[21] This happened often enough that I started thinking that saying someone had disappeared without saying goodbye was a euphemism for a person who had left the camp and did not send news, not someone who had literally vanished. On at least one occasion, I figured that in interacting with refugees, I was contributing to the revision of accounts. I had asked the journalism students to write an article about asylum seekers arriving from South Sudan. Reading articles mentioning that people had fled because of a lack of access to education in their country, I asked what made someone a refugee. They were uncertain, so I explained why refugees were granted international protection. I noted that the unavailability of education alone would probably not be valid grounds for refugee protection. A few days later, one of the students, a twenty-five-year-old who had arrived in Kenya alone when he was twelve, came to tell me that in fact, he was not a refugee: "I came to Kenya because I wanted to study. I could have stayed in Somalia. Life was difficult, but I was not really unsafe. I just wanted to go to school and there were no schools." I clarified that because he was Somali and Somalis were *prima facie* refugees in Kenya, and thus recognized as refugees in the absence of evidence to the contrary, he was considered a refugee. I added that if he had undergone refugee status determination and said that the only reason for his flight was the lack of access to education in Somalia, he might indeed not have been recognized as a refugee. I imagine that if he were ever interviewed by the UNHCR or a prospective resettlement country, he would rewrite his storyline.

Whether they were there or not, youth often alternate between "we" and "they" when talking about the family's life in Somalia and the departure. Of course, they know that they were not there, but the use of "we" might express the strong relationship between their family history and their current presence in a camp. Bloch (1995) understands the use of "we" in historical family accounts as a way of marking the continuity found between people united by a moral bond.

The Past is a Foreign Country

> Somalia is a foreign country to me, even though I am Somali.
> I know nothing about that place. My parents told me terrible
> things about it. They faced a lot of stress and trauma. Some
> of my relatives were killed. My parents fear to go back and
> think that some people who created problems are still active.
> My parents came from the same tribe as Siyad Barre. That
> is why we were attacked and came here. They are afraid
> that if they went back, they would be attacked again. Maybe
> things have changed: it is now al-Shabab that's killing people.
> Their main target is the youth. I would be afraid to be
> recruited by force as a soldier. Me, I have never carried
> a knife. If I went there, I would fear to be killed.
> —Warsame, twenty-three years old

When I asked young people how they imagined Somalia, they usually began by mentioning violence, tribalism and al-Shabab, blending the past into the present. It is only when I inquired how they imagined the country before the war and what memories their parents had shared with them that they spoke of the magnificence of the country. But the account was generally short and tended to focus on two key periods: when the family fled and the last few years, characterized by indiscriminate violence.

Youth who arrived in Kenya before the age of five usually have no recollection of Somalia and often warned me they had limited knowledge of the country and its history. Having spent their lives in Kenya and been educated according to the Kenyan curriculum, they have learned the history and the geography—and the national anthem—of their country of asylum. In many cases young people also have a limited awareness of their families' path into exile. They attribute this to their fear of reviving bad memories by questioning their parents about the past. A number of parents confirmed these views. The mother of twenty-three-year-old Aziz, for example, said: "I don't like to think about the past. Sometimes, I tell them how we lived and how life changed, how my eldest sister was killed in front of me, how I lost track of their three eldest brothers, my sons, when we fled ... But these are painful memories." Other youth stress that it is not usually the role of parents to transmit family stories, but that of grandparents, who are often absent from the camps: "It is true that the Somali culture is one of storytelling, but normally, it is your grandparents who tell you those stories. If they are not around, you miss the whole thing," explains twenty-five-year-old Hajiro.

Yet in most families I met, youth were acquainted, at least to some extent, with their family history. Miller et al. (2008: 71), speaking of Holocaust survivors, mention three patterns of family communication regarding the parents' experience: a "conspiracy of silence," overdisclosure, and parents who share their experience in a manner that is suited to the children's interest and capacity to understand and tolerate difficult stories. While Somali parents in Kakuma might not enjoy narrating their flight and talking of the past, their children are not completely left in the dark. Similarly, overdisclosure does not seem to be common. In most families, the topic is deemed sensitive, because it is likely to yield sorrow, but not to the extent of being beyond the bounds of discussion. Whereas youth usually speak of Somalia and the departure of their family with a fair degree of detachment, the same cannot be said of older people who have experienced the flight. Young people are sharing a story they have been told. Older people are remembering episodes of a difficult past. In a few instances, older people cried when talking about the life they had in Somalia and the one they were now offering to their children. This sense of loss did not come through in interviews with the youth in regard to Somalia.

The Old Days

Every youth's account of the past is different and individualized, but they also commonly share a number of features. Like their parents, they typically begin their accounts with the description of a beautiful and generous country. They frequently mention that their parents had a good occupation and owned a house, so their families were comfortable. The country attracted tourists and was "the way America is today. There was freedom, you would find women moving around freely at night" (Yasin). Stressing that their families have been better off seems to lessen the disgrace of living in a camp with very limited means, making the story of the past a key device for coping with the present. Once, after spending a full day at home with Aziz's family, I thanked them for their invitation. Aziz responded that they deserved no thanks: they could not invite me to a proper house and drive me home, as they could have done if this had taken place in Somalia. The theme of a "lost paradise," along with the loss of social standing, seems widespread in narratives of exile (Grayson 2009; Meintel 1990: 62–64).

Deeqa was a few months old when her family fled from Kismayo. Her account captures a number of elements that would customarily be brought up when speaking of the past: Somalia's good life, the fighting and the family escape:

[My father] says everything was good, there were cattle and milk, there was the ocean. There was a good president. I think his name was Mohammed Siyad. He was not discriminating people. After that, the people started contesting and fighting. There was tribalism. My grandmother and grandfather were killed in front of my father. He could not do anything. He was hiding. His brother was also killed. My father says we are lucky to be here, that if we had stayed there, we could have been killed. When my parents were coming to Kenya, they were walking. When they reached some place, they got a lift. They lived without registration in Kenya for about two months, looking for a place to settle. Then they heard that some refugees had been registered in the main office and that is when we went to camp Barawa [or Hatimy].

Deeqa's positive description of Siyad Barre is not at all atypical. Such nostalgia for the Barre era, which is usually depicted as a brutal and murderous dictatorship, can in part be explained by the fact that his removal from power signaled the end of what youth describe as a peaceful life in Somalia. It might also reflect the fact that their parents, and the Somali population in general, initially welcomed Barre's 1969 military coup and his socialist agenda—and his expressed will to eliminate tribalism and revive Somali nationalism, as well as to promote the country's self-reliance.[22]

Even though the old Somalia is portrayed in rather positive terms, these accounts are not about yearning for Somalia; quite the opposite. One day, I was discussing their arrival in Kenya with Khadra and Faarax, both in their early twenties. Khadra was explaining that back in Somalia, her father had a good job as a mechanic and a driver. Her parents owned a house:

Khadra: They had everything. But the war came and they ran away. They even left their property there. We no longer have it. They took everything. I hate that place.

Faraax: Do you dislike the country or the fighting?

Khadra: I dislike even the country. I just want a cool place, without any fighting. I don't trust it there. Even if it became peaceful, I would never want to go back.

This reflects a very widespread view of Somalia as an unknown violent country. A number of young people had nothing positive to say about Somalia. Such focus on violence could be in part shaped by young people's will to justify their desire to move abroad rather than return to Somalia. Some would add that they belonged to a minority group, which already made their lives difficult before the war and would make return impossible. The quick leap from the past to the present in Khadra's account is common, possibly because many are more familiar with the recent history of Somalia than that of the early 1990s, but also because the two are closely connected, the past structuring the present.

Unlike Meintel (1990: 64), I did not encounter many narratives that stressed the heroic character of the flight. Displacement is somehow part of life and thus is not an act of courage. It is lived through with stoicism. Nuradin's account of his mother walking for eighteen days without food is rather exceptional. Nonetheless, the resourcefulness of parents in finding a little money or food once they had reached the camp is a common feature of these accounts, as is the idea that they have lost a dignified way of living. The Mombasa camps hardly exist in their narratives. They are only mentioned in passing, possibly because the episode has little relevance in their present lives: most were too young to remember whether life was better there and they are just other camps, a short chapter in their long exile that does not have much to do with the reasons why they are living in Kakuma. Only older youth have more detailed recollections of the camps.

The Past Present

During the period in which I conducted my fieldwork, the situation in Somalia was improving slightly. A new prime minister had just been elected and the government of Kenya had started to call for the creation of a safe zone where refugees could return inside Somalia. This seemed strongly inspired by the unsuccessful Cross-Border Operation of the early 1990s. But violence was still leaving civilians dead or wounded and forcing people to flee. Young people's depiction of the circumstances in Somalia was often oblivious to recent improvements and summarized in a few snapshots: indiscriminate violence; lack of education; early, forced marriage; forced recruitment and ludicrous governance. They would usually not paint an all-embracing picture, but would focus on specific events that they had heard from newcomers to the camp and through the media.

One of the incidents that seemed to epitomize their view of Somalia was the bomb blast that killed more than twenty people during a Benadir University graduation ceremony in Mogadishu in 2009 (AP 2009). The attack was referred to surprisingly often, as if it exemplified not only how ruthless the violence was, but also how improbable education had become. The incident would also be used to illustrate that it would have been impossible for them to grow up, go to school and stay alive in Somalia.

Youth fairly frequently compared notes about the extreme lawlessness of the country and the fanaticism of al-Shabab. I once sat with Nuradin and Mahdi, who were swapping stories. Nuradin related that combatants would sometimes go to someone's house and ask for their daughter. If the father refused, the whole family would be killed: "So you give her instead of having all your family killed. They use her for a month or two and then bring her back saying they no longer want her." Mahdi quickly responded with a story about al-Shabab's farcical zeal: "The silliest story I heard is that samosas [a popular fried pastry usually filled with minced meat] had been forbidden because they are for Christians. It is a triangle. I was surprised, I laughed." I thought this was a made-up story, but it had actually been in the news in July 2011.[23]

Representing Somalia

I realized during my photography classes that while students were perfectly able to identify Somalis on pictures through their features and dress codes, the same could not be said for the country of Somalia. During our first class, while discussing information that can be gleaned from pictures, I showed the students photographs from Somalia and southern Sudan, the countries all but one of the students' families came from. I asked them what the picture was about, who was in it, where it was taken and so on. We started with a picture taken by a displaced teen, showing women and children sitting in a small room made of fabric. I knew these people had fled relatively recently and were living in a makeshift shelter on the road between Afgoye and Mogadishu, so I saw the picture as dire.

Figure 1.1 Displaced people in Afgooye. Courtesy of the Danish Refugee Council/ Zahara

The students said it was a happy picture of Somali women and their children in their home:

Me: How do you know they are Somali?

Students: From their clothing, their features and the way their house is made of fabrics.

Me: What is happening?

Students: Not much, they are resting. They are fine, they are smiling. They are home.

Then we looked at a picture of a Sudanese burial. Again, they had no hesitations: the picture was showing Sudanese men digging a grave in the sand. They knew because of the clothes and the skin color of the men, and they recognized the ritual.

I continued with a picture of the half-destroyed Mogadishu cathedral. I thought they would recognize the building, as it is one of the widely known historical buildings in Somalia. No one knew what the picture was about or where it could have been taken. Once I explained what it was, they looked at the picture attentively and asked about the cathedral. Similarly, when we looked at a photograph showing Somali women carrying loads of grass on a sandy street of Beletweyne in central Somalia, they knew immediately that the women were Somali, but found it hard to believe that the sandy windy

Figure 1.2 The Mogadishu Cathedral. Courtesy of J. Nga

environment they were seeing in the picture, which bore a resemblance to Kakuma, was in fact Somalia.

I later asked the students if they had an old family portrait that they could bring to our next class. Only one student from South Sudan had one. Most of them have never seen photographs of their families before they fled or of the place where they lived. They have mental images based on their parents' stories, but most have not completed them with actual pictures, apart from images about the latest violent incidents they sometimes see in the media. Never having seen the country, they sometimes refer to familiar spots to bring their imaginary Somalia to life. When trying to describe what he thought Somalia would look like, Faarax asked if I had ever been to the area of the camp where new (and better-looking, but still very modest) houses were being built for refugees arriving from Dadaab: "That's how I imagine it." As means of communication are readily available in the camp, their lack of visual familiarity with Somalia was somehow unexpected.

The Way We Would Have Been

> I heard Somalia is a dirty country. It is a bad country. What I
> have seen on TV is miserable. Some people are being slaugh-
> tered like goats. If I had grown up there, I could be a killer.
> —Yusri, nineteen years old

Somalia's recent history has been marked by violence and instability that have forced millions of people to leave their homes. A long journey with multiple incidents and stops brought some to Kakuma. Told in youth's words, this turbulent history becomes a succinct, fluid one that focuses on the period when their families fled and the indiscriminate violence of the last few years. Their account seems to help them cope with the present and guide their aspirations for the future. While their parents' path into exile has affected their own lives and justifies their present situation, the violence of the recent years accounts for their limited desire to return to Somalia. In general, their short narratives are not tales of yearning for their homeland, but tales of relief. They are structured in a way that makes the present bearable by making it clear that Somalia, a paradise that has become a hell, was not the right place to grow up. Indeed, a very consistent feature in their accounts is that their parents' exile was morally justified: Somalia is described as a dangerous place and, had their parents stayed there, they would not have gone to school; they would have become accustomed to violence, been married very young or forcibly conscripted, and might be dead.

Positive developments in Somalia do not significantly alter their perception, possibly because most focus on events that are in line with their narrative.

While a number of family stories are not commonly shared because of their painful character, I do not think they are forgotten. They are part of those postmemories that make people's condition bearable. Remarkably few commiserate on the past and having been forced to flee, although many stress that back in Somalia their parents had a decent life, which seems to restore some dignity to their refugeeness. Their narratives are fairly uniform, probably because they have been shared many times before and are consistent with those of their parents. Most do not see their parents' survival and displacement as heroic, possibly because, regardless of the conflict, Somalis have a tradition of movement and surviving in a challenging environment (Kleist 2004).

In fact, fleeing has not only saved their lives, but is also equated with progress. Unlike the Hutu refugees studied by Malkki (1995b), who had developed a powerful mythico-history and aimed at reclaiming their idealized native land, Somali youth who grew up in camps have little longing to return to an idyllic homeland. Going back to a country labeled as backwards does not fit into their idea of progress. If there is a mythical story about Somalia shared by young people, it is a very succinct one, highlighting that their parents were right to flee and that the further west one goes, the more modern one becomes.[24]

Notes

1. This is based on a UN population estimate of 9.8 million people (UNFPA 2012). In 2013, approximately one million Somalis were refugees and 1,117,000 were internally displaced (UNHCRb, 18 May 2013; UNHCR 2013b: 1).

2. Even though Somalis have often been depicted as a homogeneous population sharing one culture, one language and one religion, approximately a third of Somalis are not from one of the main clans and belong to minority groups. The biggest minority is the Bantu or Mushunguli (15 percent of the Somali population). Small groups (each representing between 0.2 and 0.5 percent of Somalis) include the Bravanese or Barawa, Rerhamar, Bajuni, Gaboye or Midgan/Madiban and Ashraf (UNOCHA 2002: 1).

3. For further reflection and analysis on the strategic motivations of the peacekeeping operation, its racial dimension and its impact, see Besteman (1996a); de Waal (1998); Gibbs (2000); Luling (1997); and Razack (2004).

4. The number of registered Somali refugees in Ethiopia decreased from 514,000 in 1991 to 15,900 in 2005 (UNHCRa). Large-scale repatriation from Ethiopian camps started in 1997.

5. Some returns had actually started to occur, but might have been motivated by deteriorating conditions in refugee camps rather than by improvements in Somalia. In March and April 2012, some 5,200 refugees returned to Somalia by their own means, according to the UNHCR's Somalia population movement tracking. It is not known whether such movements were temporary or permanent. Refugees returning to Somalia cited the

resumption of agricultural activities, but also reduced services and lack of livelihood opportunities in the camps, to explain their decision (UNHCR 2012a: 2).

6. For more on the impact of outside interference in the economy and politics of the country, see Doornbos and Markakis (1994: 84); Samatar (1997); Samatar and Samatar (1987); and Verhoeven (2009).

7. Utange, Marafa and Swale Nguru (commonly referred to as Benadir in Kakuma) are camps that were set up in the early 1990s on the Kenyan coast. All were closed in the late 1990s.

8. This tendency was not peculiar to Kenya. Milner (2009: 18–19) argues that, in contrast to the generally open approach of the 1960s and 1970s, African states became more reluctant to host refugees in the late 1980s and the 1990s because of a changing political context.

9. *Shifta,* a term derived from Amharic, is used in the Horn of Africa to describe bandits or rebels (Whittaker 2008: 6).

10. While Verdirame and Harrell-Bond (2005: 33) suggest that the de facto encampment policy was promoted by the UNHCR and was only adopted by the government for this reason, other authors, including Hyndman and Nylund (1998: 24), Kagwanja and Juma (2008: 220) and Milner (2009: 107), claim it was the government that refused to allow the UNHCR to house refugees in central Kenya and pushed for the encampment of refugees so as to protect itself from a "Somali invasion."

11. Section 16(2) (a) and (b) of the Refugee Act provides that the "Minister may by notice in the Gazette, in consultation with the host community, designate places and areas in Kenya to be … refugee camps" and makes unauthorized residence outside of demarcated areas an offence punishable by a fine of up to 20,000 KSh (approx. US$228) and/or six months' imprisonment. However, such areas have never been designated or gazetted (Campbell, Crisp and Kiragu 2011: 20; RCK 2012: 28).

12. Although the 1951 Refugee Convention (art. 27) obliges states to issue identity papers to refugees, the only documentation refugees registered in Kenyan camps receive is a food ration card delivered by the UNHCR. In the absence of any other document, refugees cannot move freely within the country (a right protected by art. 26).

13. Some refugees with specific health or protection problems or who are looked after by relatives are authorized to settle in urban areas (HRW 2009a).

14. *Madrassa* is the Arabic word for "school." Somalis use it to designate a religious school where children study the Islamic religion and the Koran.

15. The term "Benadiri" does not correspond to any sociological reality, but included a certain class of refugees who were seen as foreigners by the Somalis. In its strictest sense, it applied to half-caste traders who were the first inhabitants of Mogadishu and had settled in a number of coastal cities such as Barawa, Afgoye and Merka. However, it was used by refugees in a broader way, simply referring to people from Greater Mogadishu, including people from majority clans (Montclos 1999a: 2, 5–7; 2008: 296–97). The Barawa also constituted a territorial community, Barawa or Brava, rather than a social group. However, their exodus brought them together and eclipsed the heterogeneity of the group. Like the Benadiri, they define themselves as traders (Montclos 1999a: 2, 5–7, 9–11; 2008: 296–301). Bajuni fishermen were concentrated around the coastal city of Kismayo and the islands of Koyama, Ngumi, Chovayi and Chula. They were perhaps the smallest minority group in Somalia, with a population of approximately 10,000 in 1970. They organized the exile of a number of Darod by boat (Abdullahi 2001: 11; Montclos 1999a: 21).

16. The Bantus, considered non-Somalis and second-class citizens descended from slaves, originated for the most part from Tanzania and settled in the riverine and interriverine

area between the Jubba and the Shabelle. Three-quarters of those who sought refuge in Kenya wanted to "return" to Tanzania. More than three thousand succeeded in getting there, while some 3,300 stopped south of Mombasa (Abdullahi 2001: 10; Montclos 1999a: 11–15).

17. This impression could have stemmed from the targeting of two Somali groups, the Benadiri and the Barawa, for resettlement. Some 3,300 Barawa first left for the United Kingdom in 1995. In the next two years, some 7,900 Benadiri and Barawa went to the United States (Montclos 1999a: 4). The Bajuni complained that they were never considered for resettlement (Verdirame 1998: 13).

18. The first to close was the biggest coastal camp, Utange, home to some 26,000 refugees and nicknamed Mogadishu for its primarily urban, middle-class population from the capital and Kismayo. It was followed by the second biggest, Marafa (UNHCR n.d.: 3). Next was Majengo, a waste ground that accommodated up to 3,800 Benadiri. When Swale Nguru closed in 1997, its population numbered approximately 15,000 people (Montclos 1999a: 3, 5; UNHCR 1998). Hatimy, a camp hosting mainly Barawa refugees, closed in February 1998. Most of its 4,500 residents were resettled in the United States. The remaining refugees were transferred to Kakuma (IRB 1998; Montclos 1999a: 5). In October of the same year, Kwa Jomvu, the last formal camp, hosting more than five thousand Bajuni, was destroyed. Most of its residents opted for repatriation to Somalia (Montclos 1999a: 3; UNHCR 1998: 1–2; Verdirame 1998: 13). St. Anne's School, which hosted up to 2,500 Barawa refugees until August 1999, closed last (IRB 1999; IRIN 1999a and 1999b; Montclos 1999a: 5).

19. For more on postmemory, see Hirsch (1998).

20. In speaking of memories, I am usually referring to social memory, an individual memory that is built on shared information and social and historical milestones. It is a form of memory that varies from one person to another and is in constant transformation through interaction (Connerton 1989: Chapter 1). Collective memory refers to an institutionalized memory that is fixed through an ideological apparatus (Halbwachs 2002 [1925]: 196, 206).

21. Polygamy is customary to the Somali society. Men can marry up to four wives.

22. Socioeconomically, the first years of the revolution are often depicted as positive, with the expansion of education through a literacy campaign (that turned into a drought-relief campaign) and the construction of infrastructure (Besteman 1996a: 587; Samatar 1997: 701–2). The regime's popularity started shrinking in the late 1970s and Barre's rule became increasingly repressive (Horst 2006a: 52–53; Samatar 1985: 24).

23. Reasons mentioned for the ban varied. Some said samosas were banned because of their shape, "linking it to a Christian symbol" (*Daily Nation,* 25 July 2011). Others reported that the ban was imposed because al-Shabab accused traders of using cat meat (BBC 2011b).

24. The uncritical adoption by youth of a language that associates the South with an uncivilized state and progress and civilization with the West is rather disconcerting. I have not found a satisfactory explanation for this, but it would be worth further investigating the influence of aid organizations (and their advocacy against a number of "traditional" practices) and of the dream of resettlement (and the resulting tailoring of speech, especially with a Western researcher) in that respect. Grabska (2011: 87) reports similar thinking from Nuer refugees in Kakuma who "often interpreted the experience of being in Kakuma as the arrival of 'modernity' and 'civilization' into their lives. The English words 'modern' and 'civilized' were often used by young refugee women and men to distinguish their new sense of their identities, and modes of behaviour, from those of people who had stayed behind in southern Sudan."

Chapter 2

KAKUMA IS ANOTHER PLANET

⤶⟡•⟡⤷

> We came to Kakuma from camp Barawa [or Hatimy, one of
> the coastal camps] in 1997. It was such a surprise when we
> arrived here. We were expecting high buildings. There was only
> grass, sand, dust, snakes, scorpions and naked people. Those
> Turkana, we thought they were going to eat us. The same day
> that we came, the robbers came at midnight, shooting with
> guns. Bullets were flying. We didn't know where to run. There
> were not even houses. We were expected to build them. We
> slept under the tree for many nights. We just had to survive.
> —Deeqa, twenty-one years old

The first time I heard this story from Deeqa, I did not know I would be listening to so many variants of the same tale that I would come to understand
it as a foundational story. In addition to highlighting the bareness of the
land, young people speaking of the early days of Kakuma typically related
that the local Turkana community was so destitute and hungry that people
would break into refugees' homes at night not to steal their valuables, but to
drink fermenting *injera*[1] batter. They also told of tall, dark southern Sudanese
refugees fighting them because they believed the Somalis had a brotherly connection with northern Sudanese they were fleeing, due to their similar light
skin and shared religion.[2] Somali refugees recounted that upon arrival, the
hardship was so great that many refused to leave the buses they had boarded
on the coast and that anyone who had the means to do so left the camp
immediately. The story was about how enlightened Somalis, mostly arriving

from urbanized areas on the coast, tamed the "barbarians" and the hostile climate.[3] They would often go on to speak of learning to live together peacefully, establishing successful businesses and becoming the camp's most important national group, while phone networks were being established, contributing to the impression that Kakuma was increasingly connected to the world.

In Dadaab, I had often listened to refugees depicting the early days of the camp in a fairly positive light. A common account would follow that of Isaac, interviewed at the end of 2010 when he was twenty-four: "When we arrived in 1992, life was okay. We received meat, oil, sugar, fish and good education. It started getting bad in 1998. Now, food is bad and not enough and the teachers are not well trained. We used to have land for farming, but it is no longer possible because the locals refuse." In Kakuma, Somali refugees do not idealize the early days of the camp; quite the opposite. This may be because the coastal camps they came from were more hospitable, but also because they turned up in Kakuma in a period when camp conditions throughout Kenya were getting tougher due to budget reductions (Verdirame and Harrell-Bond 2005: 35).

Arriving in Kakuma in the late 1990s, Somalis are a minority in a primarily Sudanese camp. Over the years, the landscape of the camp changes and they become the majority. They do not necessarily feel part of a united community upon arrival. Although they speak the same language and share a nationality, they come from different places and are members of diverse families and clans. In this chapter, I argue that Somalis developed a broad sense of community by joining forces to face adversity together and overcome the camp's foreign and isolating environment, but also by developing a collective narrative of this experience. The process of civilization included triumphing over insecurity, opening businesses and benefiting from functional communications. An increasing Somali presence also played an important role by changing Kakuma's configuration and dynamics. In comparison to the past, the camp has improved remarkably. I contend that the development of a collective narrative of the shared experience of overcoming Kakuma's harshness and the formation of a community are intertwined. While the shared experience brought people together, the collective interpretation and shaping of that experience strengthened social bonds and their feeling of interdependence, which in turn gave rise to an ever more consistent collective narrative.

Hyndman (2000: 139–40), referring to Kenyan camps, writes that "a refugee camp is not a community," but notices "evidence of communal interest and refugee cooperation—organized, for example, among refugees of common nationality, sub-clan affiliation, or proximate physical location." She claims that, unlike citizens who live in communities, refugees who are forced into camps where their movements are restricted and who have no historical relationship to the place where they live (the camp) or any access to land, jobs, resources or livelihoods cannot constitute a community, as the latter must be based on voluntary association. While agreeing that a camp as a whole may not be or become a community, I believe, as Agier (2008: 200–19) or Malkki (1995b: 242–46) have suggested before, that multiple communities are likely to come to coexist in such a setting—probably not from the outset, but as time passes and people develop social ties, share experiences and a common space. Although refugees are not citizens and, while living in Kenyan camps, face serious restrictions to their rights in terms of freedom of movement or livelihood, these are debatable criteria for defining communities. In fact, the shared feeling of alienation may contribute to the formation of a community. McMillan and George (1986: 4) define "sense of community" by four elements: the feeling of membership; influence or the sense of mattering to the group's members; integration and fulfillment of needs or the feeling that as a member of a group, one's needs will be considered; and shared emotional connections through a common history and shared time, places and experiences. I hope to show that these are applicable to the Somali community that has formed in Kakuma and that this formation is closely linked with people's initial experience in the camp, as collectively interpreted and narrated. A number of authors have underlined the role of narratives and memories in the configuration of communities (e.g., Candau 2005: 433; Halbwachs 2002 [1925]). Others, such as Vigh (2006: 19) and Bourgois (2003: 433), have maintained that war and violence can generate a community of experience and bring lasting changes to the social landscape. However, while it has been noted that communities might come to exist in camps, that a shared experience of hardship might be conducive to community formation and that narratives contribute to the construction of cohesive community, the interweaving of these three elements has not been studied as such.

In this chapter, I first present an overview of the changing human geography of the camp over the years. I then consider the remarkably consistent narratives of refugees about the insecure environment in which they first found themselves and its evolution, notably in terms of businesses and communications. Finally, I discuss the cohesive effect of facing a harsh existence together. Although I am mainly presenting the perspective of young people, it is worth noting that their narratives correspond to those of their parents, probably because of the collective nature of their construction. However, their feeling of belonging to a Somali community that at least partly transcends clans is not fully shared by the older generation.

A Changing Landscape

In 1991, about 17,000 boys from southern Sudan, aged ten to seventeen, crossed the border into northwestern Kenya, fleeing the civil war between the northern-dominated national Islamic state and the Sudan People's Liberation Army from the south (HRW 1994: 18–20; Verdirame 1998: 15).[4] In 1992, a camp to house them was set up in Kakuma, located about one hundred kilometers away from the southern Sudanese border and one thousand kilometers from Nairobi. Until then, this poor locality in the Turkana district, with its inclement weather and persistent droughts that rendered agriculture difficult, had been inhabited by between two thousand and eight thousand people (Montclos and Kagwanja 2000: 209; Otha 2005: 231). Within a few years, Kakuma's landscape had radically changed. Not only did trees grow, but shelters also sprang up, as the camp and the village rapidly expanded. By 2000, the town was home to some 40,000 Kenyans attracted by job and business opportunities and the camp provided shelter to 65,000–80,000 refugees. The density of population in inhabited areas of the camp was high: in some blocks, it reached four hundred people per hectare, a stark contrast with the 0.02 inhabitants per hectare in the area (Montclos and Kagwanja 2000: 208). The boys had been joined by other southern Sudanese, as well as 15,000 Somalis transferred from the coastal camps and refugees from Ethiopia and the Great Lakes region (Jamal 2000: para. 15; Montclos and Kagwanja 2000: 209). With the large-scale repatriation of South Sudanese from 2006 to 2008 and the progressive arrival of groups of Somali refugees, the latter became the most populous group in the camp.

Hence, in its first few years of existence, the camp went from a small Sudanese population of 17,000 to over 65,000 refugees of various origins. Some of the first Somali refugees came when Thika camp, on the outskirts of Nairobi, closed in 1995. They were settled with the Ethiopian Oromo and the Sudanese, close to the NGO and UNHCR compound. Unhappy with the locality, many moved to the other side of the main road, around an area that is now known as the Somali market. During the next two years, they were joined by refugees relocated from the coastal camps as a result of the closure of Utange, Marafa and Swale Nguru (or Benadir) (Verdirame 1998: 12). The newcomers were mostly Benadiri and Darod. The Barawa from Hatimy camp came next, in 1998. They were joined by Bajuni refugees from Kwa Jomvu. Somali Bantus and other minority groups were also part of the movement. A number of families quickly left to settle in urban areas. As a result of the growth of population, two new sections, Kakuma II and III, were opened in 1997 and 1999 (the oldest part of the camp being known as Kakuma I). According to the UNHCR, by 2000, 12,000 Somalis were living in Kakuma. In 2002, they were joined by another 12,000 Somali Bantus relocated from Dadaab by UNHCR and the International Organization for Migration (IOM) for purposes of resettlement to the United States—officials feared that conducting interviews in Dadaab with refugees who were targeted for resettlement could create dangerous tensions with those who were not part of the process (IRIN 2002; USCR 2004). Kakuma IV was set up for them. Most of this group departed in the following two years, but those whose applications were rejected usually stayed in that part of the camp (Kagwanja and Juma 2008: 229). Each new section that was opened to accommodate arriving refugees was established next to the one most recently opened, always a little further from the offices of humanitarian organizations and from the town of Kakuma, expanding the camp over more than ten kilometers. Even though all additions were completed by 2002, there are still stark differences between the earlier and later parts of the camp. Kakuma I is undeniably the most populous and richest area, with bigger and livelier markets. The further one gets from the older parts of the camp, the less populated and the less green it becomes.

For a number of years, no significant arrivals of Somalis took place. In fact, following the resettlement of the Somali Bantu, three other Somali minority groups, the Madiban (or Midgan), the Barawa and the Ashraf, were picked out for resettlement from Kakuma. In 2006, a large-scale resettlement program to the United States got under way, targeting Somalis who had been in the camps for a long time. Thousands of refugees left and are still leaving. Thus, Somalis were and remained a minority in a Sudanese camp. Then, following the signing of the Comprehensive Peace Agreement between the Sudan People's Liberation Movement/Army and the Government of Sudan in 2005, the Sudanese started going home. At first, the camp's population shrank quickly enough for NGOs to start scaling down and even to discuss pulling out. "In 2007, the landscape of the camp was totally different," remarked an elected camp leader, Dayib. The population had gone down to just over 60,000, with more than 30,000 refugees having left the camp in the previous two years (UNHCR 2005, 2007b). Another 10,000 would leave in the coming year, before the camp population started growing again (UNHCR 2008, 2009a). "It felt very empty past the main hospital. Former southern Sudanese neighborhoods were suddenly very quiet. Then Somalis started coming. Now, it is crowded again." Starting in 2007, thousands of arriving Somalis, many of them members of the Hawiye clan family, began to arrive on their own from Dadaab, Nairobi and Somalia, advised by refugees in Kakuma that living conditions and resettlement opportunities were better than in Dadaab. They settled in Kakuma I, on plots vacated by departing Sudanese. Others went to Kakuma II, III and IV. The combined movements led to swift demographic change. At the beginning of 2006, 74,000 Sudanese made up 80 percent of Kakuma's population. Numbering 12,600 or 14 percent of the population, Somalis were the second largest national group (UNHCR 2005). By the end of 2009, the balance had tipped. Sudanese were down to some 17,000, or 27 percent of the population, and were outnumbered by the 38,000 Somalis (over 60 percent of the population) (UNHCR 2009a). Some 13,000 of them had been transferred to Kakuma from Dadaab to decongest the crowded camps by the UNHCR, the Department of Refugee Affairs and the IOM during the year (DRA n.d.; UNHCR 2009b). Among the newcomers, some had previously been in the Mombasa camps, had repatriated once and were fleeing again, confirming to long-term inhabitants that their parents' decision to stay in Kenya was a wise one. In late 2012 and early 2013, another two thousand Somali refugees were transferred from Dadaab to Kakuma for re-settlement purposes: Dadaab was deemed too dangerous for officials to visit to conduct resettlement interviews. A number of Somali refugees who were registered in Kakuma but living in Nairobi were also coming back to the camp as a result of a relocation directive by the government. In December 2012, following grenade attacks in Eastleigh and northeastern Kenya, the government of Kenya, holding refugees collectively responsible for insecurity in Nairobi, stated that they should be living in Dadaab and Kakuma camps (Chonghaile 2013; GoK 2012). Kenya did not go ahead with the forced re-location plan, but the directive unleashed a wave of abuses in the form of ha-rassment and extortion against refugees by security forces, compelling many refugees to leave the city (HRW 2013b). Thousands decided to repatriate to Somalia, while others returned to camps where they were already registered (Reini 2013). At the same time, South Sudanese started arriving again in significant numbers. By 2013, the camp had surpassed its full capacity of one hundred thousand people. Somalis remained the largest group, but were no longer the majority, making up 44.5 percent of the population (UNHCR 2012b, 2013a).

A Fluid Human Geography

Kakuma's physical and social landscape has changed significantly since the camp was set up in 1992, as refugees have been arriving and leaving, reflect-ing the ups and downs of Somalia, South Sudan and other countries in the re-gion. The camp not only went from being predominantly southern Sudanese to largely Somali, but also became ever more ethnically diverse. The various groups of arriving Somalis have altered the clan dynamics and intergroup equilibrium over time. Ranking upon arrival often comes up in conversations and the slightest differences count in the self-positioning of refugees. Older refugees see themselves as camp-wise, describing newcomers as unseasoned and still traumatized by their escape from Somalia. Conversely, newcomers emphasize that, unlike those who grew up in the camp, they know Somalia and the Somali culture and language, but also stress that camp residents have had a better access to education and have learned English and Swahili. Maybe more importantly, the length of one's camp stay is used to highlight how unfair the resettlement process is. For example, Xaawo, who arrived in 1995 from Marafa, observes that she is among the Somali refugees who have been in the camp the longest, as nearly all the others have left a long time ago and most of the remaining "old" ones "only" arrived between 1996 and 1998.

In considering the population of the camp, it is important to bear in mind that not all people fleeing end up in a camp, as people try to stay away from them, in part because the UNHCR avoids making them too comfortable so as not to encourage potential refugees to choose asylum (Hyndman 2000: 24). For this reason, many Somali refugees have never lived in a camp, but self-settled irregularly in the vicinity of the border or in urban areas. Some refugees end up moving to a camp many years after fleeing because they have exhausted their resources. For instance, when Aziz's family arrived from Baidoa in 1995, they went to Nairobi, where they stayed until 1998. It was only when they ran out of money that they agreed to go to Kakuma. When the Mombasa camps closed, many refused to be relocated to Dadaab or Kakuma or return to Somalia and simply stayed in one of Kenya's cities until they could no longer bear the expense of doing so. This prompted one of Kakuma's youth veterans, Mahdi, to comment: "Only poor people stay in Kakuma. If you have money, why would you stay here?" He is right: most refugees turning up in camps are poor (a few will manage to get richer while there) and have little education, as educated people are more likely to secure a job in urban areas and thus to settle outside of camps. People avoid camps, but in the absence of any compelling alternatives, after weighing their (limited) options, they may agree to go to one: in a camp, children have access to basic education and, in the case of Kakuma, there might be resettlement opportunities. In some instances, Kakuma may have been specifically chosen because minority groups considered it safer than Dadaab, since resettlement was deemed more likely to happen quickly there as the Somali population was smaller and thus the resettlement process was expected to be faster, and some people had relatives in the camp. In that respect, then, even for the poorest refugees, camps at least to some extent represent a choice (although it is often between bad and worse).

Becoming Kakumians

Somalis who arrived in Kakuma from coastal camps in the late 1990s encountered a mainly southern Sudanese population and an otherwise desolate environment that they would have to make their home by appropriating and shaping its landscape. Landscapes, writes Bender (2002: S104), "never stand still." They are always in the making and the way they are perceived depends on the position of the viewer at that point in time (2002: S106). When he first came to Kakuma from the coast, thirty-one-year-old Abdikadir saw it as "another planet." And it *was* another planet: insecurity was high, the weather harsh, there were no phones, no cars—but things were changing. For one thing, security gradually improved. Moreover, the population kept growing, and so did the proportion of Somalis. There were soon more businesses, telephones, Internet cafés and taxis. A parallel economic system developed, complementing humanitarian aid. Yet, initially, insecurity and fear prevailed and had to be dealt with. The collective narrative of arrival in Kakuma, which developed through an ongoing interactive process of retelling and remodeling the initial experience, emphasizes the ways in which Somalis joined forces to survive. This shared ordeal helped to forge an enduring sense of being part of a community of experience and to generate social cohesion between Somalis. As in any kind of narrative, the story was given a shape; events deemed meaningful were selected, while others were forgotten, reflecting the community's interpretation of a lived reality.

Triumphing over Insecurity

We were living in terror. When we came here, my parents compared the fear with that in Somalia but they said it was better there because at least we could speak with the attackers: we spoke the same language. Here, we couldn't. When you reached the age of eleven, you were put on guard duty. We were doing shifts. You kept hearing that your neighbor had been attacked, that someone was killed in Kakuma I, someone in Hong Kong, another one in Phase I [neighborhoods of Kakuma I]. You could be killed any time.

As is noticeable in Abdikadir's recollections, insecurity features prominently in accounts of the early days in the camp. Young people recount that their families fled from a war zone in search of safety, but found only insecurity. They mention the Turkana who attacked them to steal food or cooking utensils. Many speak of how neighbors were killed in crimes that were never solved. In addition, Somalis often remark that the Sudanese greeted them as potential assailants. They describe how lethal conflicts ended up affecting the whole camp, with entire neighborhoods being burned down. Then, as kids in school, they feared the Sudanese boys, who, besides being tall and the majority, they believed included large numbers of former combatants from the Sudan People's Liberation Army (SPLA) who could harm them.[5]

However extreme this may sound, it is consistent with studies from the late 1990s. At that point, the level of violence in Kakuma was depicted as "unacceptably high" by the UNHCR (Crisp 1999: 16) and merited mention in several reports and research documents (e.g., Crisp 1999; Jamal 2000; Obura

2002; UN General Assembly 2001: 18b; Verdirame 1998). Tensions were acute between the various national groups, between ethnic groups of the same nationality and with the Turkana. Security reports from that period include murders and attacks that seriously wounded dozens of people. For example, in September 1998, a clash between Sudanese and Somalis killed two, and more than fifty houses and shops were burned down in the Somali neighborhood (Crisp 1999: 11). In 2000, four arson attacks in the Somali area razed some seven hundred shelters and displaced thousands (USCR 2001). A security report from 12 August 1999 reads:

> On 6 March 1998, a 40 year-old refugee from Bahr-el-Ghazal [named Mr. []] was shot dead. In the same night, unknown gunmen invaded the Bajuni Somali community and took away 13 goats. On the evening of 9 March 1998, an inter-ethnic fight broke out between Sudanese Dinka Bahr and Dinka Bor, resulting in serious injuries to 155 persons. On the evening of 9 March 1998, Mr. [] was stabbed dead with a sword. On the evening of 15 March 1998, a lone gunman shot a Ugandan refugee in the arm while being pursued by Ethiopian community local guards. On 22 March 1998, at around 18.00 hours, young men of the Sudanese Nuer community attacked the Ethiopian community with traditional weapons and 29 people were seriously injured. (Quoted in Crisp 1999: 3)

At that time, the head of the UNHCR Policy Development and Evaluation Service wrote that the situation kept deteriorating and that, in contrast to other camps where residents spoke of their desire to go home and have better services and assistance, the refugees' focus in Kakuma was on insecurity (Crisp 1999: 3–4). Insecurity stemmed from a number of elements. The camp had been established in a chronically insecure and particularly poor region that was devoid of infrastructure and where state authority was limited (Buchanan-Smith and Lind 2005: 4). The arrival of a sizable population with whom the local community had no ethnic or cultural ties led to a "geographical concentration of the violence" (Crisp 1999: 20). Referring to the Kakuma and Dadaab camps, Crisp continued: "There are simply more items to steal, more people to rob and more women to rape in and around the camps than in other parts of the two provinces." Even though refugees' living conditions in camps were difficult, they were easier than those of the host community: they at least had access to food, water and healthcare. Some could hire Turkana as house-helps, since they had more wealth than the local population (Crisp 1999: 19). This imbalance triggered tensions between hosts and refugees. Within the camp, social cohesion, which tends to characterize peaceful communities, was limited in this very heterogeneous population. In some cases, distrust and rivalries were entrenched between ethnic groups or clans of the same nationality, notably between Hutu and Tutsi from the Great Lakes region, Dinka and Nuer from southern Sudan and Darod and Hawiye from Somalia. Conflict and tensions also developed between national groups, such as southern Sudanese Christians and Somalis, or Eritreans and Ethiopians. To some extent, war remained visible in the camp, as former combatants had settled there and SPLA commanders came to visit their families living in Kakuma. In addition, trauma from the past and frustration linked to encampment sparked violent behavior (Jansen 2011: 86, 91). The accumulation of conflicts and tensions created a very volatile atmosphere that led in turn to further confrontations (Crisp 1999: 25).

Refugees and aid workers claim that from the mid 2000s onward, things improved. The security apparatus was beefed up with an expansion of the police force and the General Service Unit (a paramilitary wing of the Kenyan military and police). Refugee communities created their own security system, protecting their neighborhoods with gates and fences and initiating community patrols, thus creating group boundaries. As a way of easing tensions with the host community, aid organizations distributed rations to impoverished people and children, and provided jobs to those with skills. As the Japanese anthropologist Itaru Otha (2005), who has been conducting research in Kakuma since 1978, notes, social and trade connections that developed among refugees and with the host community also contributed to the normalization of relations: the host community started selling animals and wood in the camp, while refugees hired Turkana for manual work, and sold goods to Turkana and fellow refugees. Thus, despite occasional conflicts, refugees and their hosts found ways of coexisting that were beneficial. These relationships were important enough that an NGO staff member working in Kakuma since 2001 mentioned that when the Sudanese returned home between 2006 and 2008, insecurity in the camp increased, which he believed was a result of the host community's attempt to compensate for their loss of income. Many say that people simply learned to coexist across ethnic and national divisions. Idris, a forty-year-old Somali from the Ethiopian Ogaden (but who grew up as a refugee in Somalia and fled with the Somalis in the early 1990s), recalls that in the coastal camps and in the early days of Kakuma, there were tribal clashes between Somalis: "If something was going on in Mogadishu, people would fight here. It stopped in 2001. People realized they had the same interests and problems. That is when they started saying that they all were brothers and sisters and had to help one another."

When refugees recount their arrival in a threatening environment, it is a story that gives meaning to their lives: they survived danger together by joining forces as a group. They overcame a harsh environment, took partial command of it and invested it with some sense. Moreover, having common experiences and ending up with a shared history and references, they created new communities of experience. Idris' comment is telling in that respect. In the words of twenty-seven-year-old Omar, this forced children in school to look beyond clans and become Somalis: "In primary school, you might find that Sudanese are 105 in a class, while we are three Somalis. This means that even though you are from different clans, you better be friends." Adversity thus led to changes in the spatial arrangement of the camp and to the formation of socially cohesive communities, as camp residents grouped together to protect themselves. "War," writes Vigh (2006: 19), "evidently leads to a (relative) polarization of the conflicting social categories, but it also works on a more subtle level generating social formations and bonds as people find themselves sharing the ordeals of flight, refuge, combat or post-war difficulties, generating communities of experience that are as enduring as they are profound."

Arriving in Kakuma and having to face the Sudanese and the Turkana is the metaphorical war that youth lived through. Even though they grew up away from Somalia, like their peers there, they also experienced insecurity. Violence made daily life difficult, and continues to do so, but, as a side-effect, has helped to recreate communities. "People do not simply 'survive' violence as if it remained outside of them," remarks Bourgois (2003: 433). Indeed, it leaves marks and shapes them. Somalis have united with other Somalis, despite internal divisions, to fight for their survival. This does not mean that internal tensions have disappeared—a number of Somalis from minority groups still feel discriminated against by majority clans, and refugees report tensions over the camp leadership between members of major clan families, the Darod and the Hawiye—but there is a push toward collaboration and unity among Somalis who, to some extent, feel that their national origin has become an important marker and implies a shared fate.

The Pervasiveness of Violence

However, insecurity is not merely a story from the past; it remains a topic of constant discussion and concern. Although people say the situation has improved, they also underline that in addition to community clashes that still occur from time to time,[6] everyday violence[7] is part of their life and impacts their lifestyles as it would in many poor and densely populated areas. When I asked the journalism students to think of possible topics for news stories and features, a significant proportion of them came up with security-related ideas. They reported patterns in insecurity. They noted that the intelligence services of several countries were present in the camp, adding to their discomfort, and that the Department of Refugee Affairs sometimes intimidates refugee leaders. They also mentioned rumors of police officers, dressed in civilian clothes, beating refugees in the camp, incidents that would go unreported owing to refugees' fears and their belief that no in-depth investigation would

What I dislike in This Camp

One thing That I dislike in This Camp is insecurity because There is no security in This Camp. At nigh if youdont closs yourgate, some thieves come They may Kill you or May take all your Properties In your house.

Figure 2.1 Metal gates at the entrance of a neighborhood. Courtesy of Suad

occur. Similarly, when I asked the photography students to illustrate something they disliked in the camp, several talked of insecurity. For example, seventeen-year-old Suad photographed the gates, which are closed at night.

There seems to be a relatively high level of "normal" everyday violence. The house of one of my Somali photography students was broken into one night. The attackers knocked down one of the gates surrounding the house. Instead of reporting the crime to the police, the family built new and higher walls of metal sheets around their compound and mentioned the incident to Somali elders. Another student showed up one day with pictures of a Congolese man who had just been seriously beaten by a mob accusing him of stealing cooking utensils. A young Rwandese once commented on his luck: the police had only abused him once since he had arrived in Kakuma less than a year before. He was beaten for not jumping off the road for a passing police car, and described this as an ordinary event. Another twenty-year-old South Sudanese refugee spent a few days in the communal jail for being in a fight on the basketball court. At food distribution centers and in the Field Posts, it is not uncommon for guards to beat people to force them to stay in line. Yet, the head of protection for the UNHCR, tasked with protecting refugees' rights, remarks that although the police-to-refugee ratio is far below the standard of one officer for 460 inhabitants, the camp is statistically safer than any city of a comparable size in the world. However, it is difficult to assess the reliability of any figures, as a number of crimes appear to go unreported.

Everyday violence means that staying home in the evening is perfectly normal, especially for girls. By 8 p.m., nearly all shops are closed and the market area is deserted. Aid workers are long gone, as they have to be out of the camp by 6 p.m. While boys say they could visit their friends in the neighborhood, eighteen-year-old Luula states that girls do not set foot outside at night: "When it reaches seven our gates are closed. You cannot go anywhere. Maybe boys can, but if you are a girl, you don't step outside to buy something. It is scary. If you go there and you have a phone, you have gold earrings, they will beat you and take them." I could not spend any significant amount of time in the camp after dark. My few visits were with the FilmAid team showing films in the camp at night. The camp was safe enough for people from the surrounding area to come to see the film and walk back afterwards, but all other streets and market areas were deserted.

In general, even during the day, girls avoid walking alone. Many explain that a number of girls have been deterred from attending high school by the long walk through sparsely populated areas that it entails. The walk from Kakuma II is deemed risky: girls say they fear being raped on the way and assert that in the past, there have been rapes in the area. I do not know to what extent this fear is founded on facts, but I do know it is real enough that girls try to always be escorted. For a young woman, living alone is unusual and seen as hazardous. Twenty-three-year-old Zahra is the only young Somali women I met who did so. She is an atypical Somali woman in her blunt refusal to conform to social rules she disagrees with, to the extent that other members of the community say that she is not a "real" Somali. She explained that everyone in the community knew she was living on her own:

> Men are always after you, because they know you are alone, with no parents. They don't have any respect. People know I come home late from work [for an NGO], around ten, when people are already asleep. You never know what will happen to you. It is stressful. I open my door very fast, I make sure everything is ok. But my door is weak. Someone could just give it a quick push and come in.

The sense of security or insecurity creates new geographical and temporal borders within the camp: some neighborhoods are deemed dangerous—more so at certain times of day—and are therefore avoided. This also leads to adjustments in rituals: weddings are sometimes celebrated early so that girls can be home before night falls. Insecurity has also led to changes in the social life of the camp and, paradoxically, has helped Somalis build some social cohesion. They have united with one another, regardless of their clan, to protect themselves from danger. Tensions still occur, but there is a stronger feeling of belonging to a community.

The Development of Business and Communication: The Ethos of Somalis

Let us look back at the arrival of Somali refugees in the late 1990s. In that deserted land, services and commodities are scarce or unaffordable. There is no electricity, no phone network and no means of transport in the camp. But things change progressively. As in all long-term camps, a parallel economy develops in which humanitarian assistance counts as one important resource among several. Because of the importance that Somalis assign to their business and networking skills, the growth of the camp's economy through the opening of shops and the development of means of transport, electricity and communication networks is an important part of the collective narrative of arrival and survival. Like many others, Warsame boasts that "Somalis, wherever they are living, start businesses. They will start with one hundred shillings [approx. US$1.15] and build a real business. People take a few months to learn and then they manage. Now, we are even giving money to UNHCR: we are closing that *lagga*."[8] Before Somali businesses blossomed, there was a thriving Ethiopian market, but Somalis tend to be oblivious to it. In showing how Kakuma gradually took on urban features, I seek to emphasize the role played by the establishment of prosperous businesses by Somalis and the development of communications that helped connect the camp to the world in the process of turning Kakuma into a Somali area.

Upon arrival, refugees had to rely on the support of the UNHCR. People quickly realized this meant being very poor and that aid was insufficient to provide a decent life. Food rations are inadequate: they are meager and contain no meat, no fruit and no vegetables. Children need books, pens and uniforms to go to school. Money is essential for dowries and marriages, and for medical fees, as the camp hospital is deemed to be unreliable. Young people, such as twenty-year-old Khadra, usually remember that period as one of extreme poverty, when they could not afford meat, had to trade a part of their food ration for vegetables and had "no money to buy shoes." Having animals was not an option, as refugees are not allowed to own them in Kakuma; it was feared that this would only increase tensions with the Turkana. And trying to grow crops in such an arid environment is virtually pointless. New arrivals first sell what they have. Aziz's family, for example, was relatively wealthy. His parents owned "a pharmacy, a big house, vehicles and shops" in Somalia. They did not trade everything when the family was in Nairobi, but did so progressively to cover extra expenses in Kakuma. More than a decade later, everything has been sold except their family house in Baidoa. His mother explained that once their belongings were disposed of, she opened a small shop where she sold sugar and water in plastic bags. She was not alone, as many exchanged anything they could. Everything is marketable in the camp, from plots of land to food rations, from tap water in plastic bags to sex. Some with education managed to get a job with one of the humanitarian organizations. They were paid an incentive amounting to a small portion of a real salary. Idris, who had been teaching in Mombasa, was hired as a teacher upon arrival in Kakuma. He received 1,875 KSh a month (approx. US$25, as of 1 January 2000). His Kenyan colleagues received more than six times that amount (Montclos and Kagwanja 2000: 218). In Mombasa, his monthly salary was 4,000 KSh. "Here, you had no other option," he explains. "Even earning fifty shillings was difficult."

In opening stores, Somalis were establishing businesses similar to those of the Ethiopian community, who already had a number of shops, including video clubs, hardware stores and coffee shops—but these were not to the taste of Somalis. By the late 1990s, significant economic activity had built up. Montclos and Kagwanja (2000: 215) wrote that if economic activity were taxed in the camp, it would yield more than two million Kenyan shillings annually (approx. US$27,359 at the end of 1999). Businesses grew and diversified over time. Now, there are butchers, secondhand clothing stores, mobile phone repair shops and cybercafés, among others. Generators were bought, bringing light and television. Changes came gradually. For a long time, bicycles were the only means of transport in the camp, as forty-seven-year-old Guleed emphasizes: "When we first came [in 1997], if someone was sick, we had to carry them on our back. Then we got a wheelbarrow. Then we got a cart, then a bicycle, then motorbikes. Now, we have cars." Dayib recalls that in 2009, a Somali brought the first motorcycle. "The year after, this person bought a taxi. Now, forty taxis operate in the camp, all owned by the Somali community. Only a few people own them, because not everyone has that type of wealth." While I was not able to verify whether all taxis were owned by Somalis, this comment reflects the Somalis' feeling that they have played a crucial role in the camp's economic development. Within a decade, the Somali market was booming and electricity, phones and transport were normal features. Since he arrived in Kakuma in 2003, Dayib says the camp has gone through a revolution:

> Everything has changed, except for the provision of food and water. There was no business in the Somali area and no Somali market, only a few people had phones. People were desperate. The camp was mostly Sudanese then. Minors

Figure 2.2 The Somali market in the early morning. Author's photographs

formed the majority. There were maybe a few thousand Somalis. The Ethiopian market was bigger than this one [the Somali one]. Ethiopians were getting loans from Don Bosco [a faith-based charity that provides technical training in support of livelihood activities] to start businesses, but Somalis don't take loans with interest for religious reasons, so the only real market was Ethiopian. Then the Sudanese started repatriating and more Somalis came. The Somali market is big now. People are doing business, but it doesn't mean that everyone is rich. It is people who went abroad who sent money that was invested into businesses. Money had to come from abroad because in this camp, you can't get capital.

Wealth on a small scale gradually accumulated, altering the geography of the camp. Not all parts are equally developed. Kakuma I is not only more crowded, it is also visibly richer, with bigger markets than other sections of the camp. More people have electricity and houses are larger, with velvet living room sets and linoleum on the floor. A number of refugees explain the prosperity of the Somali neighborhood there by the fact that many of its first residents were of the Darod clan family who had a better social network, with

relatives abroad, and they benefited from remittances that helped them start businesses. Somalis say that when the Somali Bantu started leaving in the early 2000s, the same phenomenon did not occur; money did not flow back to the camp. At a later stage, when new refugees, mostly from the Hawiye clan, arrived in Kakuma, they came with money and were also able to open shops. But as a Somali man explains, "they could not compete with the Darod who control all the banks in Kakuma, all [located] in Kakuma I. That is the only place where you can receive money. And Hawiye are scattered in the camp: they had to settle wherever space was available."

As Dayib remarked when talking about the wealth of taxi owners, disparities in the distribution of wealth are part of camp life. A Somali woman summarized the socioeconomic landscape as follows: "There are three categories of people in the camp: those who don't eat three times a day, those who have improved their living standards and those who have good lives." This illustrates once again that not all refugees rely strictly on the UNHCR's assistance, which would make them virtually equal in terms of wealth. This gives refugees a certain latitude and autonomy, particularly at the community level. For example, Somalis deem the health services offered in the camp to be inadequate. When someone is severely ill, money is raised in the community (as well as abroad) to pay for better healthcare outside of the camp.

Figures 2.3 and 2.4 A part of the Somali market and a Somali shop. Author's photographs

Even though Somalis had opened businesses previously, most say that major changes got under way in 2006 when many of their compatriots were resettled to the United States and began sending money back. Interestingly, 2006 is also seen as the point when trade began to decline for non-Somali business owners, as they were losing customers with the southern Sudanese going home. This highlights the interconnection of the camp economy with events beyond its borders. Furthermore, the widely scattered Somali diaspora[9] played an important role in the development of Somali businesses, and camp residents remarked that the 2012 relocation directive was affecting the economy. Refugees now returning to the camp from Nairobi had previously been transferring money to Kakuma to support their relatives. Their spending was benefiting Somali businesses in the camp. Once they were back in Kakuma, they were no longer sending money, which meant less money was circulating in the camp.

Somalis Call the World—and Call Home

In Kakuma in the late 1990s, there were no televisions and no phone network, which contributed to the feeling that the camp was "another planet." Abdikadir recounts:

> We didn't know what was happening in Nairobi. Someone had to come from there and tell you what was happening. At night, you might hear KBC [Kenya Broadcasting Corporation]. Sometimes you would get the BBC Somali services and Arabic BBC. That was the only way to get news. TV was not there. Star FM [the Somali-language radio station] only came recently. Later on, people brought Arabic [satellite] dishes so we would go to certain hotels to see the news. But that was just sometimes.

In the absence of cell phone communications, there were radio communication transmitters (*taar*) that could be used to contact Somalia, Nairobi and Dadaab to pass on information or wire money.[10] "You could call America, but it meant being put through to Nairobi, then Nairobi would call America by phone and put the phone on the radio. The communication was bad and expensive," explains Dayib. Some used the mail, as it was cheaper (but also much slower). It was not until 2004 that the cell phone network started covering parts of Kakuma (KANEBU 2004: 7). Initially, calls could only be made from a few spots in the camp. Then the coverage expanded. With the network came new business opportunities: phone repair and sales shops, phone charging and the sale of phone credit.

Cell phones helped to connect Kakuma to the world and, as twenty-one-year old Xaawo points out, facilitated communications "with those in Canada and the U.S. who can help by sending small amounts of money." The Internet soon followed. Internet cafés opened in the camp before NGO offices even had proper Internet connections; NGO staff would go to the camp to use the Internet. When M-Pesa, a popular Kenyan money transfer system operated through cell phones, was launched in the late 2000s, it could be used in the camp. Today, nearly everyone has a cell phone, which often gives access to the Internet, and many households have a television, thanks to the generators providing electricity. Somalis hold their oral culture in high esteem and claim that they were one of the driving forces in the development of telecommunications in the camp. Such global connectedness was key to overcoming the isolation of the camp.

Forever Visitors

Regardless of how accurate this account of Somalis overcoming a difficult and foreign environment and ending up in control of most of the camp economy may be, it is a central one in their folklore. Somalis fought their war, which bound the community together and gave them a shared experience of surviving harshness and isolation. Having been there in the old days confers experience-based authority over newcomers. The process encompassed the development of businesses and communications, as Somalis pride themselves on being entrepreneurs who dislike working for others and can thrive in any context, as well as valuing their orality. The growth of the Somali presence, which led to changes in the camp's dynamics and landscape, also contributes to the impression of having tamed Kakuma. A remarkable feature of these stories is their consistency. While everyone's experience is necessarily unique, the same elements are usually mentioned. Others are undoubtedly left out. This suggests that the account has been built collectively through the sharing of memories and stories, and does have a uniting effect.

If we consider McMillan and George's (1986) definition of "sense of community," Somalis who have been in Kakuma since the late 1990s have come to form a community. To some extent at least, most feel they are part of the Somali community rather than strictly belonging to a particular clan, and interact accordingly. The initial experience of violence has precipitated the community formation by compelling people to unite in the face of adversity. Hence, while violence can have a very disruptive and destructive effect, it can also instill solidarity. For Somalis, the development of a collective narrative of their experience has solidified this cohesive foundation and instigated meaningful relationships, which in turn has strengthened the unity of the narrative. Although clan and internal tensions have not disappeared, there is a sense, especially in the young generation, of belonging to a larger group of people, the Somalis, sharing a language and a culture and bound by their collective survival.

The fact that Somalis managed to turn Kakuma into a livable setting does not mean that they find it suitable. As an elderly woman who had arrived from Swale Nguru camp in 1997 sorrowfully remarked:

> You, you can go anywhere because you have a passport. Us, we cannot move around. Some of us have not even been to Kakuma town. If you have no fire-wood, you cannot go out to fetch some. It is a prison. These shops, these cars, all those things, it is not real business. It is entertainment. If Kenyans decide that we have to leave, we will have to. If there is a conflict with the host community, we must bend. This is not our country. During the [2013 presidential] elections, some people from the host community came and said: "If you have to go home, I will take this house or that shop." Kenya is tired of us and wants us to go home. We are forever visitors.

Notes

1. *Injera or canjeero,* a Somali staple and most common breakfast food, is a pancake-like bread made from a fermented mixture of wheat flour and water.
2. Sudanese refugees in Kakuma have mostly fled from the south of Sudan (now South Sudan) because of the civil war opposing the north and the south.
3. Although I evoke Kakuma's wilderness and I use terms such as "civilized," "barbarians" and "progress," which are strongly reminiscent of the racist dichotomy between the exotic primitives living in some state of nature and the moderns, dear to the evolutionary anthropology of the nineteenth century (or to current proponents of a clash of civilizations; see Razack (2008: 148)), I am not suggesting that human societies are expected to develop in a given direction, from a premodern state to a modern state—thanks to technology and Western influence. I am using this language as it was literally used by Somali youth, but also because it conveys their idea of progress as taking them closer to the West, but without renouncing their way of living and being.
4. The boys, popularly known as the "Lost Boys," arrived in Kenya after a long trek that had first taken them to refugee camps in Ethiopia, back to Sudan, then to Kenya. Many had fought and been orphaned during the Sudanese civil war (HRW 1994: 18–20).
5. While the perceived threat was possibly inflated, it is likely that the camp was, at least to some extent, militarized and under the command of the SPLA (Polman 2010 [2008]: 110).
6. For example, in early 2012, a fight between children playing football sparked a community conflict between Sudanese Nuba and the Dinka that killed one. In June 2013, fighting between Sudanese Murle and the Nuer killed six (email from the UNHCR, 23 June 2013).
7. I borrow the concept of "everyday violence" from Bourgois (2003: 426), who, drawing from Scheper-Hughes, defines it as: "Daily practices and expressions of violence on a

micro-interactional level: interpersonal, domestic and delinquent. [The concept makes it possible] to focus on the individual lived experience that normalizes petty brutalities and terror at the community level and creates a common sense of ethos of violence."

8. *Lagga* is the word commonly used to designate the Tarach river, a seasonal stream that runs along the camp and all the way to Kakuma village. It is usually empty, but sometimes floods, destroying refugee and Turkana shelters. Somali refugees initiated the construction of a dam to prevent flooding with their own money. They later went to the UNHCR and were given funding to continue the project.

9. The Somali diaspora beyond neighboring countries is important but precise figures are not available, as this information is not necessarily compiled in a similar manner by all countries. Key settlement countries include the United States, the United Kingdom, Canada, the Netherlands, the Scandinavian countries, South Africa and the Gulf States (Moret, Baglioni and Efionayi-Mäder 2006: 15). More than 100,000 live in the United States (Yamamoto 2011). The United Kingdom is home to an estimated 90,000 Somalis (Sheikh and Healy 2009: 9). Up to 100,000 are said to live in Toronto, Canada (Hammond 2007: 131). Another 100,000 are estimated to live in the Gulf States (Sheikh and Healy 2009: 8).

10. In *Transnational Nomads,* Horst (2006a: 141) quotes a Somali living in Nairobi relating that Somali refugees brought the first radio sets to Kenya in 1994. They have been used to stay in touch and send small sums of money, but also to trace relatives.

Chapter 3

GROWING UP IN KAKUMA

This is Home

❧⊙•☙

> I have been [in Kakuma I] since I was a baby. I have never
> been anywhere else. I went to Kakuma II for the first time for
> the journalism class a few months ago. I have been to
> Kakuma town: I went to school there for a while. I faced
> many problems here, but this was always my place, my home.
> —Mahdi, twenty-one years old

In principle, a refugee camp is conceived of as an "ideal" temporary arrangement that, in an emergency situation, makes it possible to streamline efforts to feed, care for and protect a refugee population. In practice, this translates into a setting where living conditions are so difficult that they affect people's physical, mental and social wellbeing. Many authors have underlined that conditions in camps are not only difficult, but also violate refugees' rights.[1] In *Rights in Exile* (2005), Verdirame and Harrell-Bond give a comprehensive catalog of human rights abuses faced by refugees living in camps in Kenya and Uganda. They document breaches to the right to work and to freedom of movement, insecurity, reduced legal recourse for refugees, arbitrary arrests and detentions, and constraints on political activities and freedom of expression and association. They point out that the right to adequate living conditions, including food, clothing and housing, is also violated:

> In order to gauge the standard of living of refugees, [UNHCR] has normally used as a yardstick the "economic level" of the local population, which, since all societies are economically differentiated, has in practice meant equating refugees with the poorest segment of the host population. For refugees in Kenya and Uganda, this situation—combined with the encampment policy and restrictions on their freedom to seek paid work or self-employment—meant that they were unable to achieve anything like an adequate standard of living. (2005: 226)

Respect for the right to education (understood as primary education, since that is the only portion made compulsory by the Convention on the Rights of the Child [Article 28]) is imperfect, as education is not considered a priority by humanitarian organizations in emergency situations. Access to high school is limited, and to university exceptional. Verdirame and Harrell-Bond conclude that the camp is "as irreconcilable with economic, social, and cultural rights as it is with civil and political rights" (2005: 264) and that refugees' rights are more at risk in a camp than when living illegally outside a camp.

Such human rights abuses are not negligible, since they significantly circumscribe refugees' prospects. The interdiction against moving freely makes it impossible to resume a relatively normal life by legally integrating locally. Bans on engaging in agricultural activities, operating a lawful business outside of the camp or being gainfully employed have a similar effect. The reduced educational offer affects academic development and thus occupational opportunities. Also, in the absence of a clearly defined legal status, refugees do not have the right of residence and cannot apply for citizenship in the country where they live. Finally, refugees' involvement in political activities is restricted because of the limitations placed on civil and political rights (Crisp 2003: 11–12). Even the UNHCR (2004: 1) considers that camp life boils down to a "long-lasting and intractable state of limbo."

Hence, camps are incompatible with healthy child development. However, people's experience cannot be reduced to a list of human rights violations. Somalis who settled in Kakuma when they were children and have been refugees for as long as they can remember saw the camp as an ordinary setting for a long period of time. Many only formed the opinion that it was a difficult and unusual environment in which to grow up when they became older and started looking back at their childhood and exploring their options for the future.

In this chapter, I reflect on the experience of growing up in Kakuma. I argue that youth mostly begin resenting limitations on education, freedom of movement or work when educational opportunities are exhausted and resettlement prospects remain unclear. The comparison with fellow refugees who have left often intensifies their discontentment, while changing family dynamics add a layer of stress. Having been educated in Kakuma, the young people tend to be more capable than their elders of navigating the humanitarian system and Kenya, and thus are often the ones expected to earn money for the family. At the same time, limited job openings make it difficult to become an independent adult and many feel that once they have completed their education, they must find a life outside of Kakuma. I first consider the "normality" of the camp and its routine. I then discuss young refugees' experience of education, both because going to school filled their days and also because refugees often center on education, as they see it as a means of transcending their condition and achieving a fulfilling life. In fact, young people often cite education and resettlement as the only two things that can be gained from being in Kakuma,[2] even though access to quality education for school-age children is anything but satisfactory.[3] I then look at what happens when education is over. Of the young people I came to know who had grown up in the camp, some were still in primary or secondary school, but they were a minority. Most had either completed school or had dropped out. Some were working or looking for work, while others were seeking opportunities to study further. I conclude with observations on how camp life makes coming of age difficult. Although young people's socialization is an important part of their experience of growing up in the camp, I do not develop that theme here, as it is the subject of the following chapter.

An Unlikely Home

For most parents arriving in Kakuma, the setting initially felt terribly unfamiliar. "It filled me with fear," recalls Amina, who settled in Kakuma in 1998. "I had small children who could not escape if anything happened. But we had to survive. We had no time for feelings. I made myself strong. I took my two youngest children to the nursery school and the older ones to primary school. UNHCR gave us some material and we built our house. Life was very hard. It still is." Their children were also facing difficulties. They were sometimes hungry, they did not get along with the Sudanese children, the weather was unpleasant and they disliked the insecurity, but this was the only environment they had ever really known, so there was not really any better place to compare it to. It just felt normal. They had a small house, most went to school every day, had friends and lived with their families. Although a refugee camp appears an unlikely home, it became one. To some extent, the camp was an ordinary city with schools, roads, a hospital and clinics, market areas, churches, football fields and distinct neighborhoods. In fact, if the camp were considered a Kenyan city, with a population of 115,000 people, it would be in the top twenty-five urban areas of the country by size[4] (Kenya National Bureau of Statistics 2009). "But of course," write Montclos and Kagwanja

Figure 3.1 A part of Kakuma I from above. Author's photograph

(2000: 208), "it is urban dwellers and not statistics that make a city; Rousseau would have even mentioned 'citizens', a term that hardly corresponds to the tragic fate of refugees."

Unless they were the heads of their families, as long as they were in school, children were somewhat sheltered from the camp reality and its imposed routine by their parents. When the photography students illustrated a day in their lives, school and related activities, such as washing their uniforms, doing their homework and walking to and from school, figured prominently, as did fetching water and cooking. Even though they were no longer small children, education still gave a feel of normality to their lives and occupied most of their days.

The importance assigned to education is so great that a number of young people, such as twenty-three-year-old Abdi, explain they are still in the camp because of their studies:

> I know people who left for South Africa. One of them told me that he now has a big business. He said he worked for nine months when he first arrived and he was well paid. With that money, he was able to establish his own business … [He] was encouraging me to come: "Talk to your relatives, tell them there is work for you in South Africa." But I don't want to go. I want to learn. I don't want a job without education. One day, people can rob you. Your mobile, your computer, they can be taken away. But if you are a lawyer, a doctor, no one can

take your knowledge away. So I want to learn first, materialize my ambitions. My friends say I am a dreamer and that my dreams are too far.

This focus on education is not particular to Kakuma or to refugees. Writing about refugees in the United Kingdom, Stevenson and Willott (2007: 676) make a comment that would apply equally to Somali youth in Kakuma: "All of the individuals interviewed spoke about their high aspiration for themselves and their desire to use higher education as a route out of poverty and exclusion and as a means of establishing a better and more secure way of life for themselves." Chatty (2010b: 336–37) makes a similar observation with Palestinian refugees in the Middle East, and Finnström (2006: 204) with a nonrefugee population: youth in Uganda.

Learning in Less than Ideal Conditions

Upon arrival in the camp, most children were enrolled in crowded schools where they followed the Kenyan curriculum. Somalis often describe their first years of schooling as a taxing socializing experience. They were a minority in a mainly Sudanese camp: "We had to go to school with [the Sudanese kids]," Khadra recounts. "They were always beating us. We were scared: they were tall." Sometimes there was no shared language between students, or between teachers and Somali students, as Abdikadir relates: "I went to school in Hong Kong [a neighborhood in Kakuma I that was mostly inhabited by Sudanese] and could not understand the teachers. Most of them were Sudanese. They didn't speak Swahili. They spoke English, but their English was very difficult for me." To manage, many children went to private afternoon classes taught by high school graduates.

Parents who had the financial means to send their children to nonrefugee schools outside the camp where the quality of education was deemed better did so. Abyan and Amran, aged seventeen and eighteen, are sisters who were raised by their grandmother. Amran relates: "When I was seven, I joined Gundeng primary school [in the camp]. It was not nice. We sat on the ground and the teachers were not good. In class 3, we went to a private school in town. We didn't have a scholarship. All our family members contributed so we could go." After finishing their primary school, they were admitted in two of the top Kenyan national high schools, where they completed their education.

The passage from primary to secondary school was (and still is) often difficult, as the secondary schools did not have the capacity to receive all the children graduating from primary school (UNHCR, UNICEF and Education Partners 2012: 20).[5] Thus, only the top students would be offered a place, and those who were not admitted in a given year would not be accepted subsequently either. In theory, rejected candidates could enroll in a Kenyan school, but that entailed paying school fees, which was not always an option parents could afford. Moreover, while primary schools were usually not far from the children's homes, there were only one or two secondary schools (depending on the period), which, for most, required walking a long distance at dawn. Twenty-one-year-old Awo is known throughout the Somali community as the outstanding Somali girl who got a university scholarship to Canada through the World University Service of Canada (WUSC). She describes her high school experience:

> I went to Kakuma secondary school. That year, there was no scholarship to study outside the camp, so everyone had to go there. I was lucky to be admitted. Many students were not. That is when the UN was sending the Sudanese back and they were not allowed to enroll in school.[6] It gave us space and that is how we managed to get in.
>
> Studying there was hard. Sometimes, the river would flow and you had to wait until it went down before you could reach school. Otherwise, because the school was far, you had to wake up very early and be on the road by 5:30. It was dangerous. You would hear of people being raped and robbed on the way, but you had to handle it. Most of the time our father walked with us, but he is old, so sometimes he was tired or sick.
>
> My sister and I, and another lady and her sister were the only girls from this area going to secondary school. In our class, there were two Burundian ladies who dropped out. They said they feared being raped. Many of our community members, when their girls passed their KCPE [Kenya Certificate of Primary Education], they refused to let them study further. It was hard, but with a lot of commitment, I was able to make it. I think that children go to school if their parents support them. Our parents, they always told us to continue, that it was our future. Sometimes they would not buy food or other commodities to be able to buy books for us.
>
> I was always doing my best, but performance is hard here. In Form I and II [the first two years of secondary school], you must get a good foundation to perform later, but teachers are mostly the WUSC students who leave in the middle of the term. Once they leave, you have no teacher for weeks or months. So in the end, you can't cover the whole syllabus. It is only when you get to Form III and IV that you get Kenyan teachers. They put you under a lot of pressure because they say that you have to be ready for Form IV exams [the end of secondary school exams], but you didn't get a good foundation.
>
> Now, school is held until 4 p.m. But before, it was only until 1:40 p.m. In the afternoon, you did your own work. Most days, we stayed in until 6 p.m. and organized our own classes. Sometimes we went to school on Sunday. If you were good in a subject, you taught others. Sometimes we asked teachers to help us. They would stay after hours, but we had to pay for their food and their transport. We each contributed three hundred shillings per term.
>
> The dynamic between students was fine and being a girl was not an issue. In Form IV, we were thirteen girls out of eighty-five students. I had been aware

that I could get a scholarship since I was in primary school: many of our teachers would tell us to get good grades so we could leave the camp.

Awo is unusual in that she is a girl and a Somali, two underrepresented groups in school, especially at the higher levels.[7] Teachers explain the relatively limited presence of Somalis by their lack of interest in more than basic education. While many girls go to primary school, only limited numbers continue to high school, as they are expected to help at home and marry young. A number of parents also refuse to send their daughters to mixed secondary schools, whereas most agree to do so at the primary level. Security threats and inadequate facilities to accommodate girls' health needs, early pregnancy and lack of material support are also obstacles to education. Low enrolment, attendance and levels of retention, especially for girls, are found in most camps in the world (Dryden-Peterson 2011: 6; UNHCR et al. 2012: 22–23).[8]

In addition, like her other siblings, Awo never interrupted her studies, which is also uncommon; not many children go to school continuously in the camp. Some stop because of financial problems. For example, Axlam explains that her family could not afford to send all the children to school at the same time:

School is free in the camp, but you need books, a pen and an eraser. Each book is ten shillings. You need ten. Then you need a bag. That is two hundred shillings. It makes three hundred shillings in total. We were eight children in my family. It makes for a lot of money. So you have to sacrifice and rotate. When I was in school, others were not going to school but only to the *madrassa*.[9] Now, I am helping them to go to school.

Children also put their studies on hold when a parent is sick and needs help or when the family moves out of the camp temporarily.

In other cases, young people explain that they simply lost interest. Hamra is nineteen and in her fifth year of primary school: "I stopped for some years because I didn't have the morale to study, I didn't have enough food. Some of my colleagues were leaving for Europe and it was affecting my morale." This, combined with the fact that many children start late or have had to stop studying because of war or, once in the camp, are delayed by having to learn a new language, means that many of the pupils in primary and secondary school are well beyond the normal age in the Kenyan system.[10] Many of those who interrupted their studies never went back to school, as Abdikadir recounts:

In 1998, when we started school, we were about five hundred [Somalis]. Some of the kids said they could not learn in the camp. They gave excuses: "It is hot, windy, there is insecurity." Only twelve out of the five hundred who started primary school went to secondary school. Out of those, seven finished. Some girls were married. Some went to Nairobi. Many were moving around, which meant that they kept missing class and ended up stopping.

The head of education at the LWF estimates that around a third of the students who start their secondary education in Kakuma complete it, while the vast majority of those who study outside the camp with a scholarship (and were often already top students in primary school) do so.[11] As Abdikadir underlines, not all the missing students have dropped out, as some switch to schools outside the camp or leave Kakuma. Reasons given by Somalis to explain this low level of retention include a lack of financial support, the fact that many decided to work rather than study, family problems, the dearth of opportunities after school and the availability of humanitarian assistance that deters students from working hard. "At the end of the day, you know you will eat," remarks Abdulaziz, a twenty-year-old Ethiopian. "You will have clothes and a shelter. Nothing makes you worry. Nothing makes you work extra hard."

The low level of completion is relatively surprising, as young people repeatedly underline the importance of education. Those who finished their secondary education stress that their parents pushed them to do so. "My mother used to tell us every morning at five, before we went to school: 'If your father and I die today, you will have your education to rely on,'" recalls Aziz, Awo's brother. Only a minority have parents who have studied. More have parents who regret not having been able to study for long enough.

After High School: Chasing Higher Education and Training Opportunities

For most of those finishing high school, this marks the end of their formal education, at least for as long as they are in Kakuma. Indeed, although higher education for refugees is deemed important for fostering leadership in protracted situations and for postconflict reconstruction,[12] opportunities for postsecondary learning are very limited, which is true for most camps (Dryden-Peterson 2011: 52). A few individuals nonetheless manage to pursue higher education, either with a scholarship, though distance learning or, in exceptional cases, with the support of the community or relatives. Except for the latter group, only the top students can hope for such opportunities and, while they are registered in Kakuma, most of those securing scholarships studied outside the camp thanks to a secondary school scholarship or private funding.

Some thirty students aged eighteen to twenty-five, out of approximately 130 applicants, are selected annually to go to Canadian universities through a WUSC program administered by the NGO Windle Trust. Of the students leaving in 2013, only two, a boy and a girl, Awo, had completed their education in the camp. Awo was also the only Somali who made it, the majority being South Sudanese. There again, girls are in the minority. Out of the thirty students, seven were girls, despite affirmative action measures: in order to qualify, boys must have graduated from high school with a B, while girls need a C+. When funding is available from the DAFI program (the German acronym for the Albert Einstein German Academic Refugee Initiative), the Windle Trust also awards a few scholarships to Kenyan universities. In 2012, two hundred people applied for the two available scholarships.

The WUSC scholarship is often seen as the only way to get a decent higher education and thus students who do not get the necessary grades to be eligible sometimes become incredibly distraught. Xaawo is one of them. She graduated with a D+ in 2011. As she was convinced her only hope was to get a scholarship, she managed to secure enough money to enroll in a school outside the camp so that she could repeat her final exams. But she did not get a C+. When she received her results, she sent me a desperate text message saying she no longer had a future.

Xaawo might have been able to enroll in higher education in the camp, but was not interested by the disciplines offered and, more importantly, longed to leave the camp. Indeed, since 2010, the charity Jesuit Refugee Services (JRS), in partnership with Jesuit Commons—Higher Education at the Margins and Regis University, in Colorado, has been running a pilot project, offering a distance learning university diploma in liberal studies, with a specialization in education or business. Professors are based in the United States and courses are given online. Approximately 250 people have applied each year for the thirty-five available places. There as well, the administrator of the program remarks that those who are selected "are often refugees from families with more money who studied outside Kakuma or refugees who completed their secondary education before coming to the camp." Again, although they are admitted with a slightly lower level, women are underrepresented, as not many apply. They account for one student in five. While conditions are not ideal—the learning material is sometimes delayed and refugees do not have computers or proper access to the Internet at home—students are very enthusiastic about the program and are proud that their diploma will be from a U.S. university, Regis. Even if the administrator of the program comments that students might not be able to fully apply their newly acquired knowledge in the camp, she feels it is worth it—in part because students gain skills that will be useful outside the camp, but also because students value their learning tremendously.

JRS also gives short courses in business and community-based development, psychosocial case management and primary education. Classes target high school graduates, but students who prove their ability to follow without having completed secondary school are admitted. Up to 150 students are trained every year—many more apply. LWF, in collaboration with the Kenyan Masinde Muliro University of Science and Technology, has started offering a one-year diploma in primary education to its teachers. FilmAid trains a number of students in participatory video production and the NGO International Rescue Committee offers medical and laboratory training. In addition, technical training classes in areas such as carpentry, computers, electrical and metalwork or tailoring and dressmaking are offered by Don Bosco to up to a thousand students a year. In all of these courses, Somalis and women are underrepresented.

There are thus a few options at the end of secondary school, but choices and places are limited. Many young people talk of their desire to study fields that are not offered in Kakuma: psychology, history, political science, sociology, medicine and engineering. The ambitions expressed often have little connection with what one can realistically do in the camp and, very likely, even outside of the camp. Sooner or later there comes a point when a student's education is finished. And while education is not necessarily an easy task, beyond that point, things seem to get darker.

When School is Over: The Tipping Point

> When I was in Grade 6, my refugee classmates started going abroad. I wanted to go, I was wondering why I had to stay here. We were called for a [resettlement interview], but nothing happened. Now, all the students I learned with in primary school are gone. I have no friends here. I really want to go. I know I can't study here. I want to go to a good university.
> —Amran, eighteen years old

Amran, who had just finished high school, underlines two important elements. First, the views of many on the camp changed with the large-scale resettlement of Somalis to North America that started in 2006. Leaving for the West became everyone's focus, and contacts with resettled refugees increased people's knowledge of global possibilities. Second, while the camp was imperfect before, it feels worse when education comes to an end. School was tough, but it kept people busy. When it is over, impatience sometimes becomes overpowering, as promising possibilities and resources are scarce. Without the right to work or move freely, and given the unlikelihood of naturalization, Kakuma cannot be a place where young people want to put down roots.

This is the moment when, in the words of a Somali elder, "youth start sitting idle, which might compel them to use drugs and nurture bad habits." Idleness, often coupled with drug abuse, insecurity and early pregnancy, are probably the words most commonly used to describe the young generation in the camp. A few initiatives are taken to keep them busy, mostly through short training sessions and support for sports and cultural activities, but youth and humanitarian workers say this is not enough. The UNHCR head of protection remarks:

> These are the people we worry the most about, but do so little for. We try increasing funding for education and livelihood, as the biggest enemy of youth is idle time, but prioritizing is an excruciating process. This year, we have ninety-four dollars per refugee. If the population increases, which is happening, the amount per person will decrease. Such an amount doesn't cover food, but shelter, education, livelihood, health, water and sanitation. Do you cut healthcare and provide more for youth? Life-saving activities will always come first. The youth program is always at the bottom and underfunded. And when it comes to livelihood, donors want to support women. It is difficult to find money for youth.

A number of young people are indeed killing time, but, with or without support, many also find ways to keep themselves busy, between jobs, businesses and community activities. A small proportion, usually the educated ones, find a job with one of the humanitarian organizations. Others work in the market. While no one is entirely free to move as they wish, having to deal with significant obstacles and limitations, agency is at play. Its interaction with social forces opens up various paths.

Money Matters

Having a proper career in the camp is close to impossible, as no one can be legally hired to fill a salaried position. Still, earning money is possible. Between 8 and 12 percent of the working-age population have an "incentive" job with one of the humanitarian organizations—more than 70 percent of them men, according to LWF's head of community services. Although business occasions are limited, Kakuma being far from any economic center, this does not prevent significant numbers from working in the markets, operating small kiosks and businesses or collecting *matatu* (minibus) fares. Educated youth often teach private classes for primary school pupils. Then, of course, there are other ways of earning money that aid organizations condemn: brewing alcohol, selling drugs and prostitution.

Jansen (2011) argues that the lack of access to legal employment is not particular to refugee camps, as the informal sector is generally more important than the formal one in Africa. For example, in 2006, the United Nations Human Settlements Programme reported that in Kenya there were an estimated 5.5 million workers in the informal sector, compared with 1.7 in the formal sector (2006: 11). Unlike Kenyans, however, refugees *cannot* work in the formal sector. For those who achieve higher education, it is thus almost impossible to find a job commensurate with their qualifications.

The Refugee Elite: Incentive Workers

After you finish high school, you are the king in this camp.
You can get any job. Here, UNHCR is what comes after
your mom and dad. They will give you a job.
—Aziz, twenty-three years old

It is true that, given the small number of people graduating from high school, graduates have a clear advantage in finding a job as a so-called "incentive worker" with a humanitarian organization. A vast majority of the positions in these organizations—up to 90 percent, according to the independent refugee-run media outlet *Kanere* or *Kakuma News Reflector* (21 August 2011)—are held by refugees, most often young men who studied in Kenya or in Swahili, or English-speaking countries. The head of education of LWF cites this as an argument to motivate students to stay in school: "Students know that if they finish high school, they can get a teaching job with LWF or be hired as incentive workers by us or another organization. Most end up with a job in the camp, if they want one." This is an optimistic perspective, considering the number of applicants with a high school diploma for each position posted. The Refugee Consortium of Kenya (RCK), for instance, received three hundred applications for fifteen protection monitor positions. Some two hundred people applied for five advertised outreach positions with FilmAid. About 90 percent of the applicants were high school graduates and a few even had university diplomas. As in school, girls are underrepresented in the workplace. LWF's head of community services estimates that they make up less than 30 percent of the workforce. Girls who work explain that their communities fear they will be "spoiled" and that they are expected to stay home until they marry and then look after their new home and children.

High school graduates are not equipped to fulfill specialized functions, but they constitute the core of the camp's workforce. They are schoolteachers, caseworkers, translators, community monitors and so on. While efforts are being made to boost their competence—medical assistants take a six-month class, for example, and more and more teachers are completing diplomas offered by the LWF or JRS—the average worker is inadequately trained. I knew a nineteen-year-old caseworker in the LWF Gender Unit who dealt with victims and perpetrators of conjugal violence without any training. He had to collect testimonies, which entailed having the first contact with the victim, and then refer the cases to the appropriate service. Without an adequate education and tutoring, he was constantly struggling, trying to figure out how to handle sensitive situations—and, despite his goodwill, frequently committed errors. Refugees and aid workers deem the quality of education and health services in the camp to be extremely poor, a situation where the lack of properly trained personnel is an important factor. "How can teachers not be trained?" wondered a member of the Somali council of elders. "How can someone train for six months and then work as a nurse in the hospital? [Technically, refugees are working as medical assistants and not nurses, but they are often the only medical staff a patient sees.] Have you seen that anywhere else? Those who go to the hospital only do so because they have no money to pay for healthcare outside the camp."

Incentives Instead of Salaries

Incentive workers might have the same or similar duties as salaried workers, but do not receive a salary, only a small incentive, far below the pay of their Kenyan colleagues. For example, a refugee primary school teacher is paid 5,850 KSh per month (less than US$70), while a Kenyan teacher on a contract, doing the same job, receives a salary that is nearly six times that. For secondary-school teachers, the difference is even greater. Thus, for the same workload and responsibilities, refugees receive a fraction of the salary paid to Kenyans. Aid organizations justify such policies by the fact that refugees are not legally allowed to work by the Government of Kenya, unless no national is qualified to fill the position.[13] They insist that refugees must be paid an amount that is lower than the lowest taxable income (thus not requiring a work permit), which would be approximately 12,000 KSh a month (approx. US$140; Michira 2011). However, the average incentive of 4,000–5,000 KSh does not even come near that threshold. Those who work say they struggle to make ends meet. My Swahili teacher worked for an NGO for a monthly pay of 4,000 KSh (less than US$50). He reflected on why some took two jobs:

> In the beginning, I thought it was selfish to do so, as it meant that someone else would not have a job. But I came to realize that surviving with 4,000 shillings is very difficult. I spend it in less than a week. I pay 1,500 for electricity, 500 for sugar, 400 for communications, 500 for deodorant—in a place like this, you cannot go without deodorant—and so on. It is very little, and I don't even have to look after a family. Everything in the camp costs more than in Nairobi, except flour.

Not only does such underpayment frustrate refugees, it also reduces their motivation and taints the relationships between refugees and nonrefugees, as the two groups are not treated as equals.

Incentive scales are set by the UNHCR and imposed on its implementing partners, which basically means all NGOs working in the camp. Only two organizations refused to follow suit: the RCK and the Kenyan Red Cross. The Red Cross pays the same stipend of 600 KSh a day (approx. 13,800 KSh a month or US$160) to its volunteers, regardless of their refugee or nonrefugee status. The head of the RCK, which had just accepted funding from the UNHCR for the first time and was therefore expected to follow the organization's rules, explained:

> I have always offered 9,000 shillings to our mobilizers. UNHCR is refusing to approve our salary scale and wants those salaries to be reduced to 5,000 shillings. I said I would not go lower than 6,000 and that I would give them benefits. I am told a cleaner here earns up to 20,000 shillings. How can I pay a [high school] graduate 5,000? I don't think Kenya would prevent us from paying salaries to refugees: you can justify hiring them for their knowledge of the camp, of a given language and community.

The UNHCR head of protection agreed that incentives were exploitative, but he justified them by noting that refugees' work is a community contribution and that people living in the camp are receiving assistance. When I objected that the amount of assistance did not nearly equal the difference between a salary and an incentive, and that teachers and medical staff are paid salaries in all countries and are not asked to do their work for a pittance, as a community contribution, he replied that the UNHCR had no money to increase incentives. If they were raised, services would have to be cut. I remarked that the allocation of salaries could be revised, knowing that the UNHCR national staff are paid several thousand dollars a month, a salary significantly exceeding the national average, and that a middle-level international staff member earns at least US$7,000 a month in an environment considered difficult, such as Kakuma.[14] He responded that this was impossible, as the money came from different budget lines. He added that he had internally criticized the system—and the differences between incentives in Dadaab and Kakuma—without success.

The UNHCR head of protection happened to be remarkably committed to his work and he often fought decisions that he believed were unfair, such as the nonregistration of southern Sudanese children in school at a time when the UNHCR was promoting their repatriation. His acceptance of a system that he qualified as exploitative was disconcerting. He was not alone: in fact, the only NGO workers I met who openly questioned the rules were the representatives of the RCK and the Red Cross. The head of an international NGO expressed a common opinion: "Incentives are not right. [Refugees] deserve better. Even if they are getting services in the camp, they need to get something additional. Unfortunately, this is something we found like that and we cannot change it. It is almost like it would have a domino effect and you would have to pull out" ("pulling out" stands for having to leave the camp as an organization because refusing to follow suit would jeopardize funding from the UNHCR). I pointed out that the Red Cross was paying a greater amount to refugees and was told with a great deal of self-righteousness that they "were breaking the rules." So NGOs keep quiet and apply the rules, with some systematically opposing any increase of incentives, insisting that it would make their budgets too tight.[15]

Refugees who dare to criticize incentives are harshly dealt with: in some cases, they are arbitrarily dismissed (under the incentive system, refugees have no job security); in others, their credibility is attacked and undermined. The silencing of dissent is very effective. Even so, within the camp and far from their managers, refugees are vocal about the unfairness of the arrangement and emphasize that their Kenyan colleagues may earn more than ten times their pay for doing a similar job, without even spending much time in the camp. Many, such as Abdulaziz, have resigned themselves to the situation, as they cannot afford to lose their income: "I grew up finding [incentives] here. Whenever you ask, you are told that this is UNHCR policy. So you just keep quiet. You have to accept it because you cannot lose that 5,000 shillings. We realize that there is nothing you can do. There is nowhere you can go to complain and say that this is your right."

Nevertheless, being an incentive worker brings a significant advantage: access to national and international staff members of NGOs, the UNHCR or the Department of Refugee Affairs and to resources, such as computers, food or drugs. Therefore, working for a humanitarian organization does give social capital. This affects power dynamics, as young people are more likely to be the ones benefiting from such privileges, since they are the ones working.

Shopping for the Right Job or Creating Your Own

Given the low incentives (and the frequently patronizing attitude of supervisors), refugees often feel limited responsibility toward their job. Workers commonly stay home when it is raining, many turn up late and people keep changing jobs. Most young people who have been working for a few years have occupied several positions with different NGOs, which they justify by a better access to resources, a higher incentive or a smaller workload. Many first worked as teachers before they found slightly better paid positions or less demanding ones. One of the journalism students, who was teaching geography in Kakuma secondary school, switched to an administrative job with JRS. Her reason was that in her new position, she could use a computer connected to the Internet.

Then there are refugees who decide not to work for a humanitarian organization, finding the pay too meager. Nuradin, who runs a shop in the Somali market, is one them: "If you have a job here, going there every day, jumping up and down, working under the sun, you get 4,600 shillings in a whole month. Imagine! Someone is working for you and you give him 4,600 shillings. What can you do with that? It is pocket money." Somalis are blatantly underrepresented in the workforce and I doubt this is merely a matter of discrimination: many are unwilling to work for a small incentive, which gives them a bad reputation with humanitarian organizations. FilmAid was making efforts to convince them to join the organization, since Somali workers are essential to pass on information to other Somalis. A few were part of the team, but their number was deemed insufficient. However, talks with elders and potential candidates yielded limited results. Idris, who works for an NGO, explains: "Somalis look at the incentive, then at their business options and decide to do business. There are people who are learned and could find a job, but the incentive is small, so they decide to do something else. If the incentive was greater, many Somalis would work." Yasin is a good example of this: he could have easily secured a job—he is smart, has finished his secondary education, and speaks good English and Swahili—but he rightly assessed that starting his own tutoring business would be more profitable. His story is also a good illustration of the entrepreneurship that is so highly praised in the Somali community. He left Dadaab after hearing that business opportunities were better in Kakuma. Arriving in 2009, he started teaching English and mathematics to thirteen pupils. He now has over two hundred who each pay 100 KSh a month. He therefore collects more than 20,000 KSh a month (approx. US$228), a respectable amount compared to the average incentive.

When You Don't Need to Fend for Yourself

Drug is a big problem. It attacks the youth. You end up addicted. But the real problem is that people have nothing to do. Me, I was lucky. I got to work straight from school. I don't know how these guys do it. When I was in school, I hated Sundays. I would wake up late in the morning. I had nowhere to go, nothing to do. At least, school kept me busy. I don't know how I would do it without work.
—Abdulaziz, twenty years old

Some youth search desperately for a job, but fail. Others decide that working is overly taxing. Faarax, a lively twenty-one-year-old who has finished high school, had a job with one of the NGOs. One day, he did not show up for work. He asked one of his colleagues to tell his boss he was resigning. When

I asked why he had done so, he explained that he wanted to enroll in a six-month laboratory course offered by the International Rescue Committee. He could not take the class while working, as he was expected to spend his whole day at work. He had not yet applied for the course and did not know if he would be selected, but he had had enough of his job, which he found too demanding in terms of time. He had decided that if he were not admitted, he would leave the camp and head to Nairobi, where he would try to find a decently paid job—which he did a few months later. Faarax was living in Kakuma with his mother and five younger siblings. He was the only one earning money, yet, when he no longer felt like working, he stopped. His colleague Abdullahi did the same thing because he deemed that traveling from Kakuma III to the NGO compound to work was not worth it. There was some truth to this, as his travel costs nearly equaled his incentive. However, he did not look for another job closer to his home.

Choosing not to work is not so uncommon. On the one hand, youth constantly draw attention to their boredom and poverty. On the other hand, they know they can afford to not work and rely on assistance. Responsibilities are few, especially for men, as women are expected to do the housework and look after the children. But this means dealing with idleness. On any given day, at any given time, there are gatherings of young people, usually men, playing board games or soccer, drinking tea or alcohol, chatting or chewing *khat*.[16] Girls stay and help in the house, visit one another or meet up at the water tap. But not all those who are not working are idle, as some are involved in community, dance or theater groups that keep them busy and engaged.

Coming of Age without Resources

During my stay in Kakuma, I received several desperate calls and text messages from youth who suddenly found the camp unbearable. One of them was Xaawo. After she received her unsatisfactory school results and sent a distressed text message, I paid her a visit. She talked about how unfair it was that she was still in this camp after so many years, while all her friends had long since departed for the West. She was going nowhere, as her resettlement case had been rejected. She had no intention of going back to Somalia, a country she did not know. She no longer wanted to be in Kakuma. "What can I do here? Get married and have children? I just want to leave." But all doors seemed closed. She was so distraught that I initially worried that she would consider taking her own life, even though Somalis say that however distressed they may be, they do not commit suicide, as Islam forbids it. They claim that Ethiopians are the ones killing themselves, out of despair, often after having been rejected for resettlement. While I do not think that suicides are common, I doubt they never happen.[17] In the ensuing weeks, Xaawo regained her composure and tried looking for ways to get enough money to enroll again in secondary school and take the exams yet another time.

Yasin, the young man who runs a successful private school, was also told he would not be resettled. He, too, expressed great discouragement and started calling repeatedly at all hours of the day and night, asking for help in looking for a job in Somalia. He said he could no longer stand the camp; he felt trapped. He added that he could not "waste" his whole life in Kakuma and was looking for a way out. However, he did not know where to start, had never applied for a job and was at loss as to how to proceed. A few weeks later, when he had somehow recovered his usual calm, he placidly said that if he was in Kakuma, it was God's plan. This is something I heard many times. Young people would vent their dissatisfaction with camp life and the endless wait for resettlement, but would conclude that it was God's will and should therefore not be questioned. In that respect, religious faith is a prime coping mechanism, although it can also be disempowering.

The focus on leaving is common. Youth who are done with school spend a considerable amount of their time thinking and talking about possible ways out of the camp, sometimes desperately. While this is true for those working, those who are not working seem even more preoccupied with the matter. Even though youth describe Kakuma as home and say they will miss their friends when they depart, they constantly speak of settling in a place where they can live a "normal" life.

While the period of transition from childhood to adulthood might be nearly nonexistent for girls who are married at a young age, for many young men it is a challenge. Socially becoming adult men in the camp, usually through marrying, moving to their own house, earning money and having children, is a difficult accomplishment. Faarax could not understand how some of his peers managed to marry at twenty: "I cannot even support myself. How can I support my wife and children? You cannot marry before you are independent. And how do you become independent here?" This is something Warsame experienced. Not long after I met him, he told me he was about to get married. He was very pleased with the news and was already speaking of his future children. But things did not go the way he had planned: the mother of his wife-to-be asked for a dowry of US$3,000. She felt it was necessary for the couple to move away and build their own home in the camp. "How can I find such money when I only earn 5,000 shillings a month?" he wondered [he was working for an NGO]. He tried convincing the mother of his future wife that they could both live in his family's house for a while and gradually save money so that at some point they would be able to have their own place. The negotiations lasted for many weeks and ultimately failed, which left Warsame bitter, feeling that he could not afford to get married. While the community would normally come together to fund the wedding, such a large sum could not be gathered.

Yasin explained that he only managed to marry because of the decent income he made with his private school:

> The relatives, they might only ask for a hundred dollars, but then, they will tell you to build a house, to organize a wedding party, to buy two or three goats, one sack of rice, maybe two liters of oil, one sack of sugar, vegetables. You also have to furnish your house with mattresses, sitting chairs, carpets. When the house is ready, then the girl can come. I paid almost 2,000 dollars.

Unions may also be delayed because of resettlement: getting married during the several-year process creates further delays, thus leading some to postpone marriage.

This is not peculiar to youth transitioning from childhood to adulthood in a refugee camp: similar experiences are shared by a number of youth in Africa, and by Somalis in the diaspora, who sometimes put off marriage because of their remittance obligations (Honwana and De Boeck 2005: 9; Horst 2006c: 11–12). What is particular to the camp is the feeling of being trapped with limited means and the impression of having been forgotten, which seems to deepen the desperation. Bauman's reflection on exile comes to mind (1998b: 321):

> To be in exile means to be out of place; also, needing to be rather elsewhere; also, not having that "elsewhere" where one would rather be. Thus, exile is a place of compulsory confinement, but also an unreal place, a place that itself is out of place in the order of things. Anything may happen here, but nothing can be done here ... In exile, one is pressed to stop being in exile; either by moving elsewhere, or by dissolving into the place, not being anymore out of it.

Notes

1. E.g., Chatty and Hundt (2005) on Palestinian refugees in the Middle East; Van Damme (1999) on refugees in Goma and Guinea; Abdi (2004), Hyndman (2000), Jacobsen (2005) and Moret, Baglioni and Efionayi-Mäder (2006) on refugees in Kenya; Harrell-Bond (1986) on Ugandans in South Sudan; and Crisp (2003) on refugees in Africa.
2. Compared with Somalia, where, from the 1980s to the present, the richest quintile of thirteen to seventeen-year-olds has on average studied less than six years and the poorest has been to school for less than one year, children have greater access to education in Kakuma, especially to primary school (Dryden-Peterson, Dahya and Giles 2013).
3. As education tends to be underfunded, educational facilities are insufficient to meet the needs of the population. Those that exist are in poor condition, crowded and under-

equipped. Teachers are also underqualified (UNHCR et al. 2012: 7, 20), although there might be progressive change: for the last three years, eighty teachers a year have been doing a one-year diploma in primary education offered in the camp by Masinde Muliro University of Science and Technology, in collaboration with the Lutheran World Federation (LWF).

4. Countries define "urban" in various ways. In some countries, the mere size or density of population defines a city. In other cases, definitions include economic characteristics, such as the proportion of the labor force that is not employed in agricultural activities, or the availability of specific infrastructure, such as water and sewage systems, paved streets or electric lighting (United Nations Human Settlements Programme 2006: 7).

5. In 2012, for example, of the 869 children who graduated from primary school, less than half could enroll in secondary school (UNHCR et al. 2012: 8). The camp's two secondary schools accept two hundred students each, while approximately 5 percent of the students are granted a scholarship to a Kenyan secondary school by the Jesuit Refugee Services or the Windle Trust.

6. From 2007 to 2009, the UNHCR implemented a policy preventing Sudanese refugees from enrolling in school in the camp in order to push them to repatriate. Asylum seekers from Sudan were also deprived of food aid during their refugee status determination, a process than can last for years. The policy was rescinded after a UNHCR protection officer protested that it amounted to forcing returns rather than promoting them. Speaking of the episode, he leveled the criticism that it was "not the first time that something like that happens when UNHCR is promoting returns."

7. For example, during the first term of 2013, Somalis made up 44.5 percent of the camp population, but only 31 percent of those enrolled in school. While they accounted for 36 percent of the children in preschool, in primary school they were down to 31 percent and in secondary school to 11 percent. Even though the South Sudanese constituted a third of the camp population, they made up nearly 60 percent of the students. The disparity can, in part, be explained by demographic differences between these groups, but not fully. Girls, regardless of their nationality, are less likely than boys to go to school. In preschool and during the first three years of primary school, there is no significant gender gap. After that, there is a sharp decline in the number of girls. At the end of primary school, girls are down to approximately a third of the students. In secondary school, the proportion drops to one in four, although those statistics do no fully reflect the proportion of refugee girls going to high school, as a greater number of girls than boys get scholarships. Somali girls fare a little better than the overall population in secondary school, making up 37 percent of Somali students in 2013.

8. For example, in 2012, only 68 percent of children aged between five and seventeen were enrolled in the various levels of education (preschool, primary and secondary). More than ten thousand school-age children were either out of school or enrolled in schools outside of the camp.

9. There are several *madrassas* in the camp, where children go after school and on Saturdays.

10. In primary school, where students should be between six and fourteen, 59 percent are over fourteen, according to the head of the education department of the international NGO in charge of education, the LWF. Secondary school students should normally be between fourteen and seventeen, but in the camp, only 15 percent are in that age range, while 75 percent are between eighteen and twenty-eight.

11. Two organizations provide scholarships every year for a small number of students based on performance or vulnerability. A little more than half of the JRS's forty to fifty annual primary and secondary school scholarships are given to girls whose situation is deemed precarious. In 2012, of twenty-four performance-based scholarships, only three went to

girls. The Windle Trust sponsors the secondary education of forty-five well-performing girls. But it is not necessarily refugees who studied in Kakuma who are selected, as half of the students chosen for their performance studied outside the camp. Not all parents are keen on such programs: a number of Somali parents refuse to let their girls go away to boarding schools.

12. For example, Afghan refugees who had had access to higher education repatriated earlier and took up work as civil servants or NGO managers, filling critical roles in the rebuilding of their society (Dryden-Peterson 2011: 52).

13. Kenya's national Refugee Act of 2006 (art. 16 § 4) stipulates that: "Every refugee and member of his family in Kenya shall, in respect of wage-earning employment, be subject to the same restrictions as are imposed on persons who are not citizens of Kenya." This article violates Kenya's obligation under the 1951 Refugee Convention, which states that refugees are entitled to the same right to work as nationals of their country of asylum after three years of residency (art. 17 § (2) a). Kenya has placed no reservation on the article. The RCK tried challenging the government on that basis, but to no avail.

14. For example, a single mid-level professional (P-3, step 3) based in Kakuma receives a gross salary of more than US\$72,000 and a hardship allowance of approximately US\$13,000. This is without considering the assignment grant and other advantages (International Civil Service Commission 2012 and 2013).

15. Walkup (1997: 42–43), writing about humanitarian organizations, distinguishes four possible options for workers who must apply a rule with which they disagree: quit the organization; voice their frustration (which is often countered by suppressive action from the hierarchy and could cost them their job); neglect (i.e., remain apathetic and do their jobs without asking questions); or manage to remain loyal to the organization, convincing themselves that working within the system is better than doing nothing. Individuals who choose the fourth option, according to Walkup, are those who get promotions. Questioning the inadequacy of incentives was usually unwelcome. I believe this is because most aid workers know that the system is wrong, but have decided to work with it rather than expressing their opposition. I could not help but think of how Arendt (1969) described bureaucracies as "an intricate system of bureaux in which no men, neither one nor the best, neither the few nor the many, can be held responsible, and which could be properly called the rule by Nobody … In a fully developed bureaucracy there is nobody left with whom one could argue, to whom one could present grievances, on whom the pressures of power could be exerted. Bureaucracy is the form of government in which everybody is deprived of political freedom, of the power to act; for the rule by Nobody is not no-rule, and where all are equally powerless we have a tyranny without a tyrant."

16. *Khat* or *miraa,* a plant with a mildly euphoric effect that is commonly chewed by Somalis and usually seen by them as a fairly benign substance, is described by Somali youth as a detrimental way to kill time. Scientific opinions on the effect of *khat* on health are polarized: some see it as mild and innocuous, while others describe it as the cause of health and social harm (Beckerleg 2008: 753; Carrier 2012; Pennings, Opperhuizen and van Amsterdam 2008: 205; Warfa et al. 2007: 316). Perhaps more immediately relevant in the camp environment, *miraa* is associated with income diversion (Carrier 2012). In Kakuma, people often buy five dollars of *khat* for a group of four to five, a considerable amount of money in the camp context. Moreover, *khat* money leaves the camp economy, as *khat* is produced in the central region of Kenya and not in Kakuma.

17. Suicide and suicidal thoughts are fairly common in a number of refugee populations in camps. For example, 37 percent of Cuban refugees detained in a camp before arriving in the United States reported having seen someone attempting or committing suicide (Lustig et al. 2004: 27); Sudanese children growing up in Ugandan camps had more

suicidal thoughts than other Ugandan children (Paardekooper 1999: 533); a survey of Afghan refugee mothers, who happened to also be Muslims, in Pakistani camps showed high suicidal feelings among them (Rahman and Hafeez 2003: 392). A recent media article about suicides in Dadaab gives anecdotal evidence of Somalis taking their own lives (Bosire 2013).

Chapter 4

THE SOMALI WAY

Ethnocultural Diversity and Cultural Preservation

e⟨◉⟩•⟨◉⟩ꝍ

A walk through Kakuma typically includes crossing paths with women covered in black from head to toe, others in *khanga* wraparounds or elaborate dresses made of *kitenge* (a colorful printed waxed fabric), and still others wearing tight tank tops, Turkana displaying layers of beads around their necks, teenagers in skinny jeans, Somali men in sarongs and a few in *jellabiyas*. Conversations in Somali, Swahili, English, Turkana, Arabic and Amharic are overheard, while one sees mosques and churches of various denominations: Ethiopian Orthodox, Catholic, Protestant, Anglican, Baptist, Presbyterian or Evangelical Christian, among others. Some shelters are visibly poor and run-down, with crumbling walls and no furniture. Others are relatively large, with fabrics covering their inside walls and equipped with Internet, electricity and TVs.

While social classes exist in most refugee camps (and human settlements), Kakuma is unusual in its cultural and religious diversity. Camps in Africa are generally set up close to the borders of the refugees' country of origin, in areas where newcomers and their hosts have already had regular contact and often share a common cultural background and close social relationships (Crisp and Jacobsen 1998: 29). The vast majority of refugees thus come from the same country. In contrast, refugees arriving in Kakuma were outsiders for their hosts, the Turkana, and also strangers to each other, coming from various national and ethnic groups. They were exposed to a greater cultural and religious diversity than most had encountered in their place of origin.

The camp could be seen as a social laboratory: within a five-year span, an isolated and sparsely populated territory receives people from southern Sudan, Somalia, Ethiopia, Eritrea and the African Great Lakes, in addition to aid workers from several different ethnic groups all over Kenya and from abroad. Refugees did not choose to live together, might not have a common language and might initially perceive the camp as an environment marked by adversity and alterity. The Sudanese view Somalis as enemies, Somalis see Turkana as primitive, and the Sudanese raid the Ethiopian neighborhood once in a while. Despite this, people must learn to coexist, at least minimally, as they share services and infrastructures.

Although "enforced proximity" (Tomlinson 1999: 181) may not foster a cosmopolitan disposition, one can ask whether a shared "refugeeness" might create a sense of common identity, a space of commonality, despite obvious cultural and religious differences. While the camp inhabitants may be from different countries, they are also all refugees, living in a bounded space, sharing services, receiving the same assistance and experiencing the same harsh conditions. Alternatively, might the exposure to others cause closure, as a way to protect their own culture? Considering that identity is fluid and open to relational influence rather than static (Augé 1987: 17–18), will this interaction bring a "gradual transformation from one mixture to a new mixture" (Appiah 2006)? In other words, will an interethnic environment lead to a reinvention of ethnic identity, defined by Meintel (1993: 11) as a feeling of belonging to a group with common ancestors (real or symbolic), a sentiment of unity, of a shared past and future?

In this chapter, I explore how people from different ethnic and cultural backgrounds have learned to live together, and reflect on the extent to which camp life has led to the creation of a broader interethnic community. I raise questions about adjustments that have taken place and how Somalis have sustained their cultural ways. I argue that a convivial culture (Gilroy 2006a) has emerged, especially among youth who have been in Kakuma for a long time, but that social life is still structured by people's ethnicity. I then consider the impact of coexistence on the identity of young Somalis and observe that the camp has to a certain extent become a space of resistance and transformation, in particular for young women who aspire to redefine their social role. In other words, I look at the way in which people coexist and then reflect on changes elicited by this coexistence within a group: that of young Somalis.

From "Enforced Proximity" to Learning to Live in Peace

When I joined Loma primary school [a private school in Kakuma town], there were people from everywhere.

> They would tell us: "Somalis are violent." I used to say
> that I knew nothing about Somalia, that I was born in
> Kenya and that I am not violent. Finally, we became
> friends, we understood how to live with one another.
> —Abyan, seventeen years old

Young people recall that in the early days of the camp, coexistence was challenging. They assert that even though some separation remains, things have evolved considerably, going from fearing one another to generally dealing peacefully with each other in class, at work and in the streets. Thus, over time, tensions gradually eased off and cohabitation and interaction between ethnic groups became ordinary features of life, bringing to mind Gilroy's idea of conviviality or "just living together" (2006b: 7): "Conviviality is a social pattern in which different metropolitan groups dwell in close proximity, but where their racial, linguistic and religious particularities do not—as the logic of ethnic absolutism suggests they must—add up to discontinuities of experience or insuperable problems of communication. In these conditions, a degree of differentiation can be combined with a large measure of overlapping" (2006a: 40). In such a context, cultural or ethnic differences become ordinary. This does not mean that conflict or racism is nonexistent, but this can usually be managed as part of public life.

In the 1990s, when the camp's first inhabitants settled in, relationships were tense between refugees, and between refugees and their hosts. Several people lost their lives in interethnic fighting. From the outset, however, there are unavoidable communal spaces. Water taps, the hospital, medical clinics and streets are forced meeting points or "contact zones" (Wise 2007: 1). For anyone wishing to buy goods, the market is another and, for employed refugees, so are workspaces. Parents can decide not to send their children to school (most commonly their daughters, so they will not have to share their bench with a boy)—and still, most parents do send their children to school. Schools are thus one of the prime spaces of mixed socialization for Somali youth, who commonly recall their first years of study as strained, since for the first time they were sharing their space with people of another religion who spoke a different language.

Although discord is still part of daily life, the level of conflict has decreased. This can probably be attributed in part to efforts made by humanitarian organizations to promote peaceful coexistence, especially through attempts to raise awareness about cultural diversity, and also through sports that bring communities together on a playing field. Traditional conflict-resolution and reconciliation mechanisms are also established in order to defuse tensions. More importantly, over time and through collective experiences, people establish social and economic relationships. By going to school together, children develop a space of commonality. They learn to speak Swahili and, regardless of their first language, commonly incorporate Swahili words and fillers such as *nini* and *halafu* ("I mean" and "then" or "afterwards," but both are used as filler words) into their mother tongue. They listen to the same Kenyan music, and wear the same beaded and plastic bracelets, although they may have contrasting dress codes. What was initially perceived as terribly abnormal in terms of dress or cultural practices becomes ordinary. Differences still exist and are still noticed, but they are tolerated. In the end, plain exposure probably has a major influence on attitudes toward other groups.

Learning to coexist is an achievement of which those who grew up in the camp are very proud, as they consider it a valuable gain from all those years spent in Kakuma. Several explained that one key feature distinguishing them from Somalis who grew up in their own country is their ability to engage with others, including Christians. Many also pride themselves on their knowledge of English, Swahili and sometimes Turkana or Arabic. They say that those who reject people on the basis of their cultural or religious differences are older people or newcomers to the camp. Twenty-three-year-old Warsame explains that had he grown up in Somalia, he would "only talk to Somali people. I would not share with others. When you meet with Sudanese or Congolese, you learn different things. My mind is growing. If I had stayed there, it would be locked."

Living Together or Side-by-Side?

Although young people are perfectly able to live side-by-side peacefully, there are clear limits to integration. While the population of the camp is culturally diverse, this does not mean that neighborhoods are equally mixed. In the early days of the camp, members of a given ethnic group arriving at the same time were usually established together. The way in which refugees are arbitrarily settled in a camp has been criticized by Malkki (1995b: 137) for segregating refugees by "types" or "kinds," just as a zoo keeper would not "put creatures of different species in a single cage." While it is true that new residents are arbitrarily assigned plots, subsequent movements in and out of Kakuma—especially once fairly large numbers of Somalis began to be resettled in 2006 and left or informally sold their plots to other refugees—have allowed people to move within the camp, thus reordering its social configuration. With the ongoing internal and external movements of population, neighborhoods have become more mixed. For newcomers, the camp still feels rather segregated, as most neighborhoods are home to particular ethnic groups and remain relatively homogeneous, but separation between ethnic communities used to be greater in the past, according to old-timers. Over the years, the Bajuni and Somali Bantu areas have continued to be known as such, but are not strictly occupied by those two groups. Neighborhoods could—and still can—be distinguished from one another fairly easily, mainly because physical boundaries in the form of gates and fences are set up between them and building styles differ. A decorated mud Dinka home with its low metal roof might share very little with a Somali shelter, which often combines a small mud house with additional rooms built out of metal sheets.

Moreover, violence between communities still periodically costs lives. In the words of the UNHCR peace-building officer, "basic mistrust" between the camp's two most important groups, the Somalis and the Sudanese, or between ethnic groups of the same nationality remains the norm. Spaces of involuntary coexistence, such as schools and water taps, are still prone to conflict. Preconceptions and mistrust continue to foster tensions. For example, Somalis will not drink the milk of Turkana animals: they believe it is unclean because the Turkana keep all their animals together, including dogs, an animal Somalis and many other Muslims consider unclean. Derogatory words are often used to describe other national groups—a light-skinned Ethiopian said he had seen me walking with a "gorilla," referring to a darker Rwandese. A South Sudanese block leader claimed that, unlike Ethiopians, Somali merchants raised their prices when the customers were not Somalis, and that Somalis were inclined to bribe the police. Another element that complicates interactions concerns what is perceived as acceptable or abusive behavior. One morning, twenty-four-year-old Ubax came to tell me she had been fired from the organization she was working for. She was told her attitude was wrong. She said she had been in conflict with her Kenyan manager because she felt he was abusive. She related that one day, when she was replacing her veil, her hair had showed slightly. Her manager had chuckled, "Are you stripping?" She was terribly offended. These are comments I heard regularly, just as I saw Kenyan staff and non-Muslim refugees pulling on the veils of girls in a joking manner. The person concerned did not perceive it as a joke, but as a form of abuse. Such acts highlight the fact that differences in perceptions of abuse can get in the way of peaceful coexistence and trust. Another bone of contention is that while everyone receives the same assistance, refugees regularly protest that other communities are given favorable treatment.

The recently developed camp Constitution is an attempt to encourage the development of a broader sense of community among refugees and introduce a non-ethnic-based leadership to avoid the marginalization of small ethnic groups.[1] Until 2012, the camp leadership was organized along ethnic or geographic lines. Some forty-five different communities each had their own leaders who fought for the interests of their respective ethnic groups. Refugees from smaller communities maintained that they were underrepresented, which created tensions. "A Somali person living among the Ethiopians could not really seek for assistance anywhere, as assistance was managed by the communities, which would lead to discrimination," recalls one of the current leaders. In mid 2012, block elections were held and several thousand refugees voted.[2] Many of the ninety-one elected leaders are young, which pleases the UNHCR administrators, who believe that they are likely to be more "open-minded" than older people.[3] One of the recently elected zone leaders (overseeing the fifteen blocks of a zone), a twenty-nine-year-old South Sudanese Equatorian asserts that the new structure, in trying to move out of the ethnic dimension, is forcing people to see themselves as a community of refugees who need to address problems together, rather than as separate ethnic groups fighting for scarce resources. However, her description of her zone makes it clear that ethnicity remains a central element:

> In my zone, there are fifteen blocks. Ten are Sudanese and five are Somali. For the Sudanese ones, seven are Equatorian and three are Dinka. The Constitution says we have to balance all nationalities. We try to have Somali Bantus on the board, rather than real Somalis.[4] We avoid real Somalis because they will not work with you, but for their clan. Somalis will not team up with Dinka because Dinka are dictators. So as Equatorians, we are the majority.

In fact, beyond sites of "imposed coexistence," social activities most commonly remain monoethnic and so do many community spaces. For example, awareness-raising activities usually target one specific ethnic group. The library in the compound of the Somali administration may be open to all, but only Somalis occupy the space. Soccer teams tend to bring together players of a single nationality or ethnicity, and Somalis and Sudanese have separate playing fields. The reasons for this are not strictly related to discrimination among the various ethnic groups. While "veteran" refugee youth speak English and Swahili, older refugees and more recent arrivals may not. Thus, unless activities are conducted in multiple languages, only groups with a shared language are likely to come together. There are exceptions: people of all horizons convene for events such as the youth festival and football tournaments, and a few restaurants in the Ethiopian neighborhood are frequented by refugees of many ethnic backgrounds.

Intercultural Friendship and Unions

Warsame came to see me one day to share his excitement: he had been to a Protestant church on Sunday to attend the service as an assignment in his intercultural communication class. He had discovered that men and women sit together in church and that women are allowed to be there even when they have their period, unlike in Islam. Given that he had lived in the camp since he was a child, was very curious and had been to school with several Christians, I found it disconcerting that he only made this "discovery" in his twenties. It meant that he had not discussed these subjects with Christians until then. In fact, because of the limited socialization between people of various ethnic groups, even people who have spent most of their lives in Kakuma often have little knowledge of the cultural or religious practices of others.

While many report that they had Sudanese and Turkana friends as children, friendships between youth of different ethnic groups are relatively rare, although they are accepted, especially between people of the same religion. Interestingly, many of the Somalis who have developed closer relationships to people of other nationalities are from minority groups who claim they have suffered discrimination. Yusri, for example, explains that most of his friends are Sudanese and not Somalis, as many of the latter would not cultivate a friendship with him because he is a member of the Madiban minority group. Students in the photography class were interesting to observe. They would usually sit next to students of their nationality. Camera sharing between girls of different nationalities went smoothly; in contrast, the boys often said they had no way of communicating with a boy of another ethnicity. Girls had an easier time and seemed to empathize more with one another across ethnic lines, as a result of their shared condition and unfavorable social status as young women. Even so, they would not socialize outside of school.

Unlike friendship, dating or marrying someone from another ethnic group, and particularly a different religion, is taboo—especially for girls. Nonetheless, interethnic dating does happen, generating tensions and conflict between youth and the opprobrium of the community. Boys commonly speak of the necessity of protecting "their" girls. Girls relate how their brothers are watching them and reporting on them to their parents. Gossip about Somali girls spending time with boys from the Great Lakes is common. During my stay, there was a much-publicized incident in which three Burundian boys were badly beaten in the market by Somali boys for having visited Somali girls on Somali "territory." The Burundians were later paid a significant amount in compensation by the Somali community. This was not unusual. A Somali leader recalled that in the previous year, Somalis had fought with Ethiopians and Sudanese for the same reason.

Cross-community marriage is always described as a very sensitive issue. Many Somalis concur that in theory, they can marry any other Muslim, regardless of origin, but they are quick to add that the community does not welcome this:

Ayan: We allow mixed marriages if the man is a Muslim and we love each other.

Deeqa: But people will say things that are not very good about you.

Ayan: Somalis like marrying Somalis. They think you should not go outside of the community. It is not really allowed.

Young people recount several stories about Somali women who have been forced to leave the camp to escape the abuse and rejection of their community because they have married Sudanese men, or women who married Turkana and went to live with the host community, becoming outcasts.

In other words, while day-to-day life has become relatively peaceful, tensions and mistrust remain part of the equation and intimate social interactions between youth of different ethnic groups are still restricted. It is more accurate to speak of living side-by-side rather than together, although adjustments are noticeable. It would be incorrect to qualify the social life of the camp as cosmopolitan if this is defined as "openness to all forms of otherness" (Glick Schiller, Darieva and Gruner-Domic 2011: 208). Gilroy's concept of conviviality seems more appropriate to describe it. This does not mean that differences are celebrated, but they tend to be accepted and often discussed with interest. The other might not be deemed a suitable wife or husband, but there is a curiosity about practices and customs, and a recognition of the other's humanity. While competition for resources does not encourage political solidarity among refugees, over time, a certain sense of solidarity around a shared "refugeeness" and space has emerged. Without it, even initiatives such as drafting a constitution would have failed. The openness of youth to cultural and religious differences is obvious. In addition to facilitating peaceful coexistence, openness to others is likely to provoke changes within groups living in the camp, given the fluid and dialogical nature of ethnic identity.

Preserving the Somali Way

> If I go to Somalia and people see me walking like this, dressed like this, they will think I am not Somali, but a tourist, maybe American. In Somalia, they wear a sarong and a shirt. We wear jerseys, long trousers and shoes. We adapted to the behavior of people we live with. If you go there, the food is different, everything is different, the way people are and socialize. Here you socialize with Sudanese, there you socialize with your people. Still, I am Somali and will remain Somali wherever I go.
> —Nuradin, twenty-two years old[5]

As Nuradin's remarks underline, young people who have spent their lives in Kakuma proudly say that they are different from youth who have stayed in Somalia, citing their knowledge of other cultures and language and the hybridization of their identity (Ahluwalia 2003: 141). Besides learning to interact with people of varied backgrounds, they have developed an identity that is rooted in Kenya, while maintaining a strong relationship with Somali culture. Several authors have concluded that the process of migrating and settling in a new environment can stimulate a renegotiation of traditions and social organization, and thus alter social reproduction (e.g., Boelaert et al. 1999: 168; Essed, Frerks and Schrijvers 2004: 8; Grabska 2011: 88–90). Preserving and transmitting a culture in a refugee camp entails some specific challenges. For one thing, the social landscape is radically different from that of the country of origin. Moreover, humanitarian aid creates a system in which refugees have limited economic independence, making it difficult to observe certain traditions, roles and social responsibilities, such as marriage (and the payment of a dowry) or the exercise of traditional justice (and its related material compensation).

Learning Your Language, Your Culture and Your History

Speaking of their differences with people who grew up in Somalia, young people often mention that their grandparents were not there to teach them their history and Somali proverbs. They consider that their imperfect command of the subtleties of the Somali language and of all its proverbs is such that any native Somali would know they have grown up abroad, the art of speaking Somali (the language spoken by up to 95 percent of the population) being at the core of Somali identity and culture (Laitin 1977: 23, 42; Warsame 2001: 343).[6] Listening to music, Faarax comments that while he easily understands the lyrics of Kenyan music in Swahili, when it comes to Somali music, he constantly has to ask his mother the meaning of the songs; thus, he prefers Kenyan music. A handful know the national anthem of Somalia, while all can sing the Kenyan anthem. A number say they are more comfortable speaking Swahili or English than Somali. Being unable to write Somali is the norm. They did not learn it in school and only a few have parents who are literate and thus were able to teach them. Only one said she wrote it without problems because she had learned the written language by reading newspapers in Somali. This was Abyan, the girl educated in one of the leading Kenyan high schools. Parents share the view of their children, as expressed by a member of the Somali council of elders:

> Youth born in Kenya, if they go back to Somalia, they will just be like new refugees. They don't know that country, they don't have land. They know the religion, but not the cultural dances and the cultural dresses. In addition, even though they know the language, they don't know the subtleties of it. In Somali, there are often five words to say one thing. Those born here only know one. They belong to this place.

Yet, youth stress that their religious practice is the same as that of native Somalis, which they see as a key marker of their Somaliness. Several elders note
that the transmission of religious values has been an essential task. "For Eid,
we celebrate the way we used to in Somalia," explains one. "The *madrassa*
schools are the same and the children learn the same as we did back there.
Religious leaders have made sure to teach the behaviors that should be followed." Young people have also adopted some customary practices, such as
the use of traditional healers. One day, Faarax had yellow fever and became
extremely sick. He was not recovering well, despite repeated visits to the hospital and strong drugs. So he was sent to the healer. He showed me the curing
burns on the outside of both of his wrists and his stomach, and added that as
soon as the burns were made, he was back on his feet. A few days later, when
I was sitting with an elder, I noticed his wrists had old burn scars. I asked if
he had had yellow fever. "Yes, and it was the only way to cure it in the bush."
Even in the camp, Somalis continue to engage in fire-burning, a customary
practice whereby a stick from a particular tree or a metal object is heated
and applied to the skin by a traditional doctor to cure illnesses (Kemp and
Rasbridge 2004: 321). The adoption of such practices can be partly linked to
youth's respect for their elders and their advice, a respect that they put forward as evidence of their unquestionable Somali identity.

Changing Social Dynamics: Remodeling the Authority of Elders

> I don't really know the culture of Somalia. I grew up
> in Kakuma. I know the culture of Kakuma. It is simple.
> We respect the elders. That is our culture.
> —Yusri, nineteen years old

Elders play a central role in mobilizing communities and clans, as they generally have a prominent position in Somali society: in addition to mediating
conflicts, they are at the heart of cultural transmission and are expected to
advise on community-related issues. Youth generally say they duly respect
the authority of elders, as they would have in Somalia. The perspective of
elders is often different. They feel the young generation is more liberal in its
approach to them, and dares to contradict them and speak up, as underlined
by a Bajuni elder: "Young men in Somalia, they would greet and show respect
to their elders. But those who grow up in the camp forget those things and
behave differently. Changes are brought by the difficult life here. Parents get
no time to advise their children."

Having been educated in English and Swahili, youth serve as translators
for older members of their communities and have become key breadwinners,
being able to work for humanitarian organizations. This, compounded with

their greater access to humanitarian resources, may have brought changes to the social hierarchy. Speaking of young refugees in Tanzania, Essed, Frerks and Schrijvers (2004: 11) state that "the suspension of traditional structures is not only a matter of deprivation. It may also facilitate positive change." Some become camp leaders, while others work for aid organizations or start small businesses. "Young men have thus created new spaces for themselves, thereby adding new dimensions to their identities." While the authors are referring to men, the argument also applies to women (Kapteijns 2009: 119). Hart (2008: 7) remarks that such a reorganization does not necessarily result in a shift in power relations, but that attention should be paid to negotiations of power and status based on age and generation. In Kakuma, although dynamics may have changed, youth still consider respecting elders a key element of being Somali. In addition, the recognition and support of elders is still needed to get married, just as the council of elders still solves conflicts within the community and with other communities. One could say that youth have indeed gained power in the camp through their ability to communicate and find work, but it does not necessarily follow that elders have lost their prominence. In addition, while young people may work, being accepted into the social space of elders and assuming adult roles and responsibilities—notably by having a family—is complicated by the scarcity of resources. This may have helped preserve the standing attached to being an elder (Tefferi 2008: 26). There is a subtle difference, however: while respect for elders in Somalia is often clan-related, youth in the camp commonly reject the clan system, and thus respect elders for their cultural knowledge and experience, but usually not for their role as representatives of a given clan.

Clan Matters: Becoming Somalis

Aziz: I just know Kakuma. It feels like one nationality to me.

Me: You think people make no differences between nationalities or clans in the camp?

Aziz: Not when the Hawiye and the Darod line up together to receive the same ration.

Another element that characterizes Somali identity is the lineage in a given clan. Somali children typically learn the names of their paternal ancestors going back more than a dozen generations. "Despite its lack of any significant visible markers," kinship at least partly defines one's personal and social identity (Lewis 2004: 491). "The standard question posed to a stranger in order to decide how to place him and so react to him, is 'whom are you (descended) from?', segmentary genealogical distance being ... a primary criterion in defining socio-political identity," writes Lewis (1994: 83). Genealogy is at the center of the clan, "a highly segmented group of agnates tracing descent from a common eponymous ancestor" (Lewis 1969 [1955]: 17). Starting from their common ancestor, clan-families are divided into clans, then into subclans or primary lineages that include four to eight generations. Within the segmentation of the latter are found *diya*-paying groups, which pay the "blood-wealth" involved in the settlement of disputes and all of whose members are collectively responsible for the group (Lewis 1994: 20). For example, if a member of the group kills someone outside of his group, all the members of his group will be held accountable for his action and will have to pay blood money or face retaliation.

The nation's primary division is between traditional pastoralists, the *Samale* or proper Somalis, and agro-pastoralists, the *Sab*. In addition, there are smaller ethnic communities and occupational groups, or outcastes, often referred to as minority groups and seen as second-class citizens. The *Samale*, who include the majority of Somalis, are divided into four main groups or clan families, named after their respective founding ancestors: Dir, Isaq, Darod and Hawiye. Before urbanization, they were primarily nomads. The Dir and the Isaq mostly live in the north of the country. The Darod mainly occupy the far south of Somalia and the northeastern region of Kenya. The Hawiye live in the center of Somalia, around Mogadishu, and in the Hiran region, as well as in northern Kenya. The *Sab* are a much smaller group, containing two major family-clans, the Digil and the Rahanweyn, who speak May, a language related to Somali. Unlike the *Samale,* they have a strong farming tradition. They mostly live in the fertile region between the Jubba and Shabelle rivers in southern Somalia. The same area is also inhabited by the largest ethnic community or minority, the Somalised Bantu, descended from Bantu and Swahili-speaking groups and former slave populations (Lewis 2002 [1965]: 5). There are also Bajuni fishermen and sea-traders living in Kismayo and on the islands in the vicinity, and the Amarani, a community of merchants and sailors in Brava and Merca, also known as Barawa. In addition to ethnic communities, there are low-caste occupational groups or *boon* or *sab* (not the same as the *Sab* tribes) attached through patronage to noble tribes and known as "the people without brothers": the Tumal (blacksmiths), the Yibir and the Midgan (or Madiban in Kakuma, both hunters and leather-workers) (Lewis 1969 [1955]: 51). Customarily, a *sab* cannot marry a Somali and the child of a *sab* father and a Somali mother is killed at birth. However, restrictions are being relaxed, partly because of Islam and the *sharia,* which is opposed to caste distinctions, and partly through the influence of human rights (Lewis 1969 [1955]: 51–53). Minority groups mostly live in the central and southern regions, which were among the most affected by the war and the famine of the early 1990s. With the Darod, they fled in great numbers to the coast of Kenya, before being transferred to Kakuma in the late 1990s (Montclos 1999a).

Lewis' perspective on kinship as the basis of social divisions in Somalia has been criticized for being reductionist and traditionalist in the prominence it gives to (static) clans as a driver of social and political behavior (e.g., Besteman 1996a; 1996b; Samatar 1992). Others see his work as an indispensable tool for understanding Somalia (e.g., Gundel and Dharbaxo 2006; Laitin 1977). Clan does appear as an important aspect in people's own definition of their identity, and the fixed representation of clans in the political system seems to corroborate their continued importance (Menkhaus 2010: 89). For youth who grew up outside Somalia, however, the meaning of clan has been re-shaped. Despite having learned their genealogy, young people are very critical of clan loyalty, which they describe as the trigger for the war and their parents' flight (Prunier 1997: 395–96). They claim that once in Kakuma, they became Somalis and that clans and ethnic divisions came to be of secondary importance. From their perspective, they have stepped away from the "Hidden Religion" (Lewis 2004: 511). Traditionally discriminated against Bantu and Madiban youth nonetheless maintain that segregation continues—which is hardly an issue raised by other minority groups—but still claim their Somaliness. The assertion that the community has triumphed over clan loyalties sometimes feels like wishful thinking, and youth are the first to bring this up, noting that older people remain mindful of clans, as are newcomers to the camp. It is not that they defend divisive clan dynamics, but these have deep roots in their history. Daud once related a conversation on tribalism he had just had with young men and elders:

> We agreed that it is still here because of the elders. If I say to my children that tribalism is only used to identify, but not to discriminate, they will carry that message. But we tell our daughters: "I am Hawiye, don't bring me a Darod man, we fought with them in Somalia." The elders are the ones who can transform the children and make them follow the right way, but we don't.

However, some elders say they are educating their children differently. Somali lawyer Osman is one of them. He avoids teaching his children about clans and tribes, and only wants them to understand that "clans are our worst enemy."

A few youth make the point that the camp has actually reinforced the group identity of minorities through targeted resettlement programs. Until 2006, group resettlement to a third country was based on ethnicity both in Kakuma and in the Mombasa camps. Specific groups, such as the Somali Bantus, Benadiri or Barawa, were deemed more vulnerable[7] (or less threatening) and given priority (Kagwanja and Juma 2008: 227; Montclos 1999a: 2).[8] Belonging to a minority group thus became a valuable asset and in some instances led to a reinvention of identities (Cassanelli 2001: 274–76; Montclos 1999a). To a certain extent, this could explain why members of minority groups often insist more on their filiation than members of majority clans, but it could also be because they genuinely feel discrimination. "Most people here, they have not learned, they are ignorant. The only thing they know and think about is tribe, tribe, tribe," laments Abyan, a Madiban. "Even those who came in 1997, when you walk by, they say this one is from this tribe. They label you, you are your tribe and not what you are." Twenty-year-old Muno adds: "People bother you because of your clan. No one except other Madiban come and visit us. Madiban live in a specific area, close to the Somali market. When people pass by, they pinch their nose, as if we stink. I cannot marry a Darod. They will say I am from a small clan."

I mentioned above that interethnic marriages are taboo. In fact, ostracism is the response not only to unions outside one's nationality; marrying outside one's clan or ethnic group is often equally taboo. Fartuun explains that marrying between majority clans is usually fine, unlike unions between people from majority and minority groups. Twenty-eight-year-old Saalim once showed me a picture of himself and a woman: "She was my girlfriend. We loved each other and wanted to get married. But her parents refused: I am Madiban and she is Majertin [from the Darod majority clan]. We had to listen to her parents." Still, some—such as Hajiro who, unlike Fartuun and Saalim, is from a majority clan—claim that the authority of parents on the issue of marriage is diminishing, because their offspring are often the ones earning money to support the family. But something else emerged from her discourse: she pointed out that speaking of clan was hypocritical, that the things that truly matter are means and money, which, to some extent, are often connected to one's clan:

> Our culture, as much as we hide behind culture and tribe, is all about money. If my parents know that this guy is from a well-off family, he has money, a business or he is very educated, they won't mind which tribe he is from. If he is poor and from another tribe, that is when the tribe will come up. Tribe is an excuse.

She still draws lines: marrying a Bantu is not an option: "When you marry a Bantu, you have kids with hard hair. Your parents will not want a grandson like that."

The differences in views between youth and their parents when it comes to clan resonate with Hoodfar's observations about Afghan refugees in Iran. She writes that young Afghans have forged a pan-Afghan identity, regardless of their ethnicity or class, thanks to their collective suffering and their group label as refugees in Iran (2008: 183). Their parents, however, have not adopted such a view and still define themselves as members of their respective ethnic groups. This could broadly apply to Somalis in Kakuma, with a nuance: while clan affiliation remains central, parents say they must get away from it, but find it a struggle to do so, given that clan affiliation has always structured their social life. To a lesser degree, this is also true for their children.

Social Support and Protection: A Fluid Arrangement

Changes in the importance of clan are also triggered by the sheer reality of numbers rather than the will of the community. Some clans have such a small presence in Kakuma that clan-based traditional arrangements have become nonviable and solidarity has come to rely on being part of a community. This includes group-based compensation, a key part of traditional justice mechanisms. Here is how Daud, a well-respected man in his late forties, explained the working of customary justice:

> If someone hurts your face, you will be taken to a sheikh or the camp's *qadi*.[9] The *qadi* will see the bruises … there will be a discussion on compensation … [If you have left scars on a women's face], before, you had to marry her, but that was related to tribalism. Every tribe in Somalia used to stay on their own in one area. But here, we are different tribes. No one can force you to marry into another tribe, so instead you have to compensate in camels. We don't have camels, so we translate that into money. We say a camel is 5,000 shillings. In reality, a camel is worth 25,000 shillings, but we decided it would be 5,000, because of our refugee situation. You don't pay by yourself. You go to your elders and they help with collecting the amount.

As in Somalia, all members of the group are collectively responsible. However, a Somali elder who was a traditional lawyer in Somalia makes an important distinction: in most cases heard in Kakuma, unlike in Somalia, the payment of blood money is not the responsibility of the clan or tribe, but of the community. Neighbors, regardless of their clan, are asked to contribute. Small groups would not have the means to support their members, hence the need to turn it into a community responsibility. Instead of being solely based on clans and ethnic groups, solidarity has therefore come to rely on being part of a community (although there is significant overlap, as members of a given clan or minority often live close to one another).[10] Solidarity is a crucial principle in Somali society[11] and has remained so in Kakuma, possibly because it is central to managing as a community in exile. In this respect, Agier and Bouchet-Saulnier's (2003: 316) assertion that by turning aid recipients into victims, humanitarian assistance might threaten the reciprocal rights and duties that structure social life does not fit the reality of Somalis in Kakuma.

In sum, young people not only define themselves by opposition to those who live in Somalia, but also by opposition to other camp inhabitants and Kenyans. They recognize differences that distinguish them from other youth in the camp, which makes them assert that they are and will remain Somali by virtue of their culture and religion. Still, they point out that they are also Kenyans, and apparently see no contradiction between being Somali and Kenyan. In fact, there is a noticeable tension in youth's relationship to Kenya: while they note that others keep reminding them that the soil on which they live is not theirs and that Kenyan aid workers can be unwelcoming, they nonetheless feel at home in Kakuma. They are more familiar with Kenya than with Somalia. They have spent most of their lives there and they speak Swahili and English, like educated Kenyans. Yet, they are also Somalis. Their families come from Somalia, they speak the language, know the culture, are Muslims and understand the social codes. Of course, Kenya is already home to ethnic Somalis, so being a Somali in Kenya is not a contradiction. Most have therefore developed an identity "with multiple referents" (Meintel 2008: 312) and have integrated into their new environment, in contrast to most of their parents, who remain more separated from their fellow refugees of other origins and from Kenyans. Malkki (1995b: 3, 140), studying Burundian refugees in a camp and in town in Tanzania, has proposed that those living in town inhabit "multiple, shifting identities" and have adopted a "rather lively cosmopolitanism." In contrast, those in the camp, insulated from the outside, developed a "categorically distinct, collective identity" as "Hutu refugees heroized as people in exile" and a strong mythico-historical discourse. This is very different from the reality of young Somalis in Kakuma who, in addition to being in constant interaction with the rest of Kenya, Somalia and Somalis across the world, as well as traveling outside of the camp fairly regularly, proudly nurture their Somaliness, yet treasure their capacity to interact with people of extremely varied horizons and adapt to a new environment. While parents may not display the same openness, they still see that of their children as a newly acquired strength, but worry about their "survival as a group" (Taboada-Leonetti 1989: 55).

While it is relatively easily for youth to name some changes related to their ethnic identity, there are other transformations they might not mention as openly. In the context of the camp, young women question certain traditional practices and gender-related social dynamics and roles. This provokes resistance and tensions not only between men and women but also between generations. As Nyers (2006: xv) has underlined, refugeeness can be understood as a site of political reinvention and reappropriation, "a site of struggle, a continual process of identity construction, and one that highlights how the activity and practices of refugees are recasting the terms of ethical and political discourse."

The Camp as a Place of Emancipation

One morning, I was accompanying the FilmAid team to a film screening in the Somali neighborhood. A Somali woman declared to the driver that the organization was not welcome because it was teaching Christian values and blocked the car's path. She was referring to advocacy films against female genital mutilation (FGM) (or female circumcision, depending on one's perspective (Hyndman 1998: 254)).[12] Traditionally, nearly all Somali girls are excised before reaching puberty.[13] Girls are then married at a fairly young age, even though what is perceived as young is also a matter of definition and subject to change. In 1994, Lewis (1994: 33) found that while child marriage might have been common in the past, it was no longer prevalent, as girls were marrying between the ages of fifteen and twenty by then. Lewis implies that by fifteen, girls are no longer children. However, according to Kenya's Children Act, a person is a child until eighteen (art. 2) and early marriage, i.e., marriage or cohabitation with a child, is illegal (art. 14). The same article outlawed the excision of girls in 2001, while the excision of women over eighteen was banned in 2011, with the adoption of the Prohibition of Female Genital Mutilation Bill. Once in Kenya, Somali refugees are expected to abide by Kenyan law and therefore to alter customs that are deemed harmful. This has given rise to numerous behavior change campaigns in the camp, in the form of billboards, films and group discussions.

But changes are not evident, as is apparent from Daud's comment: "In our religion, we believe that when a girl reaches fifteen, let her be married and have children. Otherwise, maybe she will become a prostitute, use *miraa* [*khat*] or alcohol." Thus, the Somali head teacher of Horseed primary school mentions that most girls are still being "cut," and often married long before they turn eighteen, especially in poor families, as the dowry constitutes a precious source of income. She is trying to convince young wives, and their husbands, to continue their education even after marriage and motherhood. Results are limited, but she keeps pushing. Prohibition and awareness-raising campaigns may have led to some unsought changes. "Because of legal awareness, marriages with very young girls are not happening in the camp and people keep them secret," notes the head of the LWF Gender Unit. "But we keep dealing with divorces involving young girls. They are expected to behave like wives and mothers, but they are still little girls. Their husbands complain that they go and play rather than prepare food."

The community pressure to follow traditional practices is strong, but there is a manifest and growing gap between the community's expectations toward the girls and their desire to conform to those expectations. Young women argue that this gradually leads to changes. They point out that the more girls are marrying late and studying, the easier it becomes to follow their path, the community gradually adapting to it. They tend to talk more easily of their fear of being forced to marry at a young age than of excision, which remains a more taboo subject. They most often allude to "cutting" to explain health problems. In some cases, they claim that those excision-related complications are influencing parents. A twenty-year-old who was bedridden every time she had her period, and had been told by a doctor she needed to undergo surgery, says her suffering has convinced her mother not to have her younger sisters excised.

It has also become more permissible for women to speak out. Amina has three daughters aged between eighteen and twenty-six. They are not married, have completed their secondary education and hold prestigious positions in the camp. She says she has paid dearly for vocally going against the tide when her children were young:

> I had different perspectives on education and wanted my daughters to be ed-
> ucated, unlike me. I didn't want them to be cut, because it gave me a lot of
> problems. I used to tell other people not to have their girls cut because of that.
> There was a neighbor's daughter who was about to be cut and I went to tell
> them it was not good. From that day, I was seen as an outcast. Fetching water
> was hard. People harassed me when I went to the tap. One day they attacked
> me. I was stoned and beaten. I had to go to the hospital and be stitched.

This assault happened over a decade ago. While being vocal may still not be encouraged, it has become less perilous and is thus more easily conceivable. Twenty-one-year-old Mulki describes to parents of girls how she has suffered from being married at fourteen, hoping that it will make them think twice before obliging their daughters to go through the same experience:

> I had just finished my primary school. I came home one day and I saw a man.
> I asked my mom: "Who is it?" She said: "This is your husband." I tried to
> refuse and run away, but I had nowhere to go. They tried punishing me. I had
> to accept, even though I was not comfortable. I just cried day and night. I had
> my first son when I was fifteen. I had three by the time I was seventeen. There
> were problems with my husband. I had found a job in the health post and he
> didn't want me to work, just as he didn't want me to study. But I refused to stop
> working. So he took my children away. He escaped to Somalia with them in
> 2009. I don't have any children anymore. I am missing something in my heart.

She says that some parents listen. Others accuse her of not respecting Somali customs and of trying to influence their daughters. But the camp is an en-vironment where women feel entitled to question and object to traditional practices, at least to some extent. Moreover, it is also a place where these prac-tices are prohibited by law, and young women know that and affirm it—al-though in practice, excision and early marriage still take place on the territory of the camp.

Renegotiating the Role of Somali Women

Mulki does not only speak of her marriage. She also denounces the outdated views that Somalis hold regarding women and their place in society. She re-marks that "many women in the camp are deprived of their rights." I encoun-tered that sort of resistance fairly often from young women who had grown up in Kakuma, where they have been exposed to a human rights discourse. They spoke of how they had no intention of getting married anytime soon and that they planned to study further, have a career and hold leading roles, no matter what their community thought about it.

A fascinating facet of the photography classes was seeing how young women of various ethnic groups showed a sense of solidarity with one another. One day, a Sudanese teenager mentioned that she was struggling to do her homework. Along with four other girls, she was expected to fetch water, cook and clean for nineteen boys at home, who, like her, were in Kakuma without their parents. It left her with very little time for schoolwork. All girls, regardless of their ethnicity, expressed compassion, but also indignation about the unfairness of the social position of women. Many commented that they knew it was not like that everywhere, thanks to the media and regular contacts with people who were resettled and visitors.

Young women may be developing a more liberal discourse, but it clashes with the often more conservative views of young men and their community more broadly. Girls talk of how boys enjoy more freedom than girls, who "are sometimes beaten if they are seen out in the evening." Unlike young men, who are generally encouraged to work, the reputation of a young woman who does so is damaged, a view that is confirmed and given approval by a youth leader:

> The community thinks that girls who work are prostitutes. Most of the Somali girls in Kenya are being spoiled. You can see it for yourself here or in Nairobi. In Dadaab, it is better. Girls here mingle with Kenyans and other nationalities, like the Sudanese, the Congolese, the Ethiopians. You see girls with white men. That is why parents don't want their daughters to work. It is the same thing with secondary school. Very few parents send their daughters there, because they think they will be spoiled: they are studying with boys. Let them stay home and be safe.

Women, and especially Somalis, are noticeably underrepresented on the staffs of humanitarian organizations (and in high school), a fact that managers explain by the burden of domestic work and restrictions imposed on them by their communities.

Mahdi and Nuradin once asked me how many children I wanted. I said maybe two. They told me I would be a bad Somali woman and that they wanted twenty each. I pointed out that that was a lot of children. They explained they only had to take more than one wife and that each of them could carry seven to ten children. I said I was under the impression that many women of their age were not thrilled by the idea of having so many children and sharing their husbands. "That is how it goes. It is Somali culture," they responded. Case closed. This dichotomy prompts the RCK's head of office to comment that although women feel empowered and challenge their subordinate position, this has not significantly altered the discourse and the expectations of men: "They are the ones needing to accept to change. Take FGM, we all know it happens in the camp. Men from Somalia or Darfur find it difficult to marry an uncircumcised woman. There is a feeling that excision tames a woman. They all know who is excised and who is not." But even there, some change seems to be occurring. Both Aziz and Faarax asserted that they did not see any justification for excision, and would never consider taking more than one wife. Thus, being in the camp has not only altered the transmission of the Somali language and made young people critical of clan dynamics; the role of women is also being renegotiated, as life in Kakuma contributes, to some extent, to reshaping young women's perception of their rights and the place they deserve in society.

Somalis from Kakuma

In short, Somali youth in Kakuma claim multiple belongings. Many assert that the camp is home, as this is where they grew up and live, and say that they are both Somali and Kenyan. Settling in a new environment characterized by cultural diversity has influenced their acquisition of some cultural practices and codes, such as the command of the language or a respect for tribalism. They more readily identify the influence of their host society than that of other ethnic groups, perhaps because the recognition between youth first emerged from common Kenyan references with regard to their education, media or laws. Also, young women are more and more explicitly rejecting traditional practices, which is provoking the resistance of their community, but also seems to be prompting changes. In that respect, migration could have a lasting effect on the dynamics between generations or genders, as Colson (1999), Essed, Frerks and Schrijvers (2004) and Kusow (2007) have emphasized.

Kakuma's "enforced proximity" (Tomlinson 1999: 181) may not have produced a cosmopolitan disposition, but a convivial culture (Gilroy 2006a) has emerged among the camp's inhabitants. They have learned to live close to one another and to deal with their differences in a way that does not create insurmountable communication problems. The pacification efforts of organizations working in the camp, as well as the establishment of traditional conflict resolution mechanisms, have helped. But social relationships that have progressively developed between the members of various ethnic groups have probably played a more important part. While cultural differences have become ordinary and are tolerated, they are not necessarily praised. Clear limits to integration exist: social life remains mostly monoethnic, even though young people value their capacity to engage with people of different backgrounds.

Interaction between various ethnic groups has also resulted in a transformation of young Somalis' ethnic identity. They highlight the influence of their environment on their sense of belonging and their cultural codes, but also stress that they feel Somali, alluding to their religious practice, their respect for their elders or their way of socializing. Hence, what has been observed in other migratory contexts is also relevant to refugee camps: ethnic identity can be conceived as a fluid social construction (Meintel 1993; Oriol 1985). Moreover, exposure to other cultures, Kenyan law and the grammar of human rights leads young people, and particularly women, to dispute some traditional practices and social structures. Their challenge meets with resistance, but also slowly influences social dynamics. Such changes make the idea of returning to Somalia especially difficult to consider for young women. Indeed, they believe that their progressive way of thinking and dressing—they remark that their veils are not as strict and all-encompassing as those worn by women in Somalia, and some have piercings hidden under their veils, despite their parents' strong disapproval—would not be welcomed back in their country of origin.

Notes

1. The will to foster a tension-free environment is central to the Constitution. It aims "to reduce the influence of clan, ethnicity and nationality based interest" and "to create and promote peace, stability and harmony amongst the members of the camp" (art. 2 § 3 and 6). So as to ensure that all groups are represented, the document states that any nationality with more than one hundred people in the camp must have a representative on the camp management committee. Thus, if no one is elected, someone will be nominated (art. 4.3).
2. I discuss the camp leadership system further in Chapter 7, on the subject of trust and mistrust.
3. By stating that all leaders must have a good command of written and spoken English and preferably Swahili (art. 5), the Constitution introduces a bias in favor of refugees educated in Kenya, and hence for young refugees, or originating from Swahili-speaking countries, such as the Democratic Republic of Congo.
4. Somalis themselves commonly make a distinction between "real" Somalis and other Somalis. So-called "real" Somalis or ethnic Somalis are from majority clans, while minority groups such as the Bajuni, the Barawa and especially the Bantu are considered as nonethnic Somalis.
5. Interestingly, while Somali youth speak of the way they dress as different from those living in Somalia, in reality, they dress pretty much like young men in Somalia who, just like those in Kakuma, usually wear Western clothes to work and *macawis*, a sarong-like patterned and colorful garment, to relax at home. Most have not adopted the trendy Westernized style of their peers from Sudan and the Great Lakes, who, with their skinny jeans, tight t-shirts, cool haircuts and skateboard loafers, would blend in perfectly with students in a big North American metropolis.

6. Laitin (1977: 42) remarks that Somalis "often consider speaking their language a sufficient condition for nationality." Long before the Somali language was written down in 1972, poetry was used as a "mass medium of communication and a repository of knowledge about the past" (Andrzejewski 2011: 9). Oral poets are among the most praised artists, in addition to being extremely influential. Their art has attracted the attention of numerous visitors, such as the scholars I.M. Lewis and Andrzejewski, and, in earlier times, the explorer Richard Burton (1987 [1856]: 81–82), who thought it strange that a language "which has no written character should so abound in poetry and eloquence. There are thousands of songs, some local, other general, upon all conceivable subjects, such as camel loading, drawing water and elephant hunting … The country teems with poets … every man has his recognized position in literature as accurately defined as though he had been reviewed in a century of magazines."

7. In the refugee regime, "vulnerable people" constitute a specific administrative category (in many recent documents, they are called "groups with specific needs," although this wording is not commonly used in day-to-day management). People deemed vulnerable may receive extra assistance or be targeted for resettlement for protection reasons. Definitions vary slightly, but usually include children up to five years old, pregnant/lactating women, the physically or mentally disabled, chronically sick people, female heads of households, child heads of households, elders, heads of households, single women, unaccompanied minors and survivors of gender-based violence (UNHCR 2007c: 234, 548). While the UNHCR does not specifically define what "vulnerability" refers to in its *Handbook for Emergencies* (2007c), it stresses in several instances that special attention should be given to "vulnerable" refugees or to "groups with special needs" (e.g., at 164, 230, 234 and 291).

8. Even though resettlement is in theory offered primarily to refugees with the most important protection needs, resettlement countries commonly select refugees according to their national interest. For example, Australia includes integration prospects among its selection criteria, while the United States tends to favor groups of refugees that are supposedly united and "docile" (Agier 2008 [2005]: 95; Kagwanja and Juma 2008: 228–29).

9. A *qadi* is a judge ruling in accordance with *sharia* law, the canon law of Islam.

10. This might not have been totally foreign to Somalis in Somalia: Besteman (1996a: 125) underlines that in southern Somalia, "villages could function as diya-paying groups, even if villagers were members of different kinship-based diya groups."

11. Rousseau et al. (1998: 404) consider that the prescription of giving, receiving and giving back "exists in paradigmatic form in Somali society, which imposes absolute rules of solidarity on family and age-group members."

12. While young women in the camp usually employ the term "cutting" to speak of excision and infibulation, humanitarian organizations systematically use the acronym FGM.

13. In 2006, 98 percent of Somali women were excised and, in most cases, infibulated, according to the World Health Organization.

Chapter 5

A WORLD IN MOVEMENT

The Camp as a Connected Space

❧⟨◉⟩•⟨◉⟩☙

> *Nin ann dhul marini dhaayo maleh.*
> He who has not traveled in the world has no eyes.
> —Somali proverb

After twenty-eight-year-old Saalim visited the photography exhibition that my students and I had organized, he invited me to his home to show me his own photo albums. I had never seen such an impressive collection of photographs in Kakuma. He had a few old family portraits, many recent photographs of friends, brothers and sisters, nieces and nephews, relatives, and a few women wearing smart outfits he had tailored. I asked who the people in the pictures were. "This is my sister, she is in Canada." "This is my cousin, he is in Australia." "This is my brother in Nairobi." "This one is my uncle who works in Dubai." "This is my childhood friend on the day of his departure to America." It went on and on. Nearly all the people portrayed lived elsewhere, often very far from Kenya and Somalia.

While most people in the camp do not have photographs to display, their relatives are also spread out around the globe. Everyone seems to know someone in Canada, have several relations in the United States, family members elsewhere in Kenya, others in Somalia, some in Sudan, the Gulf States or Europe, or maybe in Australia. Many have friends in South Africa. Those who have permanently left the camp are not the only ones on the move. Somalis in Kakuma also hit the road regularly, despite policies restricting movement. Many visit Nairobi or Mombasa during work or school holidays. Others go to major Kenyan cities to work, buy goods to sell in the camp or to seek healthcare, while some go back to Somalia for funerals or to look after sick relatives. In fact, traveling is common enough that people who have never left the camp are atypical. Aziz, who once asked me if it was true that there was no greenery in cities, says he used to be embarrassed about being untraveled: "When I was young, I felt ashamed when people talked of Nairobi. They would say: 'Do you know that street? Do you know that place?' And I would just slip away because I felt I should have known. I felt ashamed that others had money to go and we didn't. My family never left the camp during holidays. The others were always leaving."

It is not only the camp that visits the world, but also the world that comes to the camp, as people in Kakuma interact regularly with their compatriots around the globe by phone and the Internet, while the mass media bring daily news from all over the world. Some refugees who have left the camp also return periodically to see their family and friends. Humanitarian staff go to the camp to work, and government officials and other "dignitaries" pay occasional visits. Hence, despite being located in an isolated area, the camp is far from being cut off; it is "indissolubly linked to both local and extralocal places through what might be called networks" (Escobar 2001: 143).

I have alluded before to the influence of this connectedness on young people's perception of the camp. It has given them a greater understanding of the limitations imposed by their status and has fueled their dreams of moving further afield. It has also made them familiar with the recurring populist threats by politicians to force them back to Somalia. Kakuma seems like an exemplification of Appadurai's reflection on the interconnected effect of mass media and migration on people's imagination (1996). While large-scale migration is not new, its juxtaposition with "a rapid flow of mass-mediated images, scripts, and sensations" is, and it distinguishes today's movements from those of the past. Combined, the two factors "seem to impel (and sometimes compel) the work of the imagination" (1996: 4). This collective vision that is formed upon contact with the media goes beyond borders, even if people themselves are not in movement. Realms of imagined selves and worlds proliferate, whereas until recently, the avenues for social life were relatively limited. The immediate environment no longer strictly dictates social reproduction. This does not turn the world into a friendlier place where mobility is truly higher: "Instead, what is implied is that even in the meanest and most hopeless of lives, the most brutal and dehumanizing of circumstances, the harshest of lived inequalities are now open to the play of the imagination" (1996: 54). Such knowledge that might stimulate action and agency does not signal the death of the local, but makes it inseparable from the global.

While people's imagined paths may have been multiplied, real movement for undesirable populations such as refugees is subject to increasingly strict measures of control, making their travels complicated and costly. These are not desirable tourists, to borrow from Bauman, who speaks of a new polarization and hierarchization of the world between "tourists" and "vagabonds," magnified by globalization.[1] The former before whom borders disappear travel because they want to. The latter are in movement "because *they have no other bearable choice*" (Bauman 1998a: 93). They are "involuntary tourists" who often travel illegally, "sometimes paying more for the crowded steerage of a stinking unseaworthy boat than others pay for business-class gilded luxuries—and are frowned upon, and, if unlucky, arrested and promptly deported, when they arrive" (1998a: 89).

In this chapter, I explore the manifestations and effects of the camp's connectedness. I first consider movements that take Somalis outside the camp, whether permanently or temporarily. I then explore the impact of the "world" visiting the camp through the media, communications and people. I conclude with remarks on the influence of Kenya's political landscape on refugees' (lack of) settledness. I contend that constant interaction with people across the globe and awareness of their conditions are a source of frustration, but also become the motor for action by making Kakuma an even more intolerable place. Through the mass media and communications, people have developed an idea of a dream world and of the conditions (real or fictitious) in which other people live. There is no reason for refugees not to aspire to a better life. While the imagined possibilities are endless, real life is full of limitations. Noting that a familiarity with the wider world increases the state of discontent among people left at the margins is not new. However, it must be discussed, as it strongly affects people's perception of the camp.

When the Camp Visits the World

Movement out of the camp is ongoing. Resettlement is only one way of leaving, but it is certainly the most sought-after. In the absence of this option, a number of refugees leave by their own means. As return to Somalia remains unappealing for a large number of people due to the prolonged nature of the conflict, irregular migration either to a more desirable location in Kenya or another country can become the most easily conceivable option, despite its inherent risks.

When considering the movements of Somalis, it is essential to underscore their long tradition of using mobility as a survival strategy, owing to their nomadic heritage and also as a result of trade patterns and work-related migrations (Horst 2006a, 2006b; Kleist 2004; Lewis 1994: 146). Mobility may not have been traditionally central to the life of all Somalis, but primarily to pastoralists, who tend to originate from majority clans. It is possible that, once in exile, migration also became fundamental to non-nomadic groups through their exposure to fellow Somalis and the camp's interaction with the world (Zimmerman 2009: 88). Moreover, Somalis' movements are facilitated by the existence of a large diaspora and transnational networks that result from this tradition of mobility. Horst has coined the term "transnational nomads" to describe the Somali inclination toward "looking for greener pastures, a strong social network that entails the obligation to assist each other in surviving, and risk-reduction through strategically dispersing investments in family members and activities" (2006c: 14). This could equally be said about Palestinian, Afghan or Sahrawi refugees (Chatty 2007: 274–77). This belonging to networks (as well as the ability to make a living through other means than humanitarian assistance) allows some refugees to recover a degree of autonomy.

All My Friends are Gone: The Resettlement of Refugees

When I first met Khadra in October 2012, she told me, as did so many others, that she would soon be leaving for the United States. She was heading to Georgia. I knew that such assertions often said more about the speaker's dreams than about reality. She did add that her name had not yet been posted for departure, but she had completed her medical check and security clearance, and really wished her turn would come before these expired in less than six months. She also hoped the rest of her family would go before her, so she would not land alone in a foreign country. (Being twenty years old, she was considered independent, and thus her resettlement file had been separated from that of her family. Hence, although all members of her family should at some point travel to the same destination, they might leave months or years apart.) Two months later, her name appeared on the board where the names of departing refugees are listed, a board that refugees consult religiously every second day. The rest of her family was not on it. I did not hear this from her first, but from her friend Faarax. It was the news of the day and word was spreading very quickly among her peers.

Four days later, she was already leaving the camp, heading to Nairobi. Although she had dreamed of this drastic change for years, she was extremely agitated: she was boarding a plane for the first time in her life and had never been away from her family. A couple of days after she landed in the United States, she declared she hated it and wanted to be back in Kakuma. She held to that line for quite a few months. The adaptation was difficult. She was arriving on her own in a foreign country, with extremely limited means and under pressure to find a job rapidly. Then her discourse began to change: she started saying that she was doing all right, adjusting. In Kakuma, her friends remarked that it was always like that. At first, people hated it, wanted to be back in the camp, felt disoriented and kept up very regular contact with people in Kakuma. Then they got used to their new setting and phoned a little less often. In the following months, I saw a number of people leave, with the pattern repeating itself.

What I witnessed more often, however, was people endlessly waiting to go, endlessly talking about their hopes of finally seeing their names on the board or being called for a resettlement interview. I heard countless complaints about the lengthiness, unpredictability and unfairness of the process. Resettlement was a constant topic of discussion and preoccupation. I did not ask about it during interviews, quickly understanding that a vast majority of refugees would bring it up themselves, as going further west is, they believe, the only path to a decent future. Therefore, when they recount their stories, reflections on resettlement are necessarily a key element. Sometimes the tale is a very sour account of failure. Often, it is a story of waiting and seeing so many other people leaving. Faarax, for example, mentions that of the eighteen members of his former football team, all but four have left for the United States, most of them between 2008 and 2010: "Every day, I thought I was next. Now I am just tired."

This brings to mind Cindy Horst's writings on *buufis* and the article of Rousseau et al. (1998) on the "pre-migration dream of leaving" of young Somalis in Ethiopia and Somaliland. In the latter, the authors argue that through the dream of leaving, young people manage to survive and escape despair, but are also at risk of becoming increasingly frustrated and of losing touch with reality if their hopes remain unfulfilled. Horst (2006b: 143–44) explains that the term *buufis* is used by Somalis in Dadaab to refer to both the resettlement dream and resettlement itself. Furthermore, it alludes to people's longing for resettlement and the madness that sometimes affects those whose wishes do not become reality (in Kakuma, youth used the term to refer to resettlement, but not to speak of the dream of resettlement, unlike older people, who also defined it as the "endless hope for something"). While this phenomenon reflects the Somali tradition of mobility, it is also a novelty, "triggered by the fact that, due to transnational flows of remittances and information, refugees in remote camps like Dadaab can compare their lives in the camps to those of others elsewhere" (Horst 2006b: 144). The influence of global connectedness on aspiration is not unique to refugees: a young Turkana told me he really longed to move to Canada. His best friend, a Ugandan refugee, had been resettled there and after hearing from him and the media that it was a good country, he wanted to go too.

A Selected Few: Process and Numbers

Although refugees focus on resettlement, the proportion of people leaving Kakuma every year remains small. For example, approximately one thousand departed in 2012, which is comparable to the figure for 2011 (UNHCR 2011a, 2012c). While annual figures are proportionately minor, significant numbers of Somalis have left through various programs over time. Between 1995 and 2011, some 57,500 Somali refugees from Kenya were resettled to third countries, most often the United States (UNHCRa). A fair number of these most certainly left from Kakuma. Somalis who arrived in the late 1990s and claim to be among the few first arrivals still left in the camp are not wrong: in May 2012, less than three thousand of the over 12,000 Somalis who were in the camp in 2000 still lived there. Of course, not everyone who has left has been resettled. Some must have returned to Somalia or settled elsewhere, while others must have died.

Priority for resettlement is given to refugees whose lives might be at risk in the camp. Throughout the years, specific programs have focused on particular groups of refugees, either for their assumed vulnerability or for their very limited prospects of repatriation or local integration. The latter was the justification for the program launched in 2006 to resettle Somalis in protracted displacement to the United States. The project initially targeted refugees who had been registered in 1991 and 1992, and progressively expanded to those who had done so prior to 2005. In theory, all the first comers have therefore left the camp, except for those whose cases for resettlement were rejected. However, as the UNHCR head of protection explained, a number of cases were lost or forgotten when staff left. The office was in the process of cleaning up the resettlement database, which might explain why in 2013 I witnessed the departure of several people who had arrived in the 1990s. In addition, some refugees who arrived in Kenya during that time did not officially register with the UNHCR until 2006, while other cases have been put on hold because of suspected fraud. The necessary investigations, which can lead to the resumption of a case, a warning, permanent ineligibility or a referral for prosecution, are being conducted very slowly. Fraud includes registering twice with different identities; lying about one's life story, family composition, name, clan or locality of origin; or registering with fake identity documents.[2] The UNHCR claims that these acts make it impossible to determine a person's true identity. Family sponsorship programs also allowed a number of refugees to be resettled, but this route was closed down in 2004 due to fraud-related problems. When I was in Kakuma, it was expected to resume, with the incorporation of routine DNA testing. Hundreds of cases were also wiped out not because of fraud committed by refugees, but due to a major corruption scandal in the UNHCR office in the late 1990s that led to an interruption of resettlement activities. More than seventy people were found to be involved in a criminal ring extorting sums of as much as US$6,000 from refugees for resettlement-related services. Thousands of refugees whose claims were being processed when the scheme was uncovered had their cases put on hold for fear that they might be involved in the fraud. At that point, it was understood that these cases would be reopened, and a number of them were (HRW 2002: 176–82; UN General Assembly 2001: 2). However, the head of protection in Kakuma indicates that some never were.

The resettlement process itself is long and tedious. The UNHCR does screening interviews and checks for cheating, which take several months. The organization then hands over the individual or family file to the embassy of the potential resettlement country and the International Organization for Migration (IOM), which is in charge of the logistics and administration of the process. Between further interviews by country officials and preliminary security clearances by the receiving country, it takes at least two years to get a final answer for a case submitted to the United States, the most common destination for Somalis. Once a case is accepted, refugees undergo a medical examination and an in-depth security check, both with short-duration validity. Hence, if people do not leave rapidly once their case is accepted and both clearances have been given, the procedure must be repeated over and over, which commonly happens.

Creating Categories and Labels

A consequence of the resettlement process is the creation of specific labels for refugees in the camp, which in turn affects people's perceptions and identity (see Zetter 1991). There are those who are waiting to go. They have successfully gotten through the process and hope to be departing soon, the common view being that no one is sure to go before they actually leave. Then there are a selected few who have been picked by the World University Service of Canada to study at a Canadian university. These are seen as a kind of elite; unlike other resettled refugees who will have to struggle to earn their living once they land in a foreign land, they are being given a passport to education. There are those who are at some other stage of the process: perhaps they have been interviewed by the UNHCR or have had their case approved and referred to an embassy and are waiting for further interviews. Then there are those who are hoping for their name to come up for a resettlement interview. They have usually arrived fairly recently and anticipate that once all the earlier arrivals are gone, it will be their turn. And there are the rejected cases, those who can no longer hope for resettlement. The "rejected" label is heavy to carry, as it symbolizes failure. I became aware of this after an interview with a Bajuni elder who cried when I asked what lay ahead for his children. He said he had failed them. I thought he meant by fleeing his country and bringing his children to Kakuma. When we left, the young man who was accompanying me explained that he was crying because he had been rejected for resettlement and thus could not take his children abroad, and, in that respect, had failed to give them the only valuable future he could have offered. After that, I noticed that people commonly mentioned that a given refugee had been "rejected" in a tone that made it sound like a confidential and taboo piece of information.

While parents usually stay in the camp with their descendants after receiving a negative resettlement response, young people who have finished their studies often start making plans to leave under their own steam. A number of those who have little short-term hope of resettlement because of their relatively recent arrival do the same.

Searching for Opportunities: Irregular Movements

Many people, especially those with no resettlement chances, when they are tired of the life of refugees, they leave the camp. Most go to Nairobi, others to Nakuru and Eldoret [in Kenya]. A few go back to Somalia, mainly to stable places like Puntland and Somaliland, others to South Africa or Europe. I had two friends who went to Nairobi. Then they got money from a brother, so they went to Mombasa, took a boat to Mozambique and proceeded to South Africa. Some go from Sudan to Libya and then to Italy. They give money to smugglers to take them. I also had a friend who went to Sweden. One day, I no longer saw him around. Then I saw him on Facebook. I asked where he was. He was in Stockholm. I asked how he had managed to get there, if he had been resettled by UNHCR. "No, I resettled myself," he said.
—Abdi, twenty-three years old

For many, the camp is home, but a home that has little to offer, apart from education and resettlement. When these possibilities are exhausted or, in the case of resettlement, remain a faraway prospect, it is a home one should leave. Movements between the camp and Kenyan cities—for work, business opportunities, holiday, family visits or to seek healthcare—are ongoing. As Abdi underlines above, others go further, leaving for Western countries, the Gulf States or other African countries, most often South Africa and Sudan. Those who leave for nearby locations usually come back when there is a verification in order to maintain their refugee status. Those who migrate further away are less likely to do so. Although movements are relatively widespread, they are not easy or danger-free. While refugees say they can bribe their way in Kenya, traveling abroad is strenuous and expensive, and entails taking considerable risks.

The choice of a destination (when such choice is possible) depends on many factors, in particular the presence of relatives and the family's strategy— members of an extended family sometimes take up residence in different sites and countries (camps, towns, African and European countries, etc.) to be prepared to face all eventualities. The possibility of obtaining legal residency, education and employment prospects, the proximity of the country of origin, historical, cultural or economic ties and knowledge of the language will also influence people's choices. The existence of known routes and smuggling networks, as well as financial resources—a trip to Europe costs several thousand dollars—are also important factors (Moret, Baglioni and Efionayi-Mäder 2006: 86, 124; Zimmerman 2009: 78, 92). The actual destination of refugees is sometimes left to chance, decided by smugglers and agents who negotiate the passage of the undocumented (Moret, Baglioni and Efionayi-Mäder 2006: 109).

Finding Work and Business Opportunities in the Rest of Kenya

Although encampment is not enshrined in Kenyan law, refugees have been effectively required to reside in Kakuma or Dadaab by the Kenyan authorities for the last two decades. Those wishing to travel legally must obtain a "movement pass" from the government's Department of Refugee Affairs and the UNHCR. Such passes are only granted to refugees in cases involving urgent health issues that cannot be treated in the camps, further education, the death of a relative elsewhere in Kenya, the tracing of family members, embassy visits, the purchase of goods for camp-based trading or security problems in the camps. These restrictions contravene Kenya's national and international obligations.[3] Those stopped outside the camps without a movement pass can be arrested and fined (HRW 2009a: 44–47). Refugees usually describe the process of obtaining such a pass as lengthy and uncertain.

Regardless of these constraints, Somalis keep moving between the camps and urban areas in Kenya, traveling by bus and buying their way through the police checkpoints that are set up on the road. As a matter of fact, policies that limit the movement of refugees are difficult to implement systematically because they require substantial human and material resources. They often manifest themselves in periodic raids and arbitrary arrests (Jacobsen 2005: 31). Many people have found ways to integrate informally into the economy, often without government approval and almost entirely outside of the legal system (Banki 2004: 12–13; RCK 2012: 29).[4] Families might split up between the camp and Kenyan cities. Wives and children might stay in Kakuma where they have access to affordable living and education, while breadwinners, mostly men, travel to cities and send money back. Young people might also pursue further studies in Nairobi, where the Somali diaspora provides an important safety net. Several of those who receive regular, sufficient remittances have settled outside the camp and come back when they run out of money or a new registration takes place, so as not to lose their ration card and prospective resettlement opportunities. Reasons for leaving the camp are not limited to livelihood and educational opportunities; people also leave because of insecurity, inadequate medical services and the climate.

Movements to Nairobi are common enough for the Union of Somali Youth (USY), a Kakuma-based youth group, to have started a branch there, founded by members who have moved to the city. In its meetings in Kakuma, the USY always mentions the number of students in its literacy classes who have recently dropped out and the reasons why. Every week, several more move to Nairobi. Two young men who were very active USY members, Mahdi and Faarax, left for Eastleigh, Nairobi's Somali neighborhood, while I was in Kakuma. They were tired of the camp where they had both grown up and wanted to find work in the city. They hoped to earn up to 15,000 KSh (US$170) a month, which sounded optimistic. I accompanied them to the daily bus, which was, as always, crowded with Somalis traveling to the capital. They each had 500 KSh (less than US$6) in their pockets. Although they did not have movement passes, they were not worried about potential controls along the way. They explained that the bus was charging a slightly higher rate than the other company to cover payments at police checkpoints. They mentioned that the other bus company's vehicles were in better condition and thus more reliable, but that it was hard to board them without the necessary documents. They did reach Nairobi safely and hassle-free, where I saw them a few weeks later. They were staying with relatives and looking for jobs. They seemed a bit lost, but were getting used to the city. They kept running into people they knew from Kakuma on the streets of Eastleigh. Mahdi, who had never seen a city before, was spending hours in the streets, watching people, exploring his new surroundings. When we parted, the Somali Kenyan friend who had accompanied me commented that they would be just fine: "Somalis support one another." More than six months later, they were still in Nairobi, had only worked irregularly and were still looking for something more stable. While moving to Nairobi is relatively common, this does not mean that the transition is easy. Aden left Kakuma in 2009, aged twenty-seven, after he was turned down for resettlement. He recalls struggling for a full year in Eastleigh, looking for a job. "I had no relatives there. I would wait until people left the mosque to go there to sleep. Sometimes, for a full day, I would not even get a cup of tea. At some point, I started helping people writing applications. They would give me five hundred shillings. It was a very hard life."

When I visited Mahdi and Faarax in Eastleigh, I had an interesting encounter. While taking a look into a rundown shopping mall, I started talking to a young tailor with a small shop. When I said I had just come from Kakuma, he asked if I knew the Don Bosco training center. He then explained that he was a refugee from Somalia and had lived in Kakuma, where he learned tailoring at Don Bosco. Once he had completed the training, armed with his new skills, he had left for Nairobi and opened a business. I inquired about problems related to his lack of documents. He said he was earning enough money to be able to manage and preferred being independent, rather than living in the hardship of Kakuma. There was nothing exceptional about his situation. In 2011, the UNHCR and several NGOs estimated that between 80,000 and 100,000 refugees were living in Nairobi, some legally, others without papers. The greatest proportion of these were Somalis. Refugees have also established themselves in smaller cities where the cost of living is lower, such as Eldoret, Kisumu and Mombasa (Campbell, Crisp and Kiragu 2011: 25–26, 30).

However, relocation threats were changing the dynamic because living in urban areas was getting more complicated. Even before that, refugees said that settling outside the camp had become increasingly expensive. Not only was the cost of living soaring, but the bribes they had to pay to policemen were ever larger. While I had already left Kenya when the attack on Westgate Mall occurred,[5] it is likely that living without documents in urban areas became even trickier and more costly after that event. A few refugees in Kakuma claim they can solve the problem by buying identity documents (ID). For example, twenty-year-old Jamal said that if he was not picked for resettlement, he would not consider working as a refugee, as salaries are too low, but would do it as a Kenyan:

> You can just buy an ID card for twenty or thirty thousand shillings [US$230–345]. Then you are Kenyan. You can't do it here. You have to go to Nairobi. I know a man who is a driver. He was rejected for resettlement in 2010. He gave up his ration card and went to buy an ID. He works as a Kenyan and earns a lot of money. That is what I would do.

This was not news, as I had been told several times before about refugees in Dadaab who had acquired genuine Kenyan identity cards through corrupt officials and later faced exclusion from resettlement. (Since they were now registered as Kenyan citizens, they were no longer eligible for resettlement.) However, Jamal probably underestimated the price, as the media recently reported on the purchase of national IDs by refugees for up to 100,000 KSh (US$1,140; Wafula 2013). The acquisition of IDs by Somali refugees is not a new occurrence. The Kenya National Commission on Human Rights (2007: 9) wrote that the practice already existed in the early 1990s. It specified that cards were obtained by bribing elders, registration officers and the provincial administrator for sums of up to 2,000 KSh (less than US$30 in October 1993). In 2005, a re-registration with fingerprinting also revealed that a number of refugees were in possession of Kenyan identification documents (DRA n.d.). Not all refugees had to buy their IDs; politicians seeking to increase the number of their supporters have also distributed some to refugees (Lindley 2011b: 36).

In sum, movements to the rest of Kenya continue, but increased risks and costs attached to living in cities have motivated some to return to Kakuma or Dadaab. This might also lead others to migrate further afield.

Heading Abroad: Reaching the West, Other African Countries and the Gulf States

Not long after I arrived in Kakuma, Aziz came to ask for advice: he wanted tips on how to stay safe while conducting research on a sensitive topic. He had started gathering information for a documentary film on *tahriib*, or irregular migration, from Kakuma. A few days before, he had found out that one of his friends had drowned at sea trying to reach Europe. The family was gathering money to pay for the funeral. He believed people took such risks out of despair, either because the length of the resettlement process discouraged them or because their cases had been rejected. He also said that some received significant help to travel from relatives who hoped that paying for one expensive trip would be cheaper than providing monthly support. He had found a number of refugees who were planning to leave, some who had attempted to go and a smuggler who had agreed to speak with him. One of his prospective interviewees was Najib, whom I met several months later.

Nineteen-year-old Najib had tried to enter Italy via Libya from Kakuma, but had been stopped on the way, at the border between Uganda and South Sudan. He had been stranded in Uganda for a while, then managed to gather enough money to head back to Kakuma. The short trip had cost him his savings of several hundred dollars. This was not his first attempt to leave. Inspired by people who had undertaken the journey through Djibouti, he had tried to take it himself at the end of 2008, when he was fifteen, but had been stopped in Somaliland by his family. He arrived in Kakuma from Mogadishu a few months later. These episodes did not deter him from striving to reach Europe, which he saw as his only true option. All his family was still in Somalia and he desperately wanted to find a way to earn money to support them. He was not able to do so from Kakuma and therefore believed that he had to get to a country where it would be possible. He was planning to leave again as soon as he had enough money. He estimated that he needed at least two thousand dollars to pay for the trip, but could earn a part of that sum in Juba, South Sudan. Once in Italy, he would keep going, hopefully all the way to Sweden, Finland or the Netherlands, "where there is good education and good living conditions and, unlike other countries, they will not force you to learn their language before you can start working." He was remarkably well informed. I asked why he had first tried to go by Djibouti rather than Bosasso in Puntland, in northern Somalia, from which the journey was cheaper. He replied that while it was less expensive in those places, it was also riskier. He was right; something I knew from my former job.

Figure 5.1 Najib's journey. Map adapted by the author from Map No 4170 (World) of the UN Department of Field Support

Similarly, Najib had ruled out South Africa, where "Somalis are not welcomed"[6] and Saudi Arabia, as "you will be returned to Somalia." I asked how he felt about the danger related to the long journey to Europe. "Staying here is also risking my life. There is no future in Kakuma and in Somalia, there is war. There is no point in staying. All the other options are not worth it. At least, if you travel, you get rich or you die. It's a better choice."

While I heard some failed migration stories, I listened to many more successful accounts. Everyone seems to know someone who has left the camp and reached Europe or South Africa. Views on this subject are interlaced with those on resettlement opportunities. Youth who feel they have a good chance of being resettled in the fairly near future usually depict the trip as unsafe and unattractive. They also stress that once in a wealthier country, life remains a struggle. Others who have been rejected for resettlement or believe their turn will not come any time soon often see such migration in a more favorable light. Although some women undertake such a journey, it is mostly young men who seemed to consider it an option. Among the main factors motivating refugees who have the financial and physical means to travel irregularly to another country of asylum are insecurity and the lack of a legal status or IDs that can ensure protection and facilitate integration by allowing them to legally join the labor market or the education system (Moret, Baglioni and Efionayi-Mäder 2006: 9; Zimmerman 2009: 88).

This does not mean that reaching Europe, the Gulf States or even South Africa is simple. Such movements are usually described as secondary movements and are of particular concern for those in the First World, who would like asylum seekers and refugees to remain in their first country of asylum, typically neighboring the country of origin and at a "safe distance" from rich countries. As I mentioned in the introductory chapter, the desire to keep certain populations away from their borders has compelled Western countries to adopt a number of deterrence and interception measures. These include the introduction of visa requirements for people likely to seek asylum,[7] the imposition of heavy financial penalties on carriers accused of taking illegal migrants on board, the establishment of waiting, retention and detention centers, the extraterritorial review of asylum applications, the adoption of readmission agreements with the first country of asylum or transit countries,[8] and a very low and ever-declining rate of recognition of asylum applications (Agier 2008: 42, 77–78; Brouwer and Kumin 2003: 8–9; Zetter 2007: 181–82). Legal ways to seek refuge in Europe (or North America) are in practice limited to resettlement and family reunification. In theory, it is possible to seek asylum upon arrival in the territory. However, this entails accessing the territory, which is commonly done through irregular channels. The legal way is not only slow but also highly selective; hence, most people seeking asylum in Europe have entered irregularly with the help of a smuggler, either by crossing the border illegally or by using forged documents or a short-term visa, regardless of the legitimacy of their claim (Jacobsen 2005: 54; Moret, Baglioni and Efionayi-Mäder 2006: 86).[9]

Border closures, ever more sophisticated controls, and increasingly stringent asylum and migration policies do not have the desired effect of reducing overall migration (Human Rights Council 2012: 8). Instead, they force a perpetual reinvention of routes and destinations by asylum seekers. With tightening policies, travel routes become ever more complex and dangerous, and this only benefits the smugglers, who increase their prices accordingly (Basilien-Gainche 2011: 65; ICMPD 2007: 14). People are indeed often undeterred from moving by the difficulties and risks they are likely to experience both on the way and after arrival in a rich country. In the absence of any other satisfactory option, "the world within their (global) reach [being] unbearably *inhospitable*", the risks might seem worth taking (Bauman 1998a: 92–93).

Paths to reach Europe are diverse. A Somali seeking asylum in the European Union (EU) might have traveled from Kakuma to Nairobi by road, then flown to a EU country with false documents, or to Russia, whence he could have been smuggled into the EU. He may also have crossed South Sudan and Sudan, Libya and the Mediterranean Sea. He could have traveled through Somalia, boarded a boat to Yemen, then crossed Saudi Arabia and Turkey and, finally, reached Greece (ICMDP 2007: 24–27). Throughout his journey, he will have had to dodge military and police checks.

People who arrive in Europe at considerable risk and expense still face significant barriers. In 2010, nearly 258,000 people applied for asylum in a Member State of the EU. Some 55,000 of them were granted some form of protection (EC 2011: 5). Somalis whose claims are rejected may be forcibly returned, notwithstanding that the UNHCR has issued an opinion opposing this practice. Despite the fact that the UNHCR consistently advises against the forced return of failed asylum seekers to south-central Somalia, several countries, including Denmark, the Netherlands, Norway, Sweden and the United Kingdom, have lifted their expulsion ban, arguing that the situation has improved (AI 2014: 1; UNHCR 2010: 10; 2016b: 12). For those recognized as refugees, their status remains temporary and either leads to repatriation or to the acquisition of citizenship or permanent residency. Naturalization is often limited, as the right to survival is not the right to citizenship (Ong 2006: 500).[10] Even for others whose stay has been legitimized, settling in an environment marked by the attacks of September 11, 2001, which gave an increasingly menacing character to the "other", particularly Muslims, is difficult (Zetter 2007: 185). While refugees usually describe traveling to another African country as easier and slightly less risky, this option is not always appealing. Youth commonly mention that Somalis are not welcome in South Africa and that Sudan is unmerciful toward refugees. In addition, if one wants to settle permanently and have access to education, Europe is seen as a better choice.

One last, unpopular possibility is to return to Somalia and look for a job in a relatively stable part of the country. Although few consider this an option for themselves, many mention other young people who have done it. Yasin says that a number of his fellow students have gone to Puntland, where they got jobs after graduating from high school. He specifies that those who did so had clan affiliations that made it possible for them to move there safely and find some work. I was also told of a few people who have temporarily returned to Somalia for family reasons, but then decided to stay.

In short, the camp is strongly connected to the outside world. The scarcity of resettlement slots makes a number of people consider irregular migration, despite inherent perils and costs. In their search for opportunities, people display agency and awareness of the social forces at play. They are not simply waiting for an organization to provide them with a solution, but rather are constantly looking for ways to improve their condition. This search is fueled by a global cognizance that derives from transnational networks, media reports and two-way movements between the camp and other locations.

When the World Visits the Camp

Movement in Kakuma is not unidirectional. Indeed, while some leave the camp for good, others regularly travel back and forth between the camp and urban areas. New refugees are constantly arriving, former refugees come and visit friends and relatives, aid workers come from all over Kenya and the world, as do researchers, journalists, government officials, donors and other dignitaries. Resettled refugees send back news and money, and the media bring information from all over the globe to the camp. Refugees in Kakuma are thus constantly engaged well beyond the camp's limits.

Ongoing movements have significantly changed the face of the camp (and its acceptability in the eyes of its inhabitants), as well as people's expectations, and so has constant media exposure. The notion of imagination that transcends borders and multiplies imagined possibilities, while physical existence is geographically fixed, touches on the duality of the phenomenon of *buufis*. Horst writes that "on the one hand, images cannot be satisfied and only lead to frustrations about global inequality. But on the other hand, *buufis* as a form of collective imagination provides hope in quite a hopeless situation. It also increases people's level of power and choice by making resettlement thinkable and, once a number of people have resettled, improving actual living conditions in the camps" (2006b: 152).

Money Matters

Once in a while, a resettled refugee comes to visit his or her relatives and friends who are still in the camp. Such people are usually met with unrealistically high expectations. Gebre, an Ethiopian refugee who had moved to the Netherlands a few years previously, visited with a TV crew who were shooting a story of the path he took from his homeland to Europe via Kakuma. I ran into him when he had just arrived. He was very moved to be in the camp again and was eager to see people with whom he had lived for years. When I saw him for a second time on the following day, his mood had changed. He was close to tears. He explained that nearly everyone he encountered pretended to be happy to see him, but, in reality, expected a present from him and, more importantly, help with resettlement. He had come with a few hundred euros he had raised with fellow refugees in the Netherlands to give to specific refugees. He recounted handling over 2,000 KSh to one refugee who, instead of being grateful, retorted that it was nothing, not even twenty euros.

The general feeling in Kakuma is indeed that resettled refugees are successful and that they are therefore expected to bring generous presents when they visit. I was repeatedly told of relatives who had left for the United States or Canada and now held prestigious positions. It was sometimes assumed that those who had left were not sending enough money not because they were unable to do so, but because of their newly developed individualism, a flaw acquired in the West. I could point out as much as I wanted that arriving as a refugee in the West was not easy and that if so many really had good jobs, it was likely they would send enough money back to their immediate families to help them leave the camp, but my interlocutors would respond with stories of resettled peers successfully studying, owning a new car and a nice home. They had seen photographs. Some with very close friends and siblings who had been resettled had more realistic views. Ibrahim did not think his brother, who was in Salt Lake City, Utah, had it easy. He worked in a slaughterhouse. "It would be better to be a cleaner than to work with dead chickens! But he has to keep doing it to send us money. He cannot study, because if he does, we will suffer. That is life for refugees in America. Most don't have good jobs, even if they have some knowledge."

The common impression that life is relatively comfortable for refugees in the West might result in part from the discretion of resettled refugees about difficulties they are facing and the fact that remittances do flow back to the camp as a result of resettlement.[11] Horst (2006c: 19) found that Somalis in Minneapolis often felt weighed down by the expectation of financial support for their relatives in Somalia or neighboring countries. Yet they would not tell their families, either out of pride or because they found it unnecessary to burden their relatives with their own problems. However, nearly all managed to send money, whether they were financially stable or not.[12] Remittances are part of an implicit contract between migrants and their families and are not strictly about money. They have a social meaning in terms of reciprocity, but also as a way to preserve social standing. By triggering regular communication, remittances may also strengthen bonds between families living apart (Hammond 2007: 125; Lindley 2007b: 2, 15–16).

Several refugees mention receiving money from relatives on a monthly basis, but also for special events or needs, such as a wedding or a medical emergency. Amounts that they cite are usually relatively small, possibly because people receiving greater sums have settled in more comfortable urban areas. In spite of their size (one hundred dollars a month, for example), these amounts are enough to make a significant difference in people's living conditions and in their capacity to start small businesses that can grow. Remittances are not only beneficial to the direct recipients. They feed into the camp economy, as families mostly spend the money on food and other goods, and tend to share with relatives and neighbors.[13] Since it is common enough to benefit from remittances, refugees who do not receive such assistance often mention the fact, as it makes them significantly poorer than their peers. Aziz recalls: "I often felt God had forgotten us. No one was supporting us. We had no one in America. Most of the guys had people to rely on. They would always go to Dahabshiil [the largest Somali money transfer business, with branches across the globe] to collect money. We had nothing like that. We only had our parents."

Horst (2006a: 29) believes that at least 10–15 percent of refugees in Dadaab benefit from remittances. Those who receive money occasionally are generally given between two hundred and five hundred dollars up to five times a year. Those who collect money monthly usually receive between fifty and one hundred dollars. While I did not systematically compile data on the matter, I would estimate that among Somali families who have been in Kakuma since the late 1990s, the proportion receiving remittances is higher than that. This impression is corroborated by Oka (2011: 245), who wrote that, according to bankers and traders, 20 percent of the refugee families in the camp receive remittances from Western countries and the Middle East, and 60 percent benefit from money sent by relatives working in other cities in Kenya and elsewhere in East Africa.

Oka (2011: 244–45) has estimated that monthly sales from shops in the camp range from US$300,000 to US$400,000, while wages and incentives paid in the humanitarian and commercial sectors amount to about US$66,000. Thus, he argues, the main source of revenue in Kakuma is not employment, but remittances. There are four Somali banks in the camp, linked with global money transfer networks, and they receive between US$100,000 and US$150,000 in international remittances every month. Remittances from refugees working in Kenya or in neighboring countries made through the cell phone-based money transfer service M-Pesa are comparable in volume or even slightly higher. Interestingly, while remittances from the rest of Kenya and neighboring countries are at least as abundant as those from further abroad, they do not seem to have the same impact on people's imagination. This may result from refugees' awareness that their relatives working and living in these places face difficult conditions. Indeed, refugees who earn a living in closer locations visit their family and relatives in the camp fairly regularly and, when doing so, are likely to share more about their daily struggles than those who have been resettled further and, in their communications with people in the camp, often present their current situation in a relatively positive light. This probably limits the idealization of the conditions of refugees living irregularly outside the camp by those in Kakuma—although it does not prevent a number of them from leaving the camp to join them.

Remittances have made an important difference to living conditions in the camp, but have also influenced the work of refugees' imagination. It is not only money that is being sent, but also the idea that people in other countries are wealthier and lead more desirable lives. In addition, money transfers have created very strong global bonds through regular contacts and strong networks. Communications have also played a crucial role in structuring people's perception of the world.

Communication Matters: Imagining Another World

I love watching movies because they take me out of Kakuma
and connect me to the rest of the world. I like Hollywood
movies. You see people who are sixteen and driving their
car, doing all these things that you cannot imagine in a
camp. It is a completely different reality. Seeing what
you can't afford can give you hope, force you to accept
who you are or make you feel very frustrated.
—Aziz

Aziz has never left the camp, but can talk of tall buildings in cities, wealthy shopping centers, the comfort of big houses and colorful Indian fashion, thanks to the Bollywood films he enjoys as much as the Hollywood ones. He knows that people of his age elsewhere lead lives that have nothing in common with his reality. He considers his life "through the prisms of the possible lives offered by mass media in all their forms" (Appadurai 1996: 54) and is well informed about specific details. Once, as I was leaving after spending the afternoon with his family, he told me he wished he could drive me back in a BMW. He had never seen a real one, but had inferred from films that it was a sign of social standing and wealth.

In Kakuma, refugees are in constant contact with people around the globe. Telephone calls, social media, radio and television, as well as newcomers and visitors constantly bring the world into the camp—and the camp into the world—and give refugees material to picture other places. This ongoing exchange makes refugees increasingly mindful of other realities and inequalities, and makes the camp even less palatable, as refugees know that elsewhere, people have more comfortable lives, something expressed by Bauman (1998a: 23): "If the new extraterritoriality of the elite feels like intoxicating freedom, the territoriality of the rest feels less like home ground, and ever more like prison—all the more humiliating for the obtrusive sight of the others' freedom to move."

The same awareness makes a return to Somalia difficult to envision. While newcomers to Kakuma bring news from Somalia (usually very negative, given that they have fled), many refugees also speak regularly with relatives who have stayed in the country. Hence, they are informed of people's often difficult living conditions, and the episodes of relative quiet and spikes of violence. A few older refugees say that positive news makes them consider returning, but they are in a minority. For most, that is not an option, and the news they are getting from all sources consistently corroborates their views. Similarly, South Africa is described as a place where one could work, but would face xenophobia, a perspective informed by media reports and personal communications with Somalis who have moved there.

Media reports and communications also signal that irregular movements are dangerous and that living irregularly in Europe is not ideal. This knowledge sometimes exacerbates the feeling of being trapped in the camp. Nuradin once shared his thoughts on his (slender) options in the event that he was not resettled. Heading back to Somalia was ruled out and he was not drawn to Nairobi, where he believed refugees faced abuse. He was left with few other choices:

> At the end of the day, what will I do? If I go by boat to Italy, I might die. One of my friends went. He said: "What am I going to do here? Life is so bad." He went to Loki [Lokichoggio, at the Kenya-South Sudan border], then to Sudan. Then you have to deal with the Libyans and the Italians. My friend said he was tortured by the Sudanese, then he was in prison in Libya for two months, finally he left by boat. If the boat sinks, you're dead. There is no way to escape. He was lucky and he reached Italy. But even there, there are a lot of challenges. When it comes to money it is difficult. He is in Palermo. He is hiding. When he sees cops, he runs away. He is surviving with the help of others. He says he wishes he could come back to Kakuma.

It is striking how well informed people are of the differences in living conditions in various Western countries, which reflects their frequent interaction with the rest of the world. Many mention they would like to go to the United Kingdom rather than the United States, but the odds of doing so are small. In the United Kingdom, they believe there are more Muslims and mosques and a better acceptance of their religion. Life in the Netherlands, they say, is very expensive, while Italy is not very welcoming. Canada is easier than the United States because of better access to higher education and healthcare, and the availability of more social programs. However, the country is only accepting small numbers of refugees.

This awareness of other places also impels action and reflection. Regular communications with people in Dadaab make comparisons between camps possible. In some cases, it motivates refugees to relocate from Dadaab, as work and resettlement opportunities are deemed slightly more favorable in Kakuma. However, it also means that refugees are well informed that incentives are higher in Dadaab than in Kakuma, which exacerbates the irritation of being underpaid. Twenty-six-year-old Fartuun explains the difference by the fact that refugees in Dadaab mobilize when necessary. They have protested to demand higher incentives and are ready to go on strike, something unheard of in Kakuma. She feels that the greater cultural diversity in Kakuma has hindered such collective action. Similarly, when I was in Kakuma, refugees knew that a university campus where refugees would be able to study was opening near the Dadaab camp.

Not so long ago, a refugee camp might have felt like a very isolated setting where people remained relatively ignorant about global realities. However, Kakuma is now a remarkably well-connected site. This has brought a radical change in the way in which refugees envision their paths, assess their condition and plan their actions, but has also made them increasingly frustrated with their own situation. Increased knowledge not only makes the camp unacceptable, but also leads people to question social and cultural practices, such as the place of women in society, as we saw in the previous chapter.

Shifting Sands

> People are not moving so much now because life is
> getting hard in Nairobi. The government has asked to
> refugees to stay in the camps. Whenever a bomb blast
> occurs in Kenya, people say: "Al-Shabab and Somalis."
> —Mahdi, twenty-one years old

Mahdi is referring to the relocation plan, which was justified by the Department of Refugee Affairs by arguing that Somalis are a threat to national security. Movements in Kenya are indeed influenced by the country's political and social landscape. In fact, irregular migration and the obsession with re-settlement are a result of exposure to the movements of others, media reports, communications and the very limited opportunities offered by the camp, but also the difficult circumstances that refugees face in Kenya and Somalia's continuing insecurity.

A number of Somalis would consider staying in Kenya permanently if local integration were a realistic option. For the vast majority, however, it is ruled out for politico-historical reasons. This, coupled with the regular blaming of Somali refugees for the country's insecurity, has contributed to people's feeling of being unsettled and has made the status of Somali refugee an undesirable one. Refugees' movements and media reports have increased the camp residents' familiarity with the world as well as with the sociopolitical landscape of the country in which they live. The 2013 presidential election, and the twenty-six days between the elections and confirmation of contested results by the Supreme Court of Kenya, brought palpable tension not only to Kenyans but also to refugees. The matter was a topic of constant discussion: people were interested in the politics of a country where they have spent two decades, but they were also apprehensive about the possible negative consequences on their lives. People spent a lot of time speculating about which candidate seemed more favorable to protecting refugees and thus less inclined to force them to return to Somalia. It was in this context that an elderly woman told me that people from the host community had come to tell refugees that if they had to go home, Kenyans would appropriate their houses and shops.

The relocation threat had already sent a strong message to refugees. In addition to having a direct impact on movements—many refugees canceled trips to Nairobi—and on the camp economy, it reinforced refugees' impression of being unwelcome visitors. It made them feel that it was only a matter of time before they would be forced to repatriate to a country that was foreign to many of them. The government had already started claiming that people who had come due to the 2011 drought no longer had any reason to stay in Kenya. The next step, people felt, would be to conclude that if those who had come in 2011 could return safely, all the other refugees could follow and leave camps where conditions were in any case miserable.

Given that it has existed for more than twenty years, Kakuma feels like a permanent fixture. However, the lives of refugees in such a setting do not have the same fixity. On the one hand, some humanitarian organizations are making five-year strategic plans for their activities in the camp, which necessarily inscribes Kakuma in a long-term perspective. Refugees are establishing businesses, getting married, sending their children to school and improving their homes, all of which make the camp feel less like a transitory place. Yet people keep leaving, movement is a daily reality, pressures for repatriation are mounting and Kenya seems to be becoming less and less benevolent.

Notes

1. Such an interpretation echoes Duffield's observation (2007: 227) on the separation of the world between good and bad, useful and useless, the included and the excluded.

2. What qualifies as "fraud" for the UNHCR could also be understood as mere survival strategies. Registering twice, for example, is a way to obtain more food assistance. While it is indeed a violation of the rule, it is questionable to morally condemn people who are misappropriating aid not to become rich, but to feed their families. This is especially true in a context where already insufficient food rations are regularly cut because of shortfalls in funding and therefore do not meet the basic nutritional needs of the refugees. For a different perspective on the topic, see Kibreab (2004).

3. Section 16(1)(a) of Kenya's Refugee Act states that recognized refugees should be entitled to rights guaranteed by the international conventions to which Kenya is party. Article 26 of the 1951 Refugee Convention stipulates that refugees who are lawfully on a country's territory have the right to choose their place of residence and move freely within the country's territory. This is also affirmed by Article 12 of the 1966 International Covenant on Civil and Political Rights, which specifies that such rights can only be subjected to restrictions by law and that restrictions must be "necessary to protect national security, public order, public health or morals or the rights and freedoms of others."

4. A 2010 study reports that Somalis in urban areas are mostly hired informally by fellow countrymen who have businesses, or for domestic work (Pavanello, Elhawary and Pantuliano 2010: 21). It indicates that some 43 percent of urban refugees are self-employed. Businesses range from petty trade to real estate, import and export, money transfer operations or livestock trade and are extremely variable in size, ranging from street hawking to registered multinationals.

5. On September 21, 2013, gunmen laid siege to the Westgate Mall, a popular high-end shopping center. More than sixty-five people were killed in the attack, claimed by al-Shabab, who said it was in retaliation for Kenya's military involvement in Somalia. A week later, politicians started suggesting that camps for Somali refugees in Kenya should be closed and Somali refugees returned to Somalia (BBC 2013).

6. Somalis have been the victims of waves of violent attacks in South Africa since the mid 2000s. For example, at least twenty Somalis were killed in Cape Town in attacks that were described as xenophobic in nature by the South African police in 2006 (BBC 2006). In 2008, some sixty-two foreigners were killed and another 100,000 displaced because of xenophobic violence (BBC 2009). In 2011, in Port Elizabeth, more than fifty Somali-owned shops were attacked and looted by local residents who, according to Somali traders, resented their success (BBC 2011a).

7. For example, in 2001, Canada introduced visa requirements for Hungarians (targeting Roma) and Zimbabweans, in response to the large number of asylum seekers from these two countries (Brouwer and Kumin 2003: 8). The EU has set up a common list of the non-EU member countries whose nationals must have a visa to enter the EU that includes refugee-producing countries such as Afghanistan, the Democratic Republic of the Congo and Somalia (EC 2001).

8. For example, in 2008, Italy signed a "Friendship Pact" with Libya that authorized Italy to send boats carrying migrants back to Libya without determining whether the boat carried asylum seekers or refugees, despite the fact that Libya did not treat the latter in a manner consistent with international standards (HRW 2009c). Although the pact was judged unacceptable by the European Court of Human Rights in February 2012 (*Hirsi and Others v. Italy*), the two countries continue to cooperate on migration matters (MPC 2013: 7).

9. Although statistics on these migrations are limited by their very nature, the data consistently shows that the vast majority of refugees and asylum seekers who are in Europe came irregularly (ICMPD 2009: 52). For example, 94 percent of 109 Somali refugees interviewed by Moret, Baglioni and Efionayi-Mäder (2006) in Switzerland and the Netherlands had arrived illegally.

10. While little data on the naturalization of refugees has been compiled, the UNHCR observes that it is limited by restrictive national laws in several countries (UNHCR 2011d: 19).

11. A significant proportion of the Somali diaspora sends money to Somalia or to refugee camps. Remittances are believed to surpass international humanitarian aid in Somalia. Estimates on their total volume differ greatly. In 2002, Marchal (2002: 17–18) noted that these ranged from US$350 million to US$800 million per annum.

12. Research focused on remitters has shown that people struggle to meet the demands of their relatives and may feel forced to priorities work over their studies, cut their basic spending, take more than one job or incur debts (e.g., Hammond 2007: 136, 142; Lindley 2007a: 4). Some postpone getting married, as they fear it could hamper their capacity to send money back to their relatives (Horst 2006c: 11).

13. While conducting a study for the Danish Refugee Council in 2012, I actually met a few refugees in Kakuma who said they were supporting their families in Somalia by sending small amounts of money that was either a share of remittances they received or of their wage (Grayson, Epstein and Coles 2013: 33).

Chapter 6

THEY PROMISED US AMERICA

A Story of Deception and Mistrust

❧ ✦ ☙

> If you are punched once, you will feel the pain. Maybe the
> second time too. But the third time, you will feel it less.
> You get used to it. We came here hoping to leave within
> three months. Then we hoped to leave within one year. But
> we are still here, seventeen years later. I don't know what I
> am hoping for anymore. I don't know what I can hope for.
> —Aziz, twenty-three years old

Recounting their arrival in Kakuma in the late 1990s, Somali refugees often maintain that in order to persuade them to agree to their transfer from the Mombasa camps, the UNHCR had assured them that their stay in Kakuma would be brief: they would soon be resettled to the United States or Canada. This seemed logical and credible, as resettlement had already started in the Mombasa camps. However, as Aziz points out, this is not what happened. While the UNHCR did not officially promise resettlement to refugees who agreed to move to Kakuma, the story is widespread enough that it is difficult to simply discard it as an invention. "The move had to be voluntary," explains Abdikadir. "To convince us, they asked for the assistance of the chairmen of those camps. They were told that if they helped, they would be resettled and so would many families. That is what they told us and that's how we came here." The UNHCR head of operations acknowledges it is possible that, in order to lure refugees, some staff members implied that resettlement was in the plan, resettlement that did not materialize. In the process, Somali refugees lost confidence in the UNHCR and in the aid system more generally, and it became a common belief that it was in the interests of aid workers to keep refugees in the camps, where the workers would continue to enjoy well-paid jobs.

This initial episode was followed by several breaches of trust: food rations have been regularly cut;[1] refugees are rarely consulted about decisions that have a significant impact on their lives and are kept in the dark about budgets and programming; democratically elected leaders are sometimes pushed aside by the UNHCR (Jansen 2011: 158); and explanations of the rejection of resettlement cases are frustratingly concise. Refugees meet or hear of aid workers, policemen and government officials asking for money for theoretically free services, or threatening to curtail resettlement processes or fire refugee workers if they do not comply with various demands.

In fact, a general climate of suspicion reigns, merely serving to perpetuate mistrust at all levels and between all parties. Refugees are not the only ones who harbor feelings of distrust. Aid workers also suspect refugees of trying to cheat the system. Mistrust stems from an asymmetric balance of power between refugees and the aid administration, their opposing goals, and competition between the camp's inhabitants and the host community for limited resources. In addition, experiencing the violent events that resulted in exile, and the exile itself, can affect refugees' capacity and willingness to trust (Daniel and Knudsen 1995: 1–2). Mistrust that prompts certain behaviors, justifying strict measures of control, causes further mistrust. This hampers cohesion and cooperation, and contributes to an inhospitable atmosphere in the camp. This widespread lack of trust is not specific to Kakuma. In most camps where I have spent time, there were palpable feelings of distrust between ruled and rulers.

Although several authors have alluded to the centrality of mistrust in the camp experience, few have specifically studied this question. Voutira and Harrell-Bond (1995) and Kibreab (2004) stand out among those who have done so. The first pair paid specific attention to power dynamics among the camp's parties, including refugees, their hosts, aid organizations, the government of the host country and donors. They argue that in the absence of a social contract between refugees and humanitarian organizations or between the various refugee communities, there is no reason for them to trust one another. In fact, "the whole structure of the humanitarian regime is fraught with competition, suspicion and mistrust" (Voutira and Harrell-Bond 1995: 217). This mistrust is exacerbated by the incompatibility of the objectives of aid organizations and refugees: while the former wish to maintain their authority, the latter strive to acquire material goods. The authors conclude that the authority of the aid regime relies on an inherent lack of trust and reciprocity. Kibreab studied the lack of moral restraint shown by refugees in their interactions with aid organizations. Acts that would normally be considered immoral or dishonest, such as lying about the size of one's family to gain more food, pretending to be vulnerable to obtain more assistance or not repaying loans taken out from aid organizations, become acceptable. This partially explains aid organizations' mistrust toward refugees.

As will become evident in this chapter, although Voutira and Harrell-Bond's observations were made two decades ago and despite changes to the aid system that have occurred during that period, their reflections remain relevant in the context of Kakuma. The camp continues to be an unfavorable environment for sustained interpersonal and institutional trust. And while the longlasting character of the camp could have gradually induced trust, it has rather contributed to sustaining refugees' mistrust, as experiences from the past reinforce their impression that the aid administration and its representatives are unpredictable.

In the following pages, after defining the notion of trust, I focus primarily on the distrust that refugees feel for the humanitarian system, but also devote shorter sections to examining the mistrust of aid organizations toward refugees and the lack of trust within communities and between individuals living in the camp. I conclude with some thoughts on the effects of mistrust, in the context of the asymmetric power relations between the aid system and the camp's population. Although the host community and the Kenyan government are part of the web of trust and mistrust, and mistrust is also common between aid organizations competing for the same funding, this chapter focuses on the relationships between the camp's inhabitants and the aid system, which does include some government activities.

Defining Trust

Giddens (1996 [1991]: 33) defines trust as "confidence in the reliability of a person or system, regarding a given set of outcomes or events, where that confidence expresses a faith in the probity or love of another, or in the correctness of abstract principles." Thus described, trust is relational and relies on the faith that people or institutions will act in a fair and honest manner, respecting the norms and values of a society. Depicted by Simmel (1950: 318) as "one of the most important synthetic forces within society," it is essential to the functioning of societies and the maintenance of cooperation (Möllering 2001: 405; Zucker 1985: 5). While interpersonal trust is established mutually through interaction, trust in abstract systems, such as the humanitarian administration, does not necessarily stem from encounters with representatives of the system who act as "access points" (Giddens 1996 [1991]: 83).

Such trust "presumes faith in impersonal principles, which 'answer back' only in a statistical way when they do not deliver the outcomes which the individual seeks" (1996 [1991]: 114–15). People's experiences at access points can be seen as "junctions at which trust can be maintained or built up" (1996 [1991]: 88) and thus influence people's trust, as does their knowledge of the system, acquired through media reports or other people (1996 [1991]: 90). Lack of trust in a person leads to doubting their integrity, while lack of trust in a system usually produces skepticism or a negative attitude toward the system (1996 [1991]: 99). Mistrust and trust are not necessarily described as mutually exclusive or antithetical sentiments, but are interlinked. Giddens (1996 [1991]: 100) asserts that the absence of trust leads to "existential angst or dread" rather than to mere mistrust. When speaking of mistrust (a term that I will use more frequently than trust) in the camp, I will be referring to a lack of trust, while bearing in mind that the two sentiments can, to some extent, coexist.

In light of this definition, the camp is infertile ground for developing and maintaining trust. On the one hand, the humanitarian administration gives the impression of taking arbitrary decisions because of its lack of transparency, and thus appears unreliable and unpredictable. Refugees' negative experiences with aid workers, the system's access points, feed into the general mistrust, as does the absence of reciprocity in the relationship between refugees and aid organizations. Since refugees are competing for the same resources and may not have developed a sense of belonging to a community that transcends ethnicity, faith in other refugees' integrity is also limited and variable. Moreover, refugees' paths and experience can be inimical to the establishment of trusting relationships. Behnia (1996–97: 50, 54) notes that survivors of war may have become very conscious that other human beings can hurt them and thus should not be easily trusted. Similarly, refugees' trust in institutions such as the army, the police or the justice system has often been breached in the course of the events that led to exile or during exile. Finally, aid organizations have few grounds for believing in refugees' honesty, as their goals are impossible to reconcile. While the mistrust is mutual, the consequences of this mistrust are not the same for the two groups, whose political capital is radically different. Humanitarian workers have "certain credentials, political status, and cultural capital." Refugees have "far less political status and power" (Hyndman 2000: xvii).

Mistrusting the Humanitarian Regime

Since Voutira and Harrell-Bond made their observations in 1995, humanitarian organizations have commonly shifted from a needs-based to a rights-based approach[2] and have adopted numerous initiatives[3] aimed at increasing both their accountability toward beneficiaries and beneficiary participation (Dufour et al. 2004). This should have helped to redefine the nature of the relationship between aid organizations and beneficiaries, who are presented as equal rights-holders rather than passive beneficiaries of international benevolence. In this logic, beneficiaries are expected to participate in the identification of their needs and the design of aid programs, while aid organizations commit to being transparent (Armstrong 2008). This is meant to nurture trust and reciprocity, as affected populations are actively involved in the administration of aid and can understand the logic of aid programs.

Yet, in Kakuma, refugees' distrust of the humanitarian system still prevails due to a lack of transparency that gives it an arbitrary and intrusive character, as well as recurring suspicions of corruption on the part of aid workers and at times deleterious relationships between camp workers and refugees. The behavior of the camp's inhabitants is marked by this distrust, but also by their will to optimize their access to services and assistance. Hence, they adjust their life stories to conform to the perceived expectations of the UNHCR, thus reinforcing the distrust of aid organizations. I examine below aspects of humanitarian governance that provoke mistrust, namely the lack of transparency that fuels suspicions of corruption, and refugees' impressions that their freedom of speech and participation in decision making are subject to control. I then consider how refugees shape their stories.

Although the UNHCR and NGOs are not homogeneous bodies and particular humanitarian organizations have their own reputations with refugees, there are broad feelings of mistrust for aid organizations in general, as they are governing together. In theory, Kenya is the refugees' host. However, in practice, the UNHCR exerts control over the camp by virtue of funding nearly all activities, including those of the government. Symbolically, it is telling that both the Kenyan and UNHCR flags are raised during international day ceremonies.

An Obscure Regime

Refugees' mistrust is closely linked to the question of transparency. People complain that they are infrequently consulted regarding decisions that have profound repercussions on their lives, such as the organization of camp life, the formulation of programs or the use of funds. For example, refugees have no say in the recurrent cuts to food rations. The reduction of aid and basic services for Sudanese refugees when the UNHCR was trying to convince them to return to South Sudan from 2007 to 2009 was also decided without consulting the refugees. Such events make Somalis fear that they could at some point be pushed to repatriate by the system that is meant to be protecting them. The

UNHCR managers sometimes justify decisions by saying that orders came from headquarters or are imposed by funding shortages, leaving no room for refugees' priorities or concerns. Such unilateral (and unpredictable) decision making can be seen as a breach of trust, especially as the living standards of aid workers remain unaffected. In fact, funding shortages are probably difficult to believe in or accept as an excuse. Given that they receive very little or no information on organizations' budgets and spending, refugees assume that they have infinite resources, but choose to distribute aid sparingly to the people they are meant to be helping. It does not escape the attention of refugees that aid workers live and work in luxurious conditions compared to those of refugees. The UNHCR's pondering about digging a swimming pool for its employees, while refugees' consumption of water is always restricted, was the subject of caustic remarks. Refugees conclude that money is not the problem, but rather its allocation; funds that should have been spent on assisting refugees are instead used to pay good salaries to staff and ensure their welfare.

According to the camp's Constitution, the camp's inhabitants elect representatives who should act as the key interlocutors with the humanitarian governing body. But many hold the opinion that the new leadership system—which they describe as a positive change in theory—is not truly designed to give them more of a say in decision making. They believe its aim is to give refugees the impression that they are participating and being consulted, but that in reality their leaders' power is symbolic and mostly serves the interests of the UNHCR. Interestingly, while the Constitution defines in detail the obligations of the refugee representatives, those of the humanitarian administration in terms of consultation, transparency or accountability are not listed. Yet these are part of the commitments taken by the UNHCR and most of its humanitarian partners through the adoption of a rights-based approach. However, as Dufour et al. (2004) observe, genuine refugee participation might not be compatible with respecting pre-identified humanitarian priorities. Indeed, standards defining the obligations of aid organizations limit the influence of refugees on establishing priorities. Refugees' perception of such a gap between theory and practice works to subvert trust. One of the elected representatives, an Ethiopian who has been in Kakuma for over a decade, summarized his role as an information channel for the UNHCR and expressed great frustration:

> When it comes to funding, we only get a part of the information. For the sake of transparency, we need to know where the money is coming from and where it is going. Then we are somehow involved with the planning when it comes to submitting ideas, but we are not involved with the monitoring and the reporting. They are fooling people around with talks of participatory approaches. But who designs the project? Is it participatory? Unless the process changes, block leaders will be seen as useless. We lack a proper link with the agencies. We don't have access to UNHCR and don't have a counterpart.

Another added that if they are too vocal as leaders, national staff and the government threatened them. Yet some do note improvements in the system, affirming that the UNHCR is slightly more accessible to leaders than it used to be.

The lack of transparency also fuels refugees' suspicions of corruption among aid workers, especially Kenyans, which is not surprising, given that they make up most of the camp's workers. They are deemed to be untrustworthy and motivated by tribal matters, while foreign workers are seen as more honest, but inaccessible. This makes refugees complain about the insufficient oversight in the camp. "[Kenyans] come to the field with no supervisors," laments a Somali woman. "At the food distribution, if there is a visitor, you get a lot of food, but otherwise, they do what they want." Stories of corruption abound. Refugees state that they are routinely asked to pay small but nonetheless significant amounts in the camp context to book appointments or get documents. Students assert that teachers ask for money to give them their marks. People also report that even when they hold the necessary travel documents, this does not stop the police from asking for bribes to let them travel within Kenya. Moreover, they are convinced that some pay a high price for their resettlement ticket. "It is a market," exclaims Aden. "Say you need an alien card, you go to [the] DRA and buy it. If you don't pay, you don't get it. It is as simple as that. Money talks here." Such rumors are often regarded as true by refugees, as some have proved to be so over time. The UNHCR resettlement scandal of the late 1990s led to the suspension of resettlement activities; the fraudulent trade of ID cards has been documented and acknowledged by the Kenyan authorities. In 2011, an investigation finally showed that refugees were right to accuse aid workers of diverting food, which had long been a subject of complaint by refugee leaders before any serious investigation took place. These occurrences feed refugees' suspicions of aid workers and the government, and led them to believe corruption-related rumors. Interestingly, corruption not only creates obstacles for refugees, but also means that people with some financial means are able to buy identity documents, to travel in the country by bribing their way, to import goods and to sell them in the camp.

I mentioned to the UNHCR head of protection that people were saying they had to pay for everything, and could buy just about anything as long as they had money, including citizenship or their release from jail. Moreover, the prices they gave for the various services were consistent, which made me think that there was some truth to their claims. He asked if I had any proof, as he could not work on rumors. I did not, as I was not investigating corruption. He said he was only getting anecdotal information and that he lacked firsthand complaints. Nonetheless, he indicated that a police investigation on the issuance of false alien cards was ongoing and that a guard and an interpreter had been fired for asking for money from refugees to schedule fictitious appointments for them. He added that it was possible that the delivery of documents was delayed until refugees paid for them.

I do not doubt that he only heard rumors: refugees are reluctant to make reports, as they hold the view that no one can be trusted and that nothing will be done about their complaint. "You will see someone who is corrupt himself," says Abdikadir. "You cannot go and report when you know they are part of the problem. They don't want things to change." It is not only the feeling that their complaints will remain unresolved that prevents refugees from reporting corruption, but also the impression that it could be held against them, in particular because of people's tribal or family loyalties. Twenty-one-year-old Axlam reports that people bringing complaints against their supervisor can be fired, which holds dire consequences, as families need the income. The lack of organizational transparency further mars trust in the value of reporting. Refugees remark on the complaint boxes at the field posts, but say they usually get no response and thus feel they are not worth using.

Mistrust also stems from deleterious relationships with humanitarian staff. Indeed, problems at the points of connection with people representing the system, i.e., aid workers, are frequent and affect trust significantly. Refugees hired by aid organizations are at times fired without proper explanation and dismissive comments are not unusual. Refugees say that those who criticize the humanitarian governance and ask for better conditions compromise their resettlement prospects. "We are being told that we are 'just' refugees" is a common complaint that reflects the asymmetry of the relationship. Such asymmetry also derives from the fact that assistance to refugees is often seen as a form of charity rather than a right. This leads aid workers to behave as if refugees should simply be grateful for whatever they are given (Harrell-Bond 2002: 53–58). This dynamic interferes with the moral obligation of seeking reciprocity in giving and receiving, a social process that is also linked with the production of trust (Lammers 2007: 76–77).

A Controlling Regime: Silencing Refugees' Voices

Refugees' feeling that aid workers nurture an unbalanced relationship with them is compounded by the impression that the camp workers attempt to control their speech. They believe that humanitarian organizations try to prevent them from speaking freely to visitors—especially donors, whose visits are strictly controlled and organized. (Refugees spent considerable time gleefully recalling the exceptional visit of the Queen of Qatar, who had apparently refused the UNHCR's planning assistance and had focused on listening to what refugees had to say rather than meeting with officials.) A South Sudanese refugee representative who was enrolled in the journalism class remarked: "People like you don't really understand what is happening here. There are things that are not exposed. When donors come, we are given a speech by the UNHCR national staff. They tell us what to say." Camp residents also believe that humanitarian organizations fear that if refugees engage directly with potential donors, they could become their competitors. Abdikadir, the chairman of a Somali community youth group, Aliform Somali Generation, relates that the Somali embassy had agreed to provide manuals for the literacy classes that his organization was organizing: "When the embassy came to the camp with books, LWF wanted to take them away, claiming that they were the ones in charge of education. Some of our members were threatened. We are perceived as competition by NGOs who are doing business and want to increase their programs. The way they deal with us is from another era."

Refugees' freedom of speech is not only curtailed when engaging with donors. Jansen (2011: 158) asserts that the UNHCR forbade initiatives such as the launch of a Somali radio station. The independent refugee news bulletin *Kanere* reports being censored and blatantly undermined by the UNHCR and its partners. Its editor claims that he was fired from his incentive position with the LWF because he had criticized the inequality of the refugees' terms of employment. One of its journalists says that the UNHCR has threatened to close them down and that they are regularly summoned to its office to be told that their reporting is unacceptable:

> They want us to only speak of the shortages of food or water, but not of the incentives or the insecurity. They said we should not criticize the agencies. They offered to provide us with offices, but in return, they were to check what we publish. We didn't want that. We have very limited freedom of speech here. Whenever we meet, we fear the police might come. We don't write our names because we fear that we might be arrested or our resettlement cases blocked.

While the UNHCR deems these accusations excessive, the head of RCK finds them realistic: "*Kanere* wrote about corruption in UNHCR. UNHCR had to defend itself. [Employees] tried kicking [the head of the bulletin] out of the camp. They wanted to take him to court. They said he was writing rubbish. He was only writing as things are. They tried to shut him down. Would UNHCR try to close a national newspaper if they wrote something against them?" Shortly after I left the camp, *Kanere* won a significant victory: it finally managed to be registered as an NGO in Kenya, which means that it can operate legally and will, to some extent, more easily dismiss shutdown threats.

In such a context, refugees' ignorance of their rights is somewhat surprising, considering that they would have grounds for requesting changes. While such limited awareness is not peculiar to a refugee context, one could wonder why more efforts have not been made to ensure popular education, since refugees have rights under a very specific legal framework, and these rights and their freedoms are being eroded. As I mentioned earlier, none of the jour-

nalism students—all in their twenties and most with a full secondary education—knew why they were granted protection as refugees. Of course, there
are exceptions. I met a few refugees who had purposefully learned everything
they could about refugee law. Some hold the cynical view that dissemination
efforts are limited because ignorance gives more latitude to aid organizations.
The head of the RCK, who has embarked on teaching refugees international
and national law, thinks that the UNHCR feels threatened by the initiative:
"Refugees started realizing that UNHCR should be held accountable and
started asking questions. It changes dynamics, as refugees understand that
there are rules that UNHCR is meant to follow."

In short, refugees believe the aid system tries to limit their freedom of
expression and their access to the outside world. Moreover, the opacity of humanitarian organizations means that people can have difficulty making sense
of decisions that might seriously affect their lives, including those related to
refugee status determination and resettlement. This might partly explain why
refugees shape their life stories to smooth out any apparent discrepancies.

An Obtuse Regime: Getting the Story Right

I knew Abdulaziz, a twenty-year-old Ethiopian, fairly well when I sat down
with him for an interview. We had had regular conversations on this and that,
he had showed me films he was working on and I had helped him with an
essay he was writing for an application for a training course, as well as with the
narration for a short film he was making. I assume that is why he was willing
to disclose more information: we had built a relationship that entailed a degree
of reciprocal trust. He asked what I would do with the recording of the interview. I responded that I would use it to type my notes. He wondered if I would
broadcast it. I answered that I would not. That is when he inquired whether I
wanted to hear the "UNHCR story" or the "real story." He explained:

> When our parents come up with stories for UNHCR, they are not the true
> ones, because if you tell the truth, you are not resettled. For example, my par-
> ents did not come directly to Kenya from Ethiopia. They went to Somalia, as
> did most of those who fled Ethiopia around 1990–1991. Most people who left
> during that period were soldiers in the government before it was overthrown.
> When you come here, you don't say: "I was a soldier," because it automati-
> cally leads to rejection for resettlement. Before we came to Kakuma, we were in
> Marsabit. I heard we had an interview with UNHCR. At that time, my parents
> were not aware of those things. I think my father told the truth and said he was a
> soldier. We were rejected. Telling the truth makes your resettlement impossible.
>
> Here, people got to know things. People would help you come up with the
> right story, with the right structure, the one that the UN is able to understand,

one with a problem that will make the UN resettle you. Most of the guys who do the writing, they chew *miraa*. So you buy them some, a soda and cigarettes and they do the writing for you. The UN will be happy with the story. If people are here, they have problems. They cannot go back to their country. But they still can't say the truth. Sometimes when I write, I feel I want to tell the truth, but in a way, you might be doing yourself or your family wrong. It becomes scary to tell the truth.

While this was the only time that the motives were aired so candidly, I came to realize that many had an official story that was an amended version of their reality, adapted to what they believed the UNHCR wanted to hear. The commonly held view is that one has to be extremely careful with what one reveals to the UNHCR, and to the aid system generally, as it cannot understand refugees' complex reality. In addition, people want to avoid alienating the aid system at all costs so as to maximize their access to assistance and hypothetical resettlement. Illustrations of what refugees see as the institution's obtuseness in the resettlement procedure abound. Ayan talks about how her family was initially rejected because their mother was accused of not being their mother, as she was implausibly young, having been married at twelve. Five years later, the family was called back for an interview, and this time the case was approved. Aden says his case was rejected in 2009 because the interviewers believed his marriage to a woman fourteen years older than him could not be genuine. Several people mention that in the process, they discovered that people they had always considered as their siblings were in reality more distant relatives. While the UNHCR describes this as attempted fraud, Somalis see no difference between a blood sibling and someone they have treated as such for the whole of their lives.[4] It makes them feel that the UNHCR is blind to their social reality. "We were rejected in 2009 because that sister of mine, in reality, she was my mother's sister, but we didn't know," recounts Faarax. "I asked my mother why we were rejected. She said that this girl who we thought was our sister was in fact her younger sister. I was surprised. That made her my aunt, but I still think of her as my sister. Somalis do that, but it creates problems with resettlement." Deeqa found out that her parents had adopted two of her siblings in a similar way. When asked why they had lied to the interviewers, which led to the rejection of their case, they responded that they had never told their own children about the adoption because they wanted them to simply consider one another as siblings.

Many end up sharing a carefully reconstructed version of their path, one they believe meets the expectations of the UNHCR and prospective receiving countries, and will not make them ineligible for resettlement. Thus, people who were in the military, or who had a parent in the military, in their country of origin will neglect to mention the fact. Sudanese youth might declare dead parents who are in fact alive, but still in South Sudan. Somalis sometimes falsely claim that they belong to a minority clan, as members of minorities are deemed more likely to be recognized as vulnerable and hence resettled. The unpredictability of resettlement, the limited explanations provided on the rejection of cases or on reasons why a case is pending, coupled with the skepticism of interviewers all fuel the impression that stories have to be crafted. In a number of instances, people told me several months after an interview and after we had spent significant time together that they wanted to amend what they had initially told me. I assume there were many more cases where the only version of the story I ever heard was the official one, which calls attention to the obvious: mistrust also affects research and relationships between refugees and researchers.

Refugees can go to the field post for resettlement-related claims or questions, but they feel that the answers provided are unsatisfactory and that they are given no chance to explain their case. A Somali elder outlines the situation: "There are two field posts for 115,000 refugees. The officers go there three hours once a week. Sometimes they don't even show up. Now, they started giving appointments. You might wait for three or four months to see someone. When you get to see the officer, you cannot ask more than one question. They say they are too busy. If you insist, the security forces you out." In reality, the field posts are opened more often than that, but only answer resettlement-related queries once a week. The UNHCR head of protection acknowledges that field posts need to extend their hours in that respect, but objects that refugees' complaints about being kept in the dark are not always fair:

> People should be given the reasons why their case is pending or was rejected. This information is available on the computers. It is true that it does not always happen, but it is also that refugees are not always listening. As it is crowded, answers must be short. If people come with serious questions, we answer, but some are just trying to chitchat. Three minutes is plenty of time to counsel people.

A part of the problem might lie in the hastiness of the process. People hope for a detailed explanation, as they sense that their future is at stake, but are only given a laconic response, telling them they have lied about their family composition, that there are inconsistencies in their stories or that they have registered under more than one identity. It does not help that refugees sometimes suspect the UNHCR of having sold their resettlement slots in the 1990s.

Regardless of the validity of the reasons driving people to fabricate stories, being convinced that one must lie to the system that is meant to be providing one with protection is not benign. It means that one can never be transparent and must always remain on guard. In a study on refugees and asylum seekers in the United Kingdom, Ni Raghallaigh (2014: 94) reflects that while people lie because of mistrust or fears that telling the truth could have negative consequences, this ends up affecting their ability to develop trusting relationships.

Overall, the arbitrary and intrusive character of humanitarian governance impairs refugees' trust and leads to negative attitudes. Moreover, refugees doubt aid workers' integrity, as they suspect them of being corrupt and of trying to control their speech. The absence of trust toward the system and its representatives can at least partially explain refugees' belief that they must not tell the truth to aid workers. This in turn leads aid organizations to mistrust refugees.

From the Perspective of Aid Organizations: A Rational Mistrust

As I pointed out in the introductory chapter, a paradoxical dualism characterizes the aid regime's perception of refugees. On the one hand, they are seen as powerless victims. On the other hand, they are suspected of trying to cheat the system and are regarded as potentially dangerous, a view that bestows on them a capacity to act. The former depiction can turn refugees into victims who must be charitably helped, which might explain why refugees are not treated as equals by aid workers, and why their concerns about health or education are at times condescendingly brushed aside or their questions on resettlement are not satisfactorily answered. However, the second representation can contribute to the climate of mistrust and provide justification for measures aimed at controlling refugees. In the following, I use two examples to explore how the behavior and the speech of refugees may trigger the mistrust of the aid administration and then examine how such mistrust influences humanitarian governance.

When I was in Kakuma, it was not exceptional for a refugee to hold more than one ration card and to speak relatively openly about it, as people did not seem to think that it was immoral to collect more than their share of assistance. A significant change was planned to take place soon after my departure and was condemned by refugees: the UN World Food Programme was about to introduce biometric controls to prevent refugees from collecting more than one ration, but also to prevent employees from misappropriating food. The agency explained that donors who believed too much food was being diverted were demanding such a change. Aid organizations expected significant repercussions on the camp economy, as food is an important commodity for trade. From the perspective of aid organizations, regardless of the validity of refugees' reasons for cheating, it creates a situation where they are deemed "inherently untrustworthy" and justifies ever more sophisticated means of control (Voutira and Harrell-Bond 1995: 219). This results in camp management techniques characterized by "a number of surveillance practices through which refugees are continually mapped, marked, and monitored," attesting to the depth of the mistrust (Hyndman 2000: 24). In an attempt to impose order on disorder, the aid system codifies, organizes and carefully divides space, and "people become numbers without names" (Harrell-Bond 2000: 1). Such descriptions evoke Foucault's analysis on space and discipline: "Discipline sometimes require *enclosure*" (1995 [1975]: 141), but may also work "space in a much more flexible and detailed way. It does first of all on the principle of elementary location or *partitioning*. Each individual has his own place; and each place its individual" (1995 [1975]: 143). Techniques of control have evolved over time, reflecting a change in the norms and values governing the administration of aid. While it has been considered acceptable to conduct refugee registration and verification without prior notice to prevent groups from manipulating the numbers, this is no longer the case. Inhabitants of the camp could be rounded up by surprise, at night, and marked with indelible ink (Voutira and Harrell-Bond 1995: 219). The coercive nature of such an approach has been strongly criticized and the UNHCR's latest *Handbook for Registration* (2003) insists on the importance of consulting and informing populations. (However, as a UNHCR employee a decade ago, I witnessed registration planning that still entailed catching the population by surprise at sunrise.)

The perception that refugees are untrustworthy also contributes to their spoken word being ignored, as Fassin (2011: 87–88) observes is the case with asylum seekers in France. In Kakuma, this translates into a sometimes disquieting skepticism on the part of aid workers regarding refugees' accounts of corruption, violence or sexual harassment. My being white and ready to listen often led to refugees bringing me to meet people who had just been attacked or had a particularly critical problem, even though I kept repeating that I was powerless and thus did not want to give people the impression that I could be of any help. They still believed that I enjoyed easier access than they did to the UNHCR and that I was likely to speak of the incident. I did have access to the UNHCR—paradoxically, given that I was not part of the agency's population of concern—but what it allowed me to see was that the UNHCR received reports of corruption, sexual abuse or violence with suspicion. In one case, I mentioned to the head of operations that I had just met with the husband of a woman who, he recounted, had been taken to hospital after being raped when their house came under attack during the night. There were bullet holes in the wall to attest that something had indeed happened. His first reaction was one of deep mistrust for refugees' "stories," as he believed these were too often made up for resettlement purposes or, sometimes, to explain pregnancies outside marriage. His doubts were understandable: refugees do craft stories, which complicate matters as aid organizations try to distinguish between fabricated accounts and true ones. The head of the LWF Gender Unit estimates that only half the reports on gender-based violence made to her office are true. She considers the other half to be motivated by resettlement ambitions. Still, the methods used to assess the veracity of a story seem rather haphazard and it is possible that in some cases, real incidents are deemed to be untrue, while the opposite probably also happens with false stories.

Dealing with Irreconcilable Goals

The skepticism of the aid administration stems, at least in part, from its knowledge of strategies used by refugees to optimize their access to assistance or resettlement, strategies that the aid system is trying to curtail. In this case, the objectives of refugees differ radically from those of aid organizations, as do more broadly the kinds of behaviors that are deemed acceptable.

Kibreab's (2004) observations on the relatively taboo subject of prevalent refugee cheating in camps in the Horn of Africa open up an interesting line of thought. He tries to understand why refugees apply different moral codes depending on whether they are engaging with aid organizations or other refugees. He contends that refugees have a "propensity to behave in a morally unrestrained manner in their interaction with aid agencies" and thus feel no sense of guilt for behavior that would normally be considered unacceptable (2004: 1). In fact, in the camp, such behavior is laudable: "Those who succeeded in cheating aid agencies by presenting false stories (or misrepresenting themselves) were often regarded with respect and admiration by their neighbours and kin" (2004: 11). Yet the same act committed within refugee communities and "disregarding the interest of a relative, a neighbour or a villager is considered to be disgraceful and inappropriate behaviour" (2004: 1). He argues that cheating and misrepresentation have not come to be considered as appropriate because refugees "have undergone some kind of moral decay"; this is borne out by the high moral standards that prevail within communities (2004: 11). He asserts that tight social ties binding individuals to a code of honor cease to be relevant when refugees interact with faceless entities such as aid organizations and governments. This is especially true as individuals share no long-term interest with those institutions, making the principle of reciprocity meaningless. In such a context, "taking UNHCR, NGOs and host governments 'for a ride' [is] not considered immoral. On the contrary, it [is] considered heroic. Outmanoeuvring the rich and powerful organizations ... [is] seen as a valiant act" (2004: 18). He believes that another reason why moral codes are not upheld is because the rules and norms that regulate aid organizations may be alien and incomprehensible, and thus share little with the "informal institutional rules which generally regulate access to, control over and use of resources among the refugees" (2004: 24). The fact that those who manage aid share little with refugees in terms of ethnicity and religion—and the dearth of information on how humanitarian organizations raise and manage their funds—also seems to come into play. Kibreab reflects that refugees' cheating could also be understood "as being acts of defiance against the vague and often subjective criteria used by aid agencies to divide people into separate categories, e.g., vulnerable (deserving), non-vulnerable (non-deserving), internally displaced persons, local residents, refugees and returnees" (2004: 18). Given their belief that aid organizations have access to unlimited resources, refugees do not see collecting more than one's share as an especially reproachable act, but rather as a rational one, even though humanitarian organizations do not share such a view.

In such a context, it is difficult to envisage how trust can be established with refugees or how they can truly participate in the design of programs or in the management and distribution of aid. In considering again Giddens' definition of trust, the reasons for the mistrust felt by aid organizations and their workers toward refugees converge. Indeed, nothing indicates that refugees will act in a fair and honest manner in their interaction with the system and its administrators. The camp becomes the locus of tensions between control and circumvention, and between its inhabitants and its humanitarian government. Within the camp, although there is more evidence of trust, interpersonal mistrust is relatively common, as is mistrust between coexisting ethnic groups.

Mistrust in the Community

After an initial period of adjustment, "most of the internal relations within the refugee communities are characterized by mutual trust, respect and cooperation," writes Kibreab (2004: 13). "When the refugees interact with each other, they often act according to some moral principle that requires them to take account of each other's interest … mainly due to the principle of expected reciprocity." From Kibreab's perspective, refugees feel a moral obligation toward fellow refugees, and thus have entered into a social contract. At the other end of the spectrum, Voutira and Harrell-Bond (1995: 218) assert that:

> One seldom finds a sense of political solidarity among refugee populations …
> The power of the humanitarian regime over limited supplies generates inter and intragroup conflict, as individuals seek to ingratiate themselves with the

authorities in competition with their fellows ... Such conditions seriously undermine any potential for unity and solidarity of the population as a whole while at the same time introducing new grounds for cleavages and factions.

I believe that the reality in Kakuma lies somewhere between these two positions. While community and personal trust are at times lacking and are challenged by the competition for resources, they do nonetheless exist. Testimonies of trust are visible in the way people coexist, interact and cooperate, as well as in details of daily life, such as the credit granted to customers by shop owners or people's mutual lending of objects and money.

I have previously indicated that over time, communities did form in the camp and this entailed some trust, trust being central to the reconstruction of communities. I have also noted that people have learned to live relatively peacefully together. Yet trust does not prevail between the various communities coexisting in the camp. Distrust is obvious in the stereotypical views that refugees commonly express about refugees of other ethnicities or nationalities. For example, it is said that Somalis "only believe in money," "have problems with everyone" and "don't even cooperate within their community." This is not surprising, as refugees do not feel that they belong to one large community of Kakumians, but rather to a specific community within the camp, even though a broader sense of solidarity is perceptible at times. Even members of the same nationality, clan or tribe do not necessarily trust one another at a personal and group level.

Trust in a Land of Scarcity

Evident mistrust between individuals and between groups within communities is not specific to Kakuma. It exists in almost any setting, but the lack of confidence in this context can be accentuated by people's previous experiences. At a group level, Somalis fairly often criticize minority groups for using their ethnicity for resettlement purposes, while people from minority groups accuse those from majority groups of instigating the Somali conflict. In that respect, trust is limited. Similarly, trusting relationships are not the norm between community organizations competing for funding and recognition. This translates into unflattering remarks and limited collaboration between such groups. For example, the oldest Somali youth group in the camp, the Somali Youth League (SYL), has a fairly tense relationship with the two more recent associations, Aliform Somali Generation and the Union of Somali Youth. It accuses them of being tribal and interested only in money, which seems unfair: while the SYL initially received money from the UNHCR, neither of the newer groups has secured funding. In the case of Aliform, volunteers are even contributing 200 KSh (less than US$2) a month.

At a personal level, refugees are often suspicious of one another. Several say that they reveal as little as possible about themselves to others, as they fear that any such information might be used against them and that other refugees might try to steal their resettlement slot. When we talked of trust and security in the journalism class, many brought up suspicions that intelligence services from their countries of origin were operating in the camp. As a result, they believed that prudence was required at all times and that whatever they shared had to first be carefully filtered. Stories are commonly adapted for resettlement or assistance purposes, but also, in some cases, for the sake of protection. When I asked the smart and resourceful twenty-three-year-old Zahra why she had not applied for a scholarship with the WUSC, given that she had had good grades in high school and wanted to pursue her education, she responded that it could cause her problems. Her story is the most extreme that I heard, as it not only entailed making up a story for the UNHCR, but also changing her identity in everyday life:

> Zahra: Sometimes, as a refugee, you have to mix things up. You know, the names I am using, they are not my real names. The names I have on my school documents are not the ones they have in UNHCR. If I applied for a scholarship, they could see that I lied and I could be arrested. That means that I cannot use my documents.

> Me: Why did you change your name?

> Zahra: When my sister died [the person who had raised Zahra on the Kenyan coast, as both her parents died when she was young], life became difficult. I could not find money for food, I could not pay for school fees. So I decided to go and find my grandmother in Kismayo, back in Somalia. When I arrived, my family decided to find me a man. In our culture, at thirteen, you are meant to be getting married. I was fourteen. I got mad and decided that it would not happen. I had to get out of there. I went back to [the Kenyan coast]. I just wanted to go back to school. I was in Form 2 and I was planning to have a very good future. I was not thinking of going to the camp. I found a family who accepted to host me and send me to school if I worked for them. After high school, life became difficult. I met a sheikh who advised me to go to Kakuma. I did not want to, but I had no choice. I wanted to go to college, but I had no money and I could not get a job. When I arrived in the camp, I decided to register as someone else. I knew my grandmother was looking for me. If I used my real name in the camp, maybe there would be some people who knew people in Kismayo who would tell my grandmother I was here. The family could come looking for me. That is when I changed my name.

> Me: Why don't you go to UNHCR to explain the situation and ask for your name to be changed in your documents? You would not have to use your real name in the camp, but it would allow you to apply to the WUSC.

Zahra: I cannot do that. It is a very long process and they start suspecting that you are lying. I had a friend who was nearly arrested because they said she had changed her name. It was not even true. It happened because she had applied to the WUSC.

Me: Don't you think you would be able to explain your situation to UNHCR?

Zahra: Meeting with [the head of UNHCR's protection unit] is very difficult and I don't trust the national staff. They can make problems for you. I just want to avoid trouble. I have been going through a lot of shit and don't want more to happen.

Zahra's attitude and words starkly underline the consequences of the significant breaches of trust experienced by a number of refugees. She is consistently on her guard and never wants to talk of anything remotely personal in a public space because she fears other people might be listening. She says she has no friends in the camp and believes that no one can be trusted. "Everyone is after something. No one wants you to succeed before them, they will try to create problems for you if you are being resettled. They could go to UNHCR and tell that I am not using my real names, for example. There are people I say 'Hi' to, but I don't tell them who I really am. It has become difficult for me to open up and talk."

Rumors about refugees, spread by other refugees, abound. Most often, they are related to resettlement, which is probably the issue generating the most mistrust and suspicion between refugees. Several accuse others of not being bona fide refugees, but rather Kenyans who have registered as refugees to try to benefit from resettlement. A number of people hold that some youths have been falsely accused of rape by girls whose families are hoping to be accepted for resettlement on account of a lack of protection in the camp. In other cases, people accuse fellow refugees of fabricating stories about them to hinder their resettlement prospects. For example, the family of twenty-four-year-old Abdullahi was transferred by the UNHCR and the IOM from Dadaab in 2002 to be part of the group resettlement of Somali Bantus to the United States Most departed for the United States in the following years. Abdullahi's family was rejected from the process for lying to the interviewers. He is convinced that their case was in fact rejected because of strained social relations. His sister had refused to marry the secretary general of the camp's Somali Bantus. Snubbed, he may well have handed a report to the resettlement officers declaring that their mother was not their real mother. "Americans believed him because he was the secretary general. So anything he said was considered true. When we went to our appointment, the person conducting the interview said: 'This is not your mom.' [The interviewer] claimed we had agreed to take her to America because she was giving us money. It was a lie, but we were rejected." The tensions and distrust surrounding resettlement are such that refugees involved in the process as interpreters for the UNHCR, and especially for the IOM, are sometimes accused of spearheading the rejection of cases.

Although there are definitely more testimonies of trust between refugees and within refugee communities, distrust between the various communities and individuals is also manifest. This hampers the emergence of a community transcending ethnicity and, to a lesser extent, limits cohesion within ethnic groups. Persistent movements that lead to constant changes in the camp's population are also unconducive to the development of trusting and lasting relationships. Nonetheless, it is considered dishonorable to behave dishonestly in interactions with other refugees. While communities and individuals may not fully trust one another, their compliance with moral standards indicates that a social contract is respected, at least to some extent. This could explain why people commonly point the finger at the host community or policemen, rather than at fellow refugees, for the petty crimes committed in the camp.

In the Land of Mistrust

In this chapter, I have attempted to show how trust broke down early on in the process of the settlement of Somalis in Kakuma and was never restored, the camp's environment being intrinsically unfavorable to the establishment of trusting relationships. As a result, cooperation between refugees and the humanitarian system remains limited. In the absence of trust, which requires some transparency so that decisions can be predictable and intelligible, refugees nurture a negative attitude toward the aid system and doubt the integrity of its staff. This reinforces their skepticism regarding the probity of the system. Breakdowns in trust that occurred many years ago, such as the resettlement fraud of the 1990s, have long-term repercussions. While a complex and incremental process is required to building trust, it is relatively easy to destroy and is then longer and harder to restore than initially (Hynes 2009: 98; Saunders and Thornhill 2004: 496). In that sense, the long-term existence of the camp has not fostered trusting relationships. Refugees' behavior and mistrust fuel those of aid workers and organizations, who in turn doubt the honesty of refugees, whom they suspect of attempting to cheat in order to accrue resources and to play a role that might allow them to improve their condition. Although dynamics at a camp level between refugee communities and among individuals entail more trust, suspicion remains high.

While mistrust is palpable at all levels, its consequences are not the same for everyone, because of unequal power relations and influence. Aid organizations, whose decisions have a major impact on refugees' lives, have access to important means of control. In contrast, refugees have only limited influence on these organizations, which are usually held accountable to donors rather than refugees. The relationship between humanitarian organizations and refugees is thus characterized by an absence of reciprocity and a power imbalance. This dynamic limits the opportunities for cooperation between refugees and aid organizations, which, in turn, accentuates the mistrust of all parties, as well as the camp's inhospitality.

These observations show that Voutira and Harrell-Bond's (1995) remarks remain relevant, despite efforts to redefine the relationship between refugees and aid organizations. In fact, in the absence of a shared moral configuration, which becomes evident throughout this chapter, this relationship cannot truly be or become trustful and reciprocal. As Giddens writes, trust entails the confidence that people or institutions will act in a fair and honest manner. But the notions of fairness and honesty rely on a shared system of norms and moral values, which seems to be lacking in Kakuma. In this context, it might be relevant to ask how trust could prevail. In that sense, while I chose to revisit Voutira and Harrell Bond's writings, it would be interesting to study the moral economy of the camp (or, in fact, its moral economies), situating norms and values in their historical and social contexts (Fassin 2009: 1257). The example of refugees' stories is evocative. Through their accounts, refugees notably wish to present themselves as an "acceptable subject" and be recognized as refugees, but also to ensure their access to assistance and prospective resettlement, even if it entails polishing their account (Meintel 1990: 58). Assistance and resettlement allow refugees to meet their moral obligations toward their family who, in the first case, can live in better conditions and, in the second, can aspire to a "normal" life, and toward their relatives, through sharing their comparative wealth with them. Humanitarian organizations, on the other hand, try to prevent what they perceive as fraudulent acts and, in doing so, tend to discredit refugees' stories. In this way, they fulfill their moral obligations toward donors. Of course, this example would need to be further developed and nuanced to give a full account of the complexity of the social worlds of the camp, but the moral configurations underlying the behaviors of refugees and of aid organizations seem to differ considerably. It is likely that divergences between moral economies create mistrust.

Notes

1. Food rations in Kakuma have notably occurred in 2001, 2003, 2004, 2006, 2008 and 2013 (Africa News Service 2002; Hathaway 2005: 473; Jansen 2011: 213; Straziuso 2013).

2. The UN defines human rights-based approaches as "a conceptual framework for the process of human development that is normatively based on international human rights standards and operationally directed to promoting and protecting human rights." It specifies that charity "is not enough from a human rights perspective" (OHCHR 2006: 15).

3. These include the Code of Conduct for the International Red Cross and Red Crescent Movement and Non-Governmental Organizations in Disaster Relief (IFRC/ICRC 1994), the 1997 Sphere Project, or the 2003 Humanitarian Accountability Partnership.

4. Hautaniemi (2007) highlights the gap between the way in which Somalis and Finnish authorities understand who is a family member in the context of family reunification. While the Finnish definition of "family" (or the Western definition, for that matter) is usually restricted to a "household," the Somali one is broader and tends to refer to a wider kinship network.

Chapter 7

THROUGH THEIR EYES

Representation and Self-Representation

❦

> To be a refugee means that you are ruled by somebody, you
> don't have the freedom that you had in your own country.
> When you want to travel outside of Kakuma, you must
> take permission from UNHCR. It creates a bad picture.
> It's not good to be a refugee. It's not comfortable.
> —Fatuma, nineteen years old

I asked my photography students and several other young people to define
what a refugee was and explain how they felt about being one. Their responses
were surprisingly similar. In theory, a refugee was someone who had fled from
his or her country. In practice, they described refugees as people with no
rights who were perpetually reminded that the land they lived on was not
theirs. Refugees, they said, were held in contempt and treated as lesser human beings. While they strongly recognized and felt the limitations imposed
by their condition, they did not accept them, nor did they feel inferior to
others. In fact, they stressed that facing the camp and exile was an experience
that had forced them to be brave and strong so as to manage in a foreign environment and acquire new skills and knowledge. I came to notice that most
youth never used the words "refugee" or "camp" in speaking of themselves or
where they grew up. Being a refugee in a camp is not a defining characteristic
that they emphasize, possibly because of its stigmatizing connotation. The
gap between the way they believe they are perceived—as powerless victims

in need of help—and how they speak of themselves is vast, and they are well aware of the chasm. This came across clearly in the student's family and self-portrait exercises: their textual and photographic representations did not exude wretchedness and poverty. For the occasion, the students did exactly what one would expect from people having their portrait taken: they picked the finest settings and tried to look their best in front of the camera.

The first two pictures shown are portraits of their families by two photography students, Nafissa and Suad. I took the third and fourth pictures for a self-portrait exercise in which students wrote a text about themselves and decided how they wanted to be photographed.

Nafissa's siblings are smiling and laughing. Suad's family members are proudly posing inside their well-kept home. For her self-portrait, for which

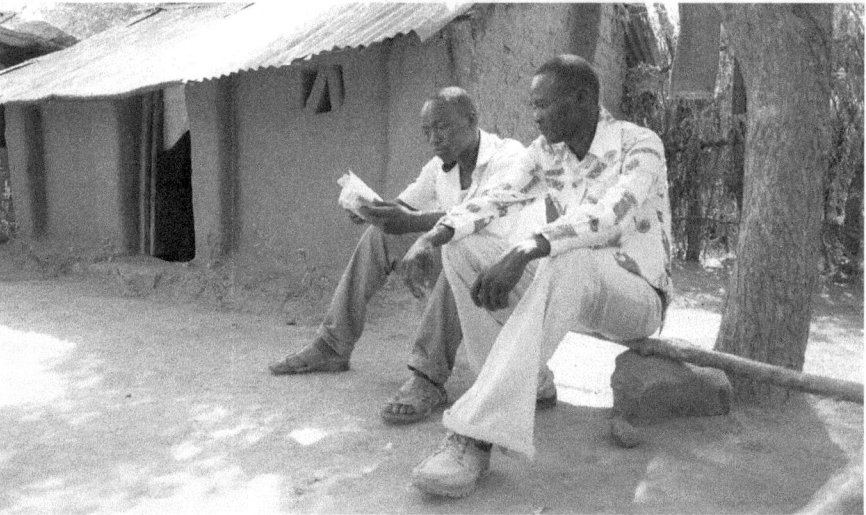

Figures 7.1–7.4 Family photographs and self-portraits. Courtesy of Nafissa, Suad and author's photographs

she wanted to be with her siblings, Suad carefully chose a spot with her mother, they covered the wall with elegant red fabric for the occasion and made sure that everyone was wearing their best attire. Yohana decided to be piously reading the Bible in his brother's company next to their home.

The following pictures of refugees in Chad and Kenya were used by the International Federation of Red Cross and Red Crescent Societies and the UNHCR to illustrate reports and news stories (IFRC 2007: 14; UNHCR 2011c). In both cases, they were accompanied by nonspecific captions that do

Figures 7.5 and 7.6 Refugee photographs by aid organizations. Courtesy of IFRC/D. Cima; UNHCR/R. Gangale

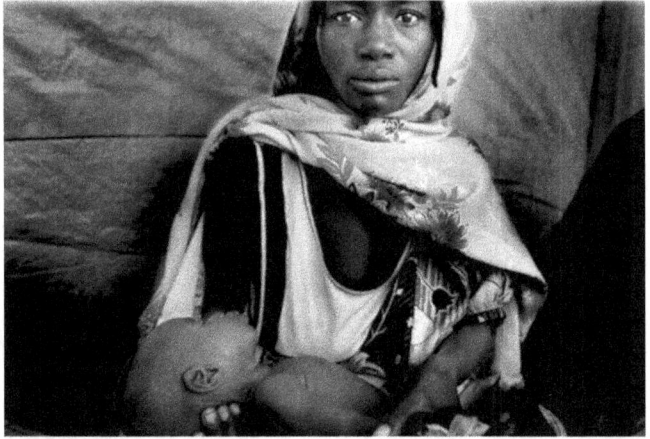

not mention people's names, where exactly they are from, why they are there or why they look distraught.

These photographs seem to epitomize the gap between the typical imagery of refugees as undifferentiated and depoliticized victims and people's self-representation as unique and capable human beings (see Berger 1980: 40). Although the "refugee" category designates people with extremely diverse stories and backgrounds who might have in common only their flight across an international border, "the refugee" has become a universal figure to which is attached a quasi-generic image of misery and suffering (Malkki 1995a: 510–11). This not only obscures people's multi-dimensionality but also their agency (Rajaram 2002: 251). Stripped of citizenship, the refugee ideal type is the very image of bare life (Arendt 1968 [1951]: 300; Nyers 2006: 61).

Such a representation may influence the prevalent perception of refugees and the way they are treated by aid organizations, but how does it affect refugees' self-representation and perception of their own capacities? To what extent does having to conform to stereotypes for assistance purposes end up shaping self-representation (Zetter 1991: 45)? Is it transformed by living in a poor and stigmatized setting where opportunities are scarce (Bourdieu 1993: 167)?

This chapter is about the way young refugees are represented and how it alters their self-perception. While the focus is on Somalis, comments by other refugees are also included as, regardless of their nationality, their observations are noticeably similar and consistent. This is a significant matter, because people's self-representation is related to their assessment of their own capacities and their belief in their ability to shape their lives. Interestingly, refugee youth occupy two potentially stigmatizing social positions. In addition to being refugees, they are youth, a category commonly perceived as problem-prone. I argue that although young people are conscious of the way they are represented, they do not accept the common view as accurate, but do in fact object to it. Such resistance forces them to define who they are, marking their distance from outsiders' expectations and perception. While one cannot help but wonder to what extent this representation insidiously alters their image of themselves, I dispute the claim that it produces a uniformly debilitating effect. Malkki (1995b) has convincingly shown that displacement and being a refugee have a significant influence on the production of sense and self-representation, but these do not necessarily tally with stereotypical images of the displaced.

In the following, I first examine the common representation of refugees and the perspective of aid workers. I then discuss how youth believe they are represented and conclude with a section on youth's self-representation.

The Way They Look at Us

The word "refugee" has become a political one,
suggesting large herds of innocent and bewildered
people requiring urgent international assistance.
—Edward Said, "Reflections on Exile"

Although it has been widely remarked that refugees are routinely depicted as powerless and voiceless victims, there is no fixed and uniform representation of refugees. Media portrayals and public reports by aid organizations are often much more simplistic and prone to subsuming refugees to their misery than are aid workers directly involved with refugees or, obviously, refugees themselves. I outline below the generic representation of refugees, before exploring the views of aid workers. I touch upon the perspective of parents and community members on refugee youth, but only briefly, as their focus on cultural change brings us back to cultural change and preservation, a theme already developed in Chapter 5.

Human Beings "in the Raw": Representing Refugees

In the aftermath of World War II, Hannah Arendt observed the reduction of refugees to their state of bare life and their exclusion from the political sphere. She wrote that refugees, stripped of their belonging to a community and denied the exercise of their citizenship, lose not only their national rights but also, more importantly, their human rights, which are in theory inalienable. They become "rightless, the scum of the earth" (Arendt 1968 [1951]: 267). "The prolongation of their lives is due to charity and not to right, for no law exists which could force the nations to feed them; their freedom of movement, if they have it at all, gives them no right to residence which even the jailed criminal enjoys as a matter of course; and their freedom of opinion is a fool's freedom, for nothing they think matters anyhow" (1968 [1951]: 296). Such complete dispossession is tantamount to "the deprivation of a place in the world which makes opinions significant and actions effective" (1968 [1951]: 296). Refugees are thus excluded from the human race, from the family of nations: "It seems that a man who is nothing but a man has lost the very qualities which make it possible for other people to treat him as a fellow-man" (1968 [1951]: 300). The legal definition of a refugee in the 1951 Convention, argues Nyers (2006: 61), assumes their state of nature by defining them as driven by their survival instinct rather than by reason. Consequently, refugees cannot "act politically, develop knowledge, or otherwise pursue a cultured form of existence."

Because of this perception, certain behaviors, characteristics and attitudes are socially expected of "authentic" refugees, who only *exist* in opposition to the norm embodied by citizens (Nyers 2006: 9). As victims devoid of speech and political subjectivity, who depend on charity rather than law, refugees are regarded as helpless and passive, ignorant of their history, their traditions and their culture (Malkki 1995b: 9–12).[1] Reduced to their biological status, refugees become a homogeneous population, usually represented in traditional gender, social and age roles (Clark-Kazak 2009: 319). Stereotypically, girls and women in camps are depicted as "feeble, vulnerable, gentle, kind and peace-loving," while men are "strong, resistant, heartless, and callous" (Verdirame and Harrell-Bond 2005: 123–24). Refugees' sole hope is to return to their country of origin, "so as to restore the conditions under which they may once again enjoy a properly human life as citizens" (Nyers 2006: 23). This representation implies that as soon as someone crosses an international border, he or she is dislocated, at a loss, a "native gone amok" because of uprooting (Malkki 1992: 34). Sedentariness is hence the only norm: the only place where human beings can live in harmony with their culture and identity is their country of origin. "Almost like an essentialized anthropological 'tribe,' refugees thus become not just a mixed category of people sharing a certain legal status; they become 'a culture,' 'an identity,' 'a social world,' or 'a community.' There is a tendency, then, to proceed as if refugees all shared a common condition or nature" (Malkki 1995a: 511).[2]

This representation—and the term itself is important, as this portrayal does not correspond to reality—conceals the specificity of individual experience and people's agency. People become bodies that must be managed, rather than full and complex human beings. This has an impact on how refugees are perceived by humanitarian organizations and their staff, which in turn influences interactions and programming.

Victims or Dangerous Outcasts

Like many refugees, the Kenyan head of FilmAid in Kakuma refused to employ the word "refugee." I asked why, pointing out that it referred to a legal status and was not in itself a derogatory term:

> I don't like using it because of how it is used by people around here. They don't use it to refer to a legal status but to subhumans. Over time, I realized that these guys [refugees] expected to be treated as inferiors because that is how they have been treated for so long. They are blamed for being here. I don't think humanitarian workers understand why they came here. I have met amazing colleagues here but also others who make comments that drive me crazy. "Refugee" has a bad meaning here. That is why I avoid using it.

It would be wrong to presume that all aid workers have an inhumane relationship with refugees. Some do, many do not. It is the management techniques that dehumanize refugees. These are influenced by the way in which refugees are represented, but also by the fact that their rights on Kenyan soil are limited in practice. The discourse of the Kenyan staff often carries more prejudice than that of the internationals, possibly because the latter spend less time in the camp directly engaging with refugees and have adopted a more proper style of speech. But in all cases, what is considered an acceptable standard for refugees would not be acceptable for most aid workers and their families: severe overcrowding in school, lack of access to decent healthcare, whipping of those who do not stay in line during food distributions, insecurity, arbitrariness or unpredictable cuts in assistance. Aid workers' acceptance of these standards suggests that refugees are not represented as fellow humans, but as recipients of charity who can be expected to be grateful.

The widespread adoption of human rights-based approaches since the early 2000s by humanitarian organizations could have led to a shift in representations. As I mentioned earlier, these approaches were meant to transform beneficiary-victims into rights-bearers and thus transfigure the charitable relationship into one between rights-bearers. But this did not materialize. Armstrong (2008: 5) claims that the prevalence of the language of human rights has not undermined previous representations, but has in fact "reinforced them by making suffering the most powerful tool of the displaced in their interface with international workers." However, not all refugees correspond to the victim stereotype, which leads to contrasting representations in Kakuma. Unlike the Sudanese, Somalis are often depicted as "bad" refugees by aid workers, seemingly because of their refusal to conform to the representation of refugees as victims.[3] They refuse to work for a miserable salary, are vocally ungrateful for meager assistance and have no respect for authority based purely on one's ranking. Remarkably, the traits that make Somalis "bad" refugees are qualities they are proud of.

The dual representation of refugees as victims and as threatening and untrustworthy outcasts seems to be encapsulated in the fact that the camp is a no-go zone after dark for aid workers and visitors. The justification for this interdiction is twofold. First, the camp is depicted as dangerous, refugees being dangerous. Then, aid workers should not have intimate relationships with refugees, because of their assumed vulnerability. Indeed, scandals of sexual exploitation by humanitarian workers have led to policies aimed at preventing sexual abuse and strongly discouraging sexual relationships between humanitarian workers and beneficiaries, as these are based on "inherently unequal power dynamics" (SG 2003: 3.2).[4] As a side-effect, social relations between aid workers and refugees have come to be closely scrutinized and often restricted. A young foreign aid worker pointed out that while these policies are justified, as they seek to prevent abuses, they also create a separate category of people with whom one cannot establish an equal relationship, since all are considered to be vulnerable, and thus any relationship would be abusive. "Back home," she said, "these are people I could have an intimate relationship with. I strongly connect with some. Here, the premise is that such a relationship would be exploitative." This boundary carries a strong symbolism, separating the realm of citizens from that of "untouchable" refugees and tainting the dynamics of socialization.

Young people have to deal with another stigmatizing attribute: they are youth, a category often described as disruptive because of its unpredictable liminality. Aid workers' representations of youth incorporate common stereotypes: they are difficult to motivate, predisposed to idleness and vulnerable to HIV infection. Girls are likely to fall into prostitution, boys into substance abuse. Those who have grown up in the camps have always depended on assistance and are therefore unable to look after themselves. Yet, these same youth are the people most commonly employed by aid organizations as incentive workers. As individuals, they are appreciated. Some are described as brilliant, full of potential, incredibly resilient and strong-willed for having survived (and in some cases thrived) in such conditions. At a group level, they are seen as a problem-prone class, especially as the scarcity of opportunities is believed to promote harmful behavior.

Parents, of course, have no prejudice against their own children for being refugees, but express concerns related to their lack of prospects after high school, which, they believe, leads to indolence and the adoption of bad habits, and triggers frustration. Some parents and community members feel that young people are at a complete loss in the camp. What concerns them, in addition to their children's limited possibilities, is acculturation. Their depiction of youth often includes Westernization, apparent in young people's clothing, tastes in music or lack of command of their own language, history and social codes. Some think young people show disrespect for cultural norms, notably by promiscuous behavior. On the other hand, parents often stress with pride that their children have managed well given the circumstances, have gained from the camp in terms of education and their ability to engage with people of varied cultural backgrounds, and have adjusted better than they themselves have to this foreign environment.

While the representation of refugees as victims and cheaters by aid organizations and the media is not part of the camp's landscape as such, it is reflected in the design of programs and the way in which aid workers engage with refugees. This generic portrayal is far from benign and contributes to the marginalization of refugees' voices, notably when it comes to consulting them on decisions affecting their lives (Harindranath 2007: 3). In the same vein, although youth are not necessarily informed about how they are represented at a global level, they are acutely aware of how aid workers view them, as manifested in the way they engage and interact with refugees.

The Way We Believe They Look at Us

When I asked young people how they were perceived as refugees, their frank and lucid responses repeatedly brought up a few elements: refugees are reduced to being nothing but refugees; as receivers of aid, they are incapable of looking after themselves and are thus dependent on other people's charity; to be a proper refugee, one has to appear vulnerable; and refugees have no rights, as they are forever visitors in a foreign land. Axlam's comment is typical of many others:

> We are only here as exiles and Kenyans despise us. They tell us that we came from a country where we bomb ourselves. They tell us that we are just refugees and have no rights in this country, that we are visitors. It kills your morale. I have been here for all my life. I came from Somalia in 1991. I was six months old. In school, we learned with Kenyans. When we did better than them, teachers would say: "How can you be less good than a refugee?" People look down on you. In order to get what you want, you don't say you are a refugee.

Many insist that being a refugee amounts to having no freedom of movement and entails always being on guard. "If a Kenyan starts a fight with you and you go to the police, they will say you don't have rights," stated Nafissa. "But this other person has the right of the country. That is why you have to be careful with everything you do."

The essentializing of people to their status is striking at times. Refugees do not fail to notice it. I once attended a farewell party organized by the UN-HCR for departing staff. Aid workers were invited, as well as some refugees who worked as incentive staff. As the formal speeches went on, the master of ceremonies called upon a "representative of the beneficiaries" to come and speak. This was an established wording to refer to inhabitants of the camp. Human beings were reduced to beneficiaries, defined by the fact that they were recipients of aid. I was sitting next to a young Rwandan I knew fairly well and who worked for the UNHCR as a translator. He said he had been asked to give the speech and had refused because he did not want to carry that label: "I am Fabrice. I am not a *beneficiary*." While people know they are unique, they are also mindful that in the eyes of the humanitarian system, they are considered as a flock of beneficiaries first and foremost and that this bears consequences.

Being a refugee or a beneficiary is seen as a sign of helplessness and destitution, points out Mahdi. "When a Kenyan calls you a refugee, it means you are nothing. You are ill and useless. You are under someone's hands, like on the UNHCR logo. You cannot do your own thing. You are being taken care of like a kid. There is no way you can take care of yourself. If you want food, the UN gives you. If you want shelter, go to NCCK [the National Council of Churches of Kenya]." Being under the UNHCR's safekeeping involves having to agree to intrusive and controlling policies, fumes Nafissa: "You must inform them of everything you are doing, even small things. If you want to have a party, you must request an authorization." It infantilizes refugees, turns them into lesser humans, something that the incentive system conveys clearly: they do not deserve the same salaries as nonrefugees. But there are more pernicious and subtle hints. Youth believe they are treated as intellectually inept. Commenting on training offered by a visiting NGO, Abdulaziz said that the course was excessively simple. "People always teach us basic things, they always simplify for us as if we were idiots."

These impressions notably arise from a lack of consideration that translates into demeaning and disrespectful behaviors. People who do not get proper answers to their questions or who are not consulted on decisions that have an impact on their lives feel that they are perceived and treated as inferiors. Some Kenyan high school teachers are blatantly rude to refugee students. In one instance, a student lent her camera to a teacher who had requested it. He did not bring it back until I went to claim it. His sole defense was: "Who is she, anyway?" Similarly, the fact that people are often not told where exactly they are being resettled creates a lot of anxiety, but is also understood as a lack of recognition of their humanness. Commenting on the latter perception, Abdikadir evokes his brothers, who, after being resettled to the United States, were amazed at no longer carrying the refugee label and being regarded as fellow humans. "They say the way they are treated and the attention they get is enough to survive even if they don't get a job. Human beings have a good feeling if they are received with an open face. It heals you internally." I am not implying that arriving as a refugee in the United States is an easy experience, but Abdikadir's comment conveys his belief that the treatment of the residents of Kakuma is dehumanizing.

Moreover, people think that they are expected to adopt behaviors testifying to their vulnerability. Speaking of the early days of Kakuma, Abdulaziz recalls that neighbors kept poultry and cultivated gardens: "But when UNHCR would come and visit the camp, refugees would hide those things because if UNHCR sees you with things that allow you to support yourself, they stop helping you. You need to look miserable if you want to be helped." This is a recurring theme: playing the vulnerability card is crucial to being assisted as a refugee.

Being conscious of being seen as inferiors, of having limited rights and of being discriminated against can negatively alter people's self-representation.

However, as Zetter (1991: 40) points out, refugees might "conceive their identity in very different terms from those bestowing the label." It is manifest that although youth find those labels painful, they reject them and regard those who convey and believe them as ignorant. Their depiction of people's perception of refugees often becomes the background against which they define themselves by opposition. They are not lesser humans; they have survived in conditions that others would have been unable to face and have managed to gain something from the experience. To a certain degree, being a refugee might not be a weakness, but rather a testimony of strength and determination.

The Way We Look at Ourselves

US
We are girls and boys.
We are Sudanese, Somalis and Ethiopians.
We are sons and daughters, brothers and sisters.
We are footballers and basketball players.
We are away from our countries.
Here is where we grew up.
—Text written by the photography students
for the exhibition of their work

Refugee youth know their condition is stigmatizing, as it constitutes a socially discrediting attribute that gives them a character that is "not quite human" (Goffman 1975: 15). But individuals are not reducible to their stigma, to their status of beneficiaries and victims. Indeed, if we subscribe to the idea that refugees are thinking individuals with a political subjectivity and not merely victims, knowing how they are perceived does not mean accepting and conforming to that perception and adopting it as their identity. In fact, refugees' portrayal has become an object of resistance and derision. One can still question how much the label influences their self-representation, possibly through opposition rather than compliance. And while they can refuse labels, they cannot ignore the limitations attached to their status.

At first sight, youth patently reject the refugee stigma and the "principle of vulnerability," thus defying the conventional representation of refugees (Agier 2008: 233). The shame of being a refugee that some felt as children is often long gone by the time they have become young adults and has been replaced by the pride of having survived harsh conditions, something that Aziz expressed repeatedly. As a child, he was embarrassed by being a refugee. "But when I grew up and I saw my sister working as headmistress, my brother working for IOM as an interpreter, and me in the film-making program, I started feeling that I had a unique experience. I became proud because I managed well in school and in those difficult conditions." This does not prevent young refugees from recognizing and profoundly resenting the disabling aspect of their condition. They persistently emphasize that with the same level of education as Kenyans, they cannot aspire to the same positions or enjoy the same salaries, and that their bosses may have less education than they do, yet be in a higher position only because they are Kenyans. But they do not accept this as something justifiable. They denounce it as neither fair nor right, and that is, in short, what they repeated over and over. What they seem to be doing, in seeing and underlining the unfairness and joking about how they are being diminished, is stressing that they are conscious of the prejudiced views people hold of them and how these influence their treatment. There is a team of young women footballers from Kakuma that was once invited to one of Nairobi's slums, Mathare, for a tournament and community work. They describe being put up in a big room with no sheets or blankets, only mattresses. The latrines were worse than in the camp. They are convinced that they were so poorly accommodated because they are refugees. They were provided with shoes and socks for the match, "so we would look smart," but had to give them back when they returned to Kakuma. Their sarcastic depiction of the trip makes clear their view that the experience might have been humiliating, but the people who treated them with such lack of consideration because of their status are blinded by labels and are not worthy of their respect, only their mockery.

In short, youth are aware that their social identity is a hindrance, as they are not oblivious to their social environment and the way they are perceived. Yet, they do not simply comply with this misrepresentation. They remain social actors who act on their environment and give meaning to their actions and experience. Being mindful of their situation means that young people know only too well that their social navigation is complicated and limited by the constraints attached to their status. The fact that several state that it is sometimes better to hide their refugee status testifies to that. And that is the frustrating part. While they intimately sense that being refugees is not their essence, they also realize that it has serious consequences on their real-life possibilities and visions for the future.

Who are We?

Since the representation of refugees has an impact on their existence, it is reasonable to think that it influences their self-representation and their identity. While identity is a subjective, dialogic and dynamic construct, it cannot be detached from people's social reality, from the objective, the given, and from the feedback of their social setting (Kaufmann 2006: 42). Given the fluidity of identity or self-representation, we can suppose that the interaction with the humanitarian system and its representation of refugees leads to adjustments. Of course, there is no direct transfer of meaning: people do not mindlessly embrace representations of themselves by others. They can reject a perception or partly accept it, a response that varies from one individual to another, as a result of people's unique personal identities. However, regardless of the reaction, the label remains entangled with people's self-representation, a label that is also constructed and imbued with meaning by refugees themselves (Nyers 2006: xv). The shame attached to the "rejected from resettlement" label testifies that categories imposed on people are not meaningless.

Swann (1987: 1038) maintains that people tend to conform to outside expectations, thus shaping their social reality based on other people's perceptions, although in some cases they vehemently refuse the labels. It is sensible to think that people's dialogue with their social world and their social world's expectations interact closely with their identity. But which social world? Which expectations? Which perceptions? Swann further notes that self-conceptions are developed from childhood from the observation of people's behavior, the reaction of other people to one's own behavior and one's comparison with other people (1987: 1039). When refugee youth were children, their interactions with humanitarian workers were limited, and thus the latter were not the ones providing them with their main feedback. In primary school, their teachers were most often fellow refugees, as were an important proportion of their high school professors. In daily life, they rarely interacted with aid workers, but mostly with relatives, members of their community and other refugees. These interactions, in which the stigma attached to being a refugee was probably absent, were quite probably more influential in constructing their self-representation. As Goffman points out, a stigma only exists in relation to others (1975: 13–14). Thus, the refugee stigma surfaced with nonrefugees, with outsiders, but probably not within the community. Later, of course, some came to interact more regularly with the humanitarian system as employees, leaders or heads of families, but even then, intimate life in the camp remains fairly disconnected from the world of aid workers, although the aid regime profoundly affects its functioning. Nor do all interactions have the same impact on people's identity. As Bisharat (1997: 204) mentions: "Some of the voices in the dialogue may be more compelling than others, speaking to deeper aspects of consciousness, and conjuring up more stirring symbols of inclusion and exclusion."

In addition, while identity is changeable and could be altered by interaction with the humanitarian system, it is not subject to constant radical change either. Swann (1987: 1044) underlines that enduring changes in people's self-conceptions typically stem from a "major reorganization in the way [they] view themselves" and from consistent feedback supporting the new perception. Such shifts are triggered by important transformations in one's life, such as a marriage or a promotion. Adults who came to Kenya as grown-ups and became refugees must have faced significant reorganization and undergone major change. On the other hand, refugee youth who were born in Kenya or arrived when they were too young to remember did not become refugees; they always were, even though it might not have been a key definer (on becoming refugees, see Loizos (1981: 120–21)). Moreover, although certain social expectations are attached to most social roles, including that of refugee, youth's social roles are plural: being a refugee is only one of them and not necessarily the most significant. Their age group, gender, nationality, clan or ethnic group, artistic talent, job or performance at football could also define their social identity. The pre-eminence of a given social identity is most likely context-specific and it would be overly simplistic to infer that young people's identities are shaped primarily by their victimhood.

I mentioned before that a number of young people stressed that refugees are expected by the UNHCR to be vulnerable. Studying the impact of human rights approaches with internally displaced persons living in camps in northern Uganda, Armstrong (2008) reflects that in the camp context, narrations of suffering had become a form of agency (or "victimcy," in the words of Utas (2005)), since being vulnerable was valued by the humanitarian system and foreigners. Victimcy thus became a strategic choice, but, argues Armstrong (2008: 24), asserting it "tends to be a limiting rather than liberating action. It encourages passiveness and the expression of helplessness that can become internalized." I would not assume such a direct transfer between acting vulnerable and internalizing vulnerability. Being capable of circumventing the system might also be empowering. However, I noticed that most youth in the camp refused, at least in public, to pretend to be victims for the sake of assistance, which could point toward their refusal to act as victims. Inhetveen (2006: 9) remarks that in Zambia, many refugees labeled themselves as "vulnerable." This is also the case for older refugees in Kakuma, but youth rejected this administrative categorization, at least in informal discussions. They are perhaps more likely to play that card in their interaction with aid organizations, particularly for resettlement purposes. In fact, one could wonder if failing at being selected for resettlement could be interpreted as having failed to represent oneself adequately as a victim. In their daily lives, they nevertheless seem to reject the "principle of vulnerability," which emerges more often in the discourse of older people.

Young people's narratives are telling in terms of self-perception. Narratives and identity are intrinsically connected, notes Ricoeur (1991: 188), situating people's identity in their narratives. Young Somalis' accounts are stories of courage and survival in taxing conditions, not of destitution and vulnerability. They are survivors, not victims—although the perceived unfairness of resettlement is beyond their control. As I have said before, most never use the word "refugee" when talking about themselves. When I asked Nuradin why he avoided the word, he explained: "Why would I define myself as a refugee? I have always been here. This is my home. Deep inside my heart, I know I am only here because we had problems, but I am not a refugee, I am a person." This echoes observations by Chatty (2010a: 29), who underlines that all refugee youth in prolonged displacement from the Middle East and North Africa who participated to their study shared "the sense of being 'different' and 'the same', of belonging and of being excluded."

I have not directly answered the question of how Somali youth represent themselves. As singular individuals, first. They are not generic refugees. They have their own nicknames and are known in their communities for particular personality traits. Their self-representation cannot be detached from their gender or their broad social, political, historical and economic context. Living in a culturally diverse environment compels them to define themselves by opposition to others: they are Muslims and not Christians; solidarity within their community is greater than in others; they do not accept authority blindly, unlike others. They also believe they have been enriched by their exposure to other cultures, ways of living and beliefs. Then, being refugees has led, at least to some extent, to the construction of new (gendered) roles and expectations, and has influenced the way they interact and build relationships. They see themselves as essential breadwinners for their families and thus as shouldering responsibilities. I have noted several times before that being a refugee is often understood as leading to a degree of emancipation and progress. Speaking of exile as a fruitful experience is not unique to Somalis. Malkki (1996: 382) made a similar observation with Burundian refugees in Tanzania who saw their exile as a "useful, productive period of hardships that would teach and purify them."

As I underlined previously, youth in the camp also define themselves in contrast both to Somalis who have stayed in Somalia and to those who have moved to Western countries. Their intimate representations somehow entail being a mix of Kenyan and Somali. They think of themselves as superior to Somalis in Somalia. They feel they are more open and better equipped to navigate the world. They are more educated, they have become acquainted with the wider world and speak English and Swahili, attributes that are also highlighted by newcomers to the camp. They are peaceful, as opposed to those in Somalia who have "grown up with the sound of bullets" (Abdullahi). However, they are not as sophisticated and worldly as Somalis in the West—or not as contaminated, depending on people's perspectives. (Warsame explained that young men preferred to marry Somali women in the camp, ideally those who had just arrived from Somalia, rather than those in the United States, as they were more "pure.") Young women believe they would have had to deal with a stricter social environment in Somalia, would have had fewer opportunities to study, and would have married and had children at a young age. But in these young people's definitions of themselves, the limitations imposed by their status also come up. Although some experience them more strongly than others, all feel they are unable to fully express themselves and their potential. In another context, their accomplishments would have been greater not only because of easier and better access to education, but also as a result of being free to move and work legally. Still, that does not necessarily turn them into victims; they have managed to live on in conditions that might easily have destroyed others.

Surviving Refugeeness

Unlike their parents who fled and became refugees, youth who have spent their whole lives in camps have not experienced a drastic change in their status. While young people dislike the restrictions attached to their situation, they have no yardstick of previous personal experiences with which to compare. Of course, they have heard stories and grievances from their parents, but it has never been their lived reality. Growing up, in the eyes of their parents and members of their community, they were not primarily refugees. They were unique individuals. The fact that they were principally refugees for others probably only became a reality when they grew older. Being a refugee and being represented as one combines two difficult-to-reconcile dimensions. On the one hand, it entails having survived, studied and learned to live with others while Somalia was crumbling, and thus being strong. On the other hand, it means being perceived as dependent on charity and thus less capable than others to look after oneself.

While the self-representation of these youth is not compatible with the typical refugee representation, the young people know that the latter carries weight and consequences in their lives, particularly in the camp, where they are, above all, considered as refugees by the aid community and lawmakers. This entails significant restrictions, turning the camp into a space of control, and limits their prospects. Their rejection of their representation as victims has turned them into survivors. This rejection also reflects their belief that they have the capacity—even the duty—to find a way out and make a better life for themselves.

Notes

1. Nyers (2006: 98) points out that refugee warriors defy "the traditional characteristics associated with refugeeness. Instead of being passive, there refugees take action. In place of voicelessness, they have clear objectives and demands. In defiance to the 'humanitarian and nonpolitical' terms that define their status, they are unmistakably political actors engaged in the deployment of violence for political ends." They are seen as an anomaly, as "failed" refugees (2006: 102).
2. This brings to mind Farah's account of a conversation with a Somali in Sweden (2000: 190): "For, apropos my own admonition, he asked if I realized that 'we were not Somalis when we were in Somalia.' 'How do you mean?' I asked. 'Because we did not tend to divide ourselves into smaller units, each of us locating our identities in one or another of the clan families? I was a member of this family, you were probably a member of another, and so on!' 'And in Sweden?' 'Here, we are refugees first, black Africans second and Somalis last.'"
3. In *Yesterday, Tomorrow: Voices from the Somali Diaspora,* Farah (2000: 32) irritatedly quotes an acquaintance, a Kenyan hotel manager, who believes that Somalis behave in a way that does not correspond to their status as asylum seekers or refugees: they are inappropriately arrogant and rent expensive hotel rooms.
4. In 2002, a UNHCR and Save the Children report described extensive sexual exploitation of refugee and internally displaced girls in Guinea, Liberia and Sierra Leone by aid workers who traded services or goods for sex (UNHCR and SC-UK 2002).

Chapter 8

IN MEMORY OF THE FUTURE

⁂

Life Is What We Make It
This is what we want to be in our future.
We have dreams and we want them to become reality.
We want to make our lives better.
We want to be known by the world.
Our lives are in our hands.
We are just waiting for the right time.
—Text written by the photography students
for the exhibition of their work

I am looking for a big future. I want to be someone big,
someone other people can look up to. I don't want to live
the life I have been living. I want a better life. A better life
in which, maybe I can wake up in the morning, go to work.
Maybe I am earning enough to take care of myself. Maybe
I have kids and I am taking good care of them. I am a role
model to my kids and others in the community. Maybe
I am doing something that helps other people.
—Zahra, twenty-three years old

When I first wondered about young people's ambitions, expectations and
dreams for their future, I imagined that they would not only focus on resettlement, but also make backup plans. I was mostly proven wrong. Although
some make backup plans, they are a minority. Most feel that no other decent

and legal way out of the camp exists or is worth considering. Once abroad, they wish to study, find good jobs and have their own families.

In previous chapters, I discussed young people's views of their past and present. This exploration leads us into the future. People's decisions on education, occupation and social relationships speak of their past and their present, but also of their future orientation, as expectations and hopes motivate choices and everyday behavior (Nurmi 1991: 1; Raffaelli and Koller 2005: 250). In addition to being shaped by the individual's personality, age and cultural setting, future orientation is influenced by the possibilities and constraints of the present and experiences from the past. The past and the present therefore feed into people's perception of their future, which, in return, conditions the present as it alters how people plan and undertake their own development (Salmela-Aro et al. 2007: 690–91; Seginer 2008: 272–73). In other words, the reality of the camp is lived in the present, a present that is structured by the past and that influences the envisioned future by affecting perspectives and ambitions.

This chapter is about Somali refugee youth's perspective on their future selves. Such a reflection is especially relevant with people in their late teens through their early twenties, as this period is filled with transitions and life decisions such as shifting from education to work or starting a family. It is a time commonly described as one of "identity exploration, self-focus, possibilities, feeling in-between, and instability" (Salmela-Aro et al. 2007: 692). Nurmi (1991: 49) distinguishes three processes related to youths' orientation to the future. First, they set goals linked to their motivation and their expectations. Then they plan how to achieve them and finally they assess whether they will be able to do so. In order to complete these steps and anticipate future events and give them meaning, people must envision a context in which goals will be realized.

Becoming, for Somali youth in Kakuma, first entails leaving the camp, where their capacity to take on adult roles is hampered by limited educational and work opportunities, and a lack of economic stability. While the camp might have allowed space for reinvention, redefinition and even learning, to benefit from the experience, one must break free. And there, an imagination fueled by mass media that transcends national borders and expands the range of possible routes (at least virtually) comes to play a significant role.

Given the unpredictability of their ultimate location, the steps of planning and assessing the feasibility of goals are hard to accomplish. In general, youth's plans are indefinite and they know it. They have big dreams, but also know that they will have to adjust to their circumstances and that they do not control a key variable: whether they will be resettled or not. Their hoped-for selves[1] are relatively clear: they want to live in North America, study, find a good job, set up house and have a family. However, their expected selves are less clear, as most refuse to consider nonresettlement as a possibility and feel that it is only in the West that they would be able to make concrete and realistic plans, as new "social horizons" would emerge.

Vigh (2006: 30–31) defines social horizons as "spaces of possibilities and spheres of orientation that constantly arise in the interaction between agents in motion and the shifting social and political circumstances they seek to move within." In Kakuma, these horizons are subject to constant negotiation and redefinition, as constraints and possibilities evolve, sometimes due to changing circumstances outside of young people's realms of control, and sometimes due to their own movements and transformation. Resettlement opportunities may open up; conditions in Somalia deteriorate or improve; new scholarships are offered, while others are suspended; controls in the rest of the country become stricter or laxer; studies are completed, a new job is secured and a family situation changes; or new smuggling routes to other countries open up. On these shifting sands, youth continually re-adjust and revise their plans, swinging between hope and discouragement. Speaking of people in crisis, Vigh (2008: 20) underlines that "people constantly produce future scenarios and terrains of action by anticipating and predicting the near and distant future through the social imaginary."

Reviewing people's future aspirations involves considering the "where," but also who and what they want to be and become. Where youths' envisioned futures will unfold is the first element I examine in this chapter. Once out of the camp, youth aspire to shape up their lives. I thus explore what they want to do and be, which are crucial aspects of "becoming." I conclude with some thoughts on the tension between a growing disenchantment with waiting and the hope that someday it will be their turn to leave, and on their overall optimism, in spite of the gap between their ambitions and their reality. Through this discussion, I wish to reflect on youth's views on their future in a context choked with restrictions, and on their ability to plan for the future when an essential variable, place, feels mostly beyond their control.

In Search of a Place to Call Home

Mahdi: Where life takes me, I will be happy. Even within Kakuma, I am happy despite challenges. There is no day where I say that I have had enough. If life takes me to America, I'll be happy. If I am not resettled, I'll be fine. I'll find a job. Maybe I'll get an opportunity in Nairobi and get some money to send to my family here. I could also go to other parts of Africa. I am sure I can help myself. I am somehow educated.

Me: Could you stay in Kakuma?

Mahdi: Staying here for another twenty years would be disgusting. Unless that is what God has written for me, I don't want to stay here.

Where people imagine they will live is an important aspect of their perspective on the future: plans, possibilities and aspirations are dependent, at least to some extent, on people's location. Ambitions can flourish in certain settings, but might be out of reach in others. In the refugee regime, the search for permanent solutions that enable refugees to secure the political, economic, legal and social conditions needed to maintain life, livelihood and dignity focuses primarily on the location where people can lead a proper life. Three durable solutions are usually acknowledged: voluntary repatriation to the country of origin, local integration or resettlement to a third country. Recent thinking has highlighted the need to be more creative in the search for solutions, notably by considering integration in the intermediate term[2] and mobility within and across borders, as migration might help a number of refugees regain physical, legal and livelihood security (Long 2014).

Repatriation has become the preferred durable solution since the 1980s, notably due to host countries' unwillingness to offer local integration to refugees—and to a sedentarist bias, according to several scholars (e.g., Al-Rasheed 1994: 202; Malkki 1995a: 508; Verdirame and Harrell-Bond 2005: 335). However, it is not envisioned as a reasonable option by Somali youth, at least in the near future. While many would consider formal local integration in Kenya a suitable option, it remains improbable for large groups of refugees. Resettlement is by far people's preference, but it is an unlikely prospect for a significant proportion of refugees. In the absence of resettlement, leaving the camp by one's own means and settling irregularly in Kenya or in another country might appear to be the only truly available option. But not all are willing or able to take such a chance.

When We Get to America

> As refugees, we always live in some kind of imaginary hope. You cannot say that you are going to the U.S. You find people who have finished the process for five or six years and are waiting for their flight. I am not waiting. I have finished all the process, but I cannot say that we will go to the U.S. So I don't know if I will go to Nairobi, Somalia or the U.S. My aim is to go to USA.
> —Aziz, twenty-three years old

For many young people, the United States is the only answer to the question of where they want to live. For those whose resettlement process is ongoing, this may possibly materialize, but it is uncertain and so is the timeframe. Once there, a number imagine that the adjustment to a new life will be challenging, but worth it. Indeed, many are mindful of the fact that they will struggle to find decent work and that life is expensive. However, the positive aspects outweigh the difficulties. One can move freely and without fear, work legally, go to a proper hospital when sick; no one has to fetch water at the tap or line up for a food ration. Somehow, while life in the camp is not easy and may not nurture hope, the prospect of resettlement helps keep youth hopeful. Some focus on the education and work experience they can acquire in Kakuma, which they trust will help them to succeed in the West, while putting off getting married, to avoid creating further delays. "We are studying here, so we are not illiterate when we get there and people don't make fun of us," explains Ayan. However, others assume that these skills will not be valued in the United States and therefore have limited motivation to work or study in the camp. They plan to study once they are abroad. For now, they are killing time and waiting for resettlement.

Such endless waiting can have a disempowering effect on youth (and people in general): their future is not in their hands, but depends on the goodwill of others. This feeling of not being in control of one's life sometimes makes planning for the future seem like a useless endeavor. "My future..." ponders eighteen-year-old Bilal. "It all depends on UNHCR. If they take me to a good place, I can perform. But if they leave me here, I don't know what will happen. I have not decided. I cannot leave the camp. I will still depend on UNHCR." Such powerlessness is somehow dire, as the absence of resettlement seems to equate to the end of hope. Yet, those who have been rejected for resettlement do not necessarily lose hope. While some live in denial, others intend to leave the camp or manage to build a life in Kakuma, while scanning the horizon for better options.

If I Don't Go to America: Immobility and Mobility

I had some plans, sometime back, but now [that I have been rejected for resettlement] I am really confused. I don't have a plan. I don't think I can go back to Somalia because I don't know that country. I don't know what it looks like. Even if I went back, I would need to work. In Africa, you find a job through knowing people. People need to know where you were born and where you came from. They can reject me because I am educated. In Kenya, I cannot live outside of the camp. In some countries, if you stay five or six years, you will become a citizen. I have been in Kenya for twenty-two years, but I am not a citizen. If I could be resettled, I would have a plan for the future. I was planning to become a politician in my country of resettlement. If not that, a doctor, since I have done a nursing course with IRC [the International Rescue Committee].
—Abdullahi, twenty-four years old

As illustrated by Abdullahi's quote, some liken being rejected for resettlement to their lives coming to a standstill. But in fact, Abdullahi's words do not fully reflect his reality. In real life, significant changes are occurring: he recently got married, has become a father and has a job, and thus is building a life in the camp. However, he cannot imagine himself being there for years to come. That feeling is common, and some who have been rejected for resettlement keep talking about it as a possibility or refuse to consider other options, even after having been told that cases will not be submitted twice. There is always the lingering hope that a decision will be reviewed or that another country will agree to receive them. Such denial might be occasioned by the scarcity of alternatives.

Unlike those who are tired of waiting for resettlement but still hope for a positive outcome, some rejected applicants seem to live in a slightly different reality, fearing "indefinite stasis" (Griffiths 2014: 2001). Griffiths (2014: 1992), writing about refused asylum seekers and immigration detainees in the United Kingdom, evokes "a sense of temporal difference [that] contributes to the experiential distance many refused asylum seekers feel from others, including those who physically share the same space." She later writes (2014: 2001) that "people's lives can also be made chaotic through a lack of change," which resonates with the reality of those who are rejected for resettlement and feel there are no other options.

Others make backup plans that typically involve leaving Kakuma by one's own means, an option that is usually set aside as long as resettlement remains a possibility, as this is the safest way to reach a Western country and obtain legal status. In the absence of such a prospect, most believe it makes sense to try their luck. This is what Nuradin stated when his close friends Faarax and Mahdi left for Nairobi: they were right to go and try to work in Nairobi even if it entailed being in an irregular situation, as their resettlement was forever pending. Moreover, if Somalia became safer, Faarax wanted to move there and start a business (a year later, he was actually resettled to the United States). Zahra, who holds little faith in resettlement, is actively looking for a suitable country in Africa to move to, one where refugees face fewer restrictions. But how she will manage to reach that country is unclear. Yasin, who, like Abdullahi, has married and started his family in Kakuma, has no intention of staying in the camp indefinitely, but no longer counts on resettlement. He hopes to find a way to study, which would allow him to successfully settle elsewhere: "What I would like to do if I get the money is to join a university in Kenya, or maybe in Uganda. I like Makarere University [in Kampala, Uganda]. My English teacher used to tell me about it." Again, however, he can hardly explain how this will become reality. Somehow, he has managed to successfully navigate his environment since finishing high school. In fact, citing the example of an acquaintance who managed to open a shop in Nairobi, he holds that refugees "have matured: many people have the concept that they can change their life without depending on UNHCR." He therefore feels confident that he will reach his goal, although he also has moments of great despair when he fears being trapped in Kakuma.

I mentioned in Chapter 6 that settling elsewhere in Kenya appears to many as a possible option, even though the government has been persistently opposed to formal local integration. Regardless of the absence of legal status, a number of refugees do live and work informally in Kenyan cities, de facto integrating into the country. However, living in an irregular situation is not only stressful but also costly, as refugees are commonly asked to pay bribes. Similarly, everyone knows of refugees who have left Kenya for another country where they either live irregularly or have claimed asylum. But this entails paying high fees for travel and taking significant risks, something that youth are well informed of. This limits people's desire and capacity to move out of the camp, turning mobility into a relevant strategy only for those who can gather sufficient financial or social capital. Young people often point out that they cannot afford to live elsewhere, although many manage to spend some time in other parts of the country. Moving by one's own means also appears harder to envisage for young women than for men: their families are more reluctant to let them leave and many, having married young, have to look after their children.[3] If settling legally outside of the camp were possible, many would do so rather than wait in the camp in the hope of a hypothetical resettlement. After all, youth commonly say they feel like Kenyans. But for the time being, only informal local integration (or further movement) can be envisioned.

Discovering Somalia

There is another option: "returning"[4] to Somalia, a country that they do not know, but where they could move and work in complete legality. During the period when I was in Kakuma, repatriation was a sensitive topic, partly because of the growing political support for the quick return of refugees that made people fear that they could be forced to go back. After pointing out that people were still fleeing Somalia, youth repeatedly remarked that returning to an unknown country notorious for its violence held little attraction.

It is often assumed that refugees long to go home. But not all refugees want to repatriate. According to Al-Rasheed (1994), who studied the myth of return among two groups of Iraqi refugees in England, this desire is influenced by people's relationship with their country of origin and its population. While young Somalis in Kakuma consider themselves culturally Somali, they do not necessarily feel a strong connection to Somalia, as noted by Warsame:

> If I am not resettled, my philosophy would be to stay in Kenya. There is no way I would go back to Somalia. I came from Mogadishu. I know nothing about that place, which is why I can't go back. I have never seen it, but I have heard and learned some history, saw things on the Internet. If I go back to Somalia, I will be a foreigner. It is just like going to the U.S. It would mean starting another life.

Repatriation may be the preferred international response to refugee movements, but it might not be the optimal solution for all refugees, especially in protracted situations (Kibreab 1999: 390). It might entail significant losses, notably in terms of livelihood, access to education and services. This would probably be the case for refugees returning to south-central Somalia, where, after two decades of conflict and instability, and in the absence of a functioning government, public amenities are very limited and in a poor state (UNOCHA 2012: 22). The prospect of repatriating to the rural areas that their families left, with their limited public facilities, seems difficult to envisage for youth born and raised in camps that, in comparison, feel like cities. For many, going back would be perceived as a form of regression rather than progression, a failure. Like Afghan youth in Iran, Somalis believe that gains made in exile, notably in raising their status and having greater access to education, will be lost if they move to Somalia (Hoodfar 2008: 181). The fact that many refugees come from minority groups who felt excluded from the Somali sociopolitical landscape is another factor that makes repatriation unappealing.

While moving to Somalia is hardly conceivable in the near future, this does not mean that returning to Somalia will never be an option. A few speak of their desire to visit the country or imagine that they could live there at some point. Youth often plan to be resettled first. Then, after completing their studies, they would work and, once they had gained sufficient experience and resources, would consider returning to Somalia to establish themselves if it had become peaceful. Resettlement and mobility could thus become a step toward an eventual return, rather than an end in itself, something that Chatty, Fiddian-Qasmiyeh and Crivello (2010) also observed with Sahrawi refugee youth. While returning is not excluded, it is not envisioned as the next move and remains highly hypothetical, as it is usually contingent upon having studied and then finding a good job, as well as security and stability in Somalia. Abdi is one who speaks of such plans. He rejects the idea of going back to Somalia directly, even though it is where he ultimately wants to live: "I first want to go to a place where I can get enough education ... I am expecting that one day, I will be resettled to Canada, America or another country. There, I can get education and plan my future. Once I am established, then I will be able to go back to Somalia." The discourse of those rejected for resettlement often shows slightly more openness to a quicker return than that of those who have either been accepted or are still in the process of having their case examined and thus, still hope to get a positive response.

A number, such as Awo, underline that their studies would be useful to re-build Somalia and help Somalis, but have ambiguous feelings toward Somalia:

> If my dreams come true, I can study medicine and then I would like to go back. Going back would mean I can be of assistance to my people. For now, I can't think of going because of many fears. Most of the time, people who are educated, when they go back, they are considered like spies. Al-Shabab doesn't like people who speak other languages. That scares me, but as time goes, I will see how the situation is.

Somali youth interviewed in Australia and Finland also expressed the will to help people in Somalia and play a role in rebuilding their country (Omar 2008: 74, 86). Others, especially young women, are adamant about never wanting to set foot there. As I noted in Chapter 4 they believe not only that it would be a foreign land, but also that it is one where, as women, their free-dom would be further restricted. Several also express doubts about the like-lihood of Somalia becoming peaceful and stable, as underscored by Ibrahim: "I don't hope to go back. That land is not a safe place. If you go, you don't know if you will come back safe. If I am resettled, I will just be a Somali U.S. citizen." Many stress that they do not have to be in Somalia to remain Somali and that being elsewhere will not alter their identity.

In their hopes for a future abroad, young people continue to see them-selves as Somalis and not as Westerners. At some point, returning to Soma-lia could make sense. Hoodfar (2008: 181) made similar observations about Afghan refugees in Iran. While they felt pride in being Afghan, they had no desire to move to Afghanistan, at least not before finishing their education. Like Somalis, they did not see a contradiction in claiming their Afghan iden-tity and not wanting to live in the country. However, a number of them did hope to finish their education and then return to Afghanistan to contribute to the reconstruction of the country. The desire to finish their education was actually given as the main reason why they needed to postpone their return. In Kakuma, there is at times a visible tension, even a contradiction, between youth's strong stand that returning cannot be envisioned and their expressed will to help "their people," to visit and possibly return to live in Somalia in some elusive future.

I have already referred to how media reports and frequent interaction with the rest of the world and with their immediate environment feed youth's imagination. This certainly comes into play when they assess where they want to settle. Such interaction sometimes seems to motivate agency and to compel youth to seek a way out of the camp. In other instances, it has the opposite effect and the constant awareness of the fact that people have better lives in places that are not easily accessible induces despondency. Moreover, there is a clear link between the vagueness of where they might end up living and the difficulty they have concretely planning for who and what they will become in the future.

Becoming Who We are

I want to become one of the best engineers in the world.
I want to have a company of my own, like Safaricom
[a leading Kenyan mobile network operator], probably
in Canada. I want to fight against wars. I want Africa to
stop having refugee problems. I have had an experience
in a camp since I was born and I don't want people to
experience that. I would love to fight for peace and
education for women wherever I will be. I always feel
that women are underestimated by men. I want to prove
to the world that women can be as great as men.
—Amran, eighteen years old

Writing about Palestinian youth, Chatty (2010b: 318) underlines how they "consistently express a willingness to act to improve their situation as well as a cautious and measured optimism for their future." Despite experiencing difficult living conditions and events beyond their control, they manage to "maintain a sense of agency against all odds and hold on to aspirations for a better personal and community future." Similar observations can be made about Somali youth in Kakuma, whose discourse on the future is, at times, not only one of "measured optimism," but one that is truly hopeful. In setting ambitions, parents, peers and teachers are influential. Youth often share and coregulate their goals with their peers, notably when it comes to education and trajectories, which could be why young Somalis in Kakuma often have similar views on their future (Salmela-Aro 2010: 17–18).

Few can describe how they intend to achieve their ambitions, probably because these are so dependent on where they will find themselves, something over which they commonly feel they have little or no control. The lack of "temporal predictability" (Griffiths 2014: 2005) makes it difficult to imagine the future in concrete terms. This might explain why they often have more to say about where they want to be and what they dream of being once they leave the camp than about what they will (realistically) be and do, or fear to become.

Dreaming of the Unknown

I want to be an oncologist. In Kenya there are only eight.
In Somalia, there is none. Africa has only a few. Most
people who die of cancer, they just know what they
have at a late stage. You could do something at an
early stage, before it goes to other parts of the body.
I just want to help them and Africa.
—Abyan, seventeen years old

In speaking of the future, Somali youth most frequently focus on their desire
to get a good education. Career goals are also regularly mentioned. Family
and marriage, as well as wealth, come up relatively often. Such themes are
similar to those listed by youth in other contexts (Raffaelli and Koller 2005:
257). As I mentioned earlier, education is key because it is often seen as the
only way to have a proper future, to become someone "respectable" or, in
Yasin's words "a big person." Most youth underline that they want to study in
another country rather than in Kenya. This could stem from the limited access to higher education that they have in Kenya. In point of fact, many also
affirm that if they were offered a scholarship to study at a Kenyan university,
they would happily do so. However, in the absence of such an option, studying abroad after resettlement becomes a more reasonable aspiration. While
they know that it may not be easy for refugees to pursue higher education in
a new country, this remains one of the big gains expected from such a move.
Many have great educational and work ambitions—they will become doc-
tors, nurses, professors, ambassadors or engineers. Given that a good number
have not managed to complete high school, it is difficult not to deem their
plans unrealistic.

While there is not necessarily a mismatch between their hoped-for location
and where they will eventually settle—a significant number of them will be
resettled at some point—there is discordance between the studies and career
path they hope for and their expected reality. Clearly, they know their ambitions are not always realistic, as they mention that studying in the United
States is expensive and that refugees have to earn their living, which gets in
the way of education. Even so, their hoped-for future remains rather optimistic, although nonspecific. There is a kind of magical thinking associated with
moving to the West. Although they have all heard about the difficulties faced
by refugees resettled in the United States, they still believe that once there,
education will somehow become possible and wealth accessible.

In all their vagueness, their ambitions convey that they do not see themselves as mere victims, and their optimism may help some to keep going and
stay engaged. They are looking for a way out of a life that does not suit them

and aiming for a proper future, but they also have to confront limitations and elements far beyond their control. It has been pointed out that expectations concerning the future tend to vary according to sex. In a review of the literature on youth's ambitions, Nurmi (1991: 30) writes that males focus more on the material aspects of life, through education and career, while females place importance on family, religion and making a contribution to society. Such a stereotypical divide is not obvious in Kakuma. Although women speak more often of their desire to have a family, men also regularly mention it. Religion seems important for all, as do education and having a career.

Children's Duty

Children's ambitions and views on the future are greatly influenced by their parents and family. Parents play a role in shaping their children's interests and goals, serve as models and inspire their children's attitude toward the future. Peers and the school environment are also determining elements, although they may have more of an impact on short-term than on long-term decisions (Nurmi 1991: 11, 32). Stevenson and Willott (2007: 683) observe that refugee parents tend to have great educational ambitions for their descendants, for the same reasons as their children: they see education as the best route out of poverty and as critical to their integration. In Kakuma, parents' perspectives on the future are often darker than those of the younger generation and, even more strongly than their children, they consider resettlement the only solution that can lead to a bright future. In its absence, there is little hope, and parents are concerned, as highlighted by Khadija:

> Our greatest worry is our children. They are the most unsettled. They have no idea of their future. They only want to go to Europe or America ... Some stop going to school, they have no motivation. It is difficult to be motivated when you live in a camp. They think: "I was born here, I will die here." Some want to become Kenyans, so they can be citizens and be free. But they cannot become Kenyans. Most of those who have been here for long were sure that they would go [to a third country through resettlement]. They were waiting and still are. But those who have been rejected sometimes decide to go by themselves. They don't want to be like us, become old in the camp.

Parents worry, but also see their children as their future, which is common in refugee situations (Dryden-Peterson and Giles 2010: 2). They hope that their descendants will be capable of looking after them properly if they are resettled. Faarax's mother says that she is expecting her children to study in the United States, so that they can "work hard, have a good career, help me and help other people who are in need. I am tired and I need some rest. I will eat the food they bring." Youth are conscious of their parents' expectations and feel a responsibility toward them. Hence, their certainty that they have to leave the camp and be successful is also motivated by the recognition that their parents count on their support.

Between Hope and Frustration, Constraints and Opportunities

While youth obviously have different ambitions and views regarding their future, they share the belief that in order to achieve their dreams, they must leave the camp, ideally through resettlement to the United States. In fact, most refuse to consider the possibility of not being resettled and appear unable to make alternative plans. This does not stem from a lack of imagination. Young people know that opportunities are scarce in Kakuma and that their rights are limited outside the camp. They are well informed that they can navigate Kenya, but at their own risk. Similarly, if they can muster sufficient means and are willing to gamble with their lives, they might reach other countries, but do not know if they will be able to secure legal status. Moreover, Somalia can hardly be seen as home by people who have never visited the country and have heard mainly about its perils.

In a context where uncertain prospects of resettlement are the only decent exit, youth's hopeful but vague ambitions and future orientations are somewhat surprising. Still, they seem to prevent many young people from giving up. The environment in which people live and grow influences their development of values and expectations for the future. Violence and poverty may limit one's ability to plan for the future (Stoddard et al. 2011: 2). Kakuma is a poor and insecure environment, but it is also one that offers youth some potential, although this is limited and, sometimes, beyond their control. While the camp is a place of constraints, it can, paradoxically, become a land of opportunity, as it gives access to possible resettlement, basic education, other facilities and even work, albeit poorly paid. Young people know others who have left the camp through resettlement or by their own means and who manage relatively well. They also know of people who have secured scholarships or have started their own reasonably successful businesses. This may have helped in shaping some positive expectations, despite the limited options. Their optimism could yield positive outcomes, as being hopeful about the future during adolescence is linked to the capacity to adjust to circumstances and initiate action toward goals, and to the belief that things can change (Stoddard et al. 2011: 2).

Nonetheless, the picture is not always rosy and many live through moments of great despair and disempowerment. Twenty-year-old Abdulaziz, talking about how he imagined his future, observed: "Sometimes it is mixed up because you don't have the assurance that you will actually be someone, somewhere. When you are a refugee, you don't know if you will go back to your country, stay here, or go elsewhere, so it is a bit confusing." The older youth become, the less optimistic they appear to be, probably because time is passing and nothing is happening. They feel caught in a suspended time during a period of their lives where they should be preparing their future and establishing themselves as adults. Despite this, most manage to hold on to fairly optimistic views, maybe because otherwise, they would have to consider themselves as stuck in an "indefinite stasis," a thought that is either inconceivable or would lead to great distress. Youth keep scanning their broad network for possibilities, but also realize that essential elements remain beyond their control: resettlement, Kenya's policy toward refugees and Somalia's instability, all of which greatly influence their lives, but are unaffected by their views, dreams and ambitions.

Notes

1. The possible selves theory distinguishes between "hoped-for selves," "expected selves" and "feared selves." The first designates what someone would like to become, the second what someone could realistically become and the third what someone fears becoming. Hoped-for selves tend to be grounded in little concrete knowledge and may have limited impact on behavior. Expected selves do influence people's plans and behavior, and feared selves may guide avoidance behavior (Markus and Nurius 1986: 954; Yowell 2002: 63–64).
2. Banki (2004: 2–3) defines integration in the intermediate term as the "ability of the refugee to participate with relative freedom in the economic and communal life of the host region." It might entail partial rather than full self-sufficiency. Unlike local integration, it might not include cultural and political participation or full legal rights. High levels of refugee integration are characterized by the fact that refugees are not restricted in their movements, may own or have access to land, can participate in the local economy, are moving toward self-sufficiency, are able to utilize local services such as health facilities and schools, and are dispersed among the population.
3. For an interesting perspective on the feminization of immobility and the masculinity attached to movement, see Hyndman and Giles (2011).
4. I am using the term "return," which is the word youth commonly use to speak of their possible settlement in Somalia. In fact, the term is not always appropriate, as many have never been to Somalia and would therefore not be returning to Somalia, but going there for the first time.

Chapter 9

A Note on Life after the Camp

It is not how I expected it. I wanted to go to university,
do interesting things, but now, I need to survive. In Africa,
I had this excuse that I would become someone in the USA.
Here, I no longer have any excuse. I have to face the reality.
You always have to pay your rent and your bills. I am
disappointed to be where I am now. The first year is over
and I am not even going to school. Maybe things will
change, but I don't know. I always used to calm myself by
thinking I'd go to the U.S. But here, it is permanent. I am
no longer going somewhere else. My mom still worries
about what she will cook. She worries that if we get sick,
we will not be able to pay the rent. Even people born here,
they have problems, unless their fathers were rich. People take
big loans to go to school. I am disappointed with things.
—Aziz, twenty-three years old

Aziz was resettled in Columbus, Ohio, in 2013. In the year that followed,
his parents and siblings joined him, except for Awo, who is studying at a
Canadian university. Aziz works as a translator and two of his siblings have
enrolled in college. Since I left the camp, I have periodically received messages
from people back in Kakuma informing me that they were being resettled or
had decided to leave by their own means. Somehow, people seem to write
most often when they are about to move, as if they finally had news worth
sharing. Fatuma has moved to Nairobi, but fears that the Kenyan authori-

ties could send her back to the camp at any time. Abdikadir first landed in California with his family, but soon moved to Minnesota, where he was told the rent would be cheaper. He has been hired by a resettlement organization to help arriving refugees find homes and schools for their children, and get access to social services. He plans to enroll in school soon and complete a liberal arts degree that he started in Kakuma. Khadra left Kakuma a few months before I did. After being in the United States for more than a year, she was still finding it difficult and described her job as miserable. A year later, her parents finally joined her and she was hoping that her life would become easier in their company. Nafissa landed in Regina, Saskatchewan, and is going to school. The two brothers Nuradin and Warsame live in Ohio, and both work long hours in warehouses to send money every month to their mother and younger siblings in Kenya. Faarax was recently resettled to the United States. Mahdi enrolled in school in Nairobi. Many more remain in Kakuma, still hoping for a way out.

In the year and a half that followed my stay in Kakuma, in addition to keeping up intermittent contact by email, Facebook or phone with several people I knew from the camp, I conducted ten semistructured interviews with Somali youth who grew up in Kakuma or in one of the Dadaab camps and who have left these places relatively recently (between 2006 and 2013). I did about half of the interviews in person and the others either by phone or via Skype. I knew two of the interviewees from Kakuma (Warsame and Aziz). Two others came to Canada with scholarships from the WUSC (Sagal and Ilhaan) and another one through family reunification (Samakab). Twenty-six-year-old Ilhaan was back in Dadaab for an internship when I spoke with her. One interviewee has moved to Somalia to work after completing his education in Dadaab (Amin). Two are dividing their time between Kenya and Somalia (Absame and Aden), and two are studying in Nairobi (Hajiro and Omar). With the exception of those who I met in Kakuma, I was introduced to all of them by people I knew from Kakuma or Dadaab or by refugees I interviewed who had already left the camp.

These exchanges corroborate observations made in the camp, but also suggest that once people no longer live there, they adopt a more critical perspective than those still in the camp. This note briefly presents their reflections.

Of Gains and Losses

In the eyes of people who have left the camp, it remains an environment that gave them access to education, allowed them to learn to coexist with people of other clans or ethnic groups, and made them strong and able to survive in challenging circumstances. "Looking back, Kakuma is not a place where one should live, but I don't regret the eighteen years I spent there because I used every opportunity," remarks Warsame one year after being resettled to Columbus, Ohio. "If you come to the U.S. with nothing, you will struggle. Without Kakuma, I wouldn't have achieved much here. Kakuma was like a military training. Once you adjust to it, you can live anywhere in the world." But the camp is also described as a repressive setting that imposes unacceptable limitations on movement, education and work. The critical stance taken by former camp dwellers may result partly from the fact that they no longer have to endure it. It may also be associated with their having a basis for comparison and enunciation through being elsewhere, and their integration of a new grammar to articulate their experience. This comes out in Ilhaan's comment:

> As soon as I came [to Canada], I was able to move from place to place. I moved from Toronto to Ottawa. I was conscious that this was something I could not do for many years and that my family could still not do, as they were still in the camp. I felt guilty for my own freedom and realized how oppressive the camp was. Still, I tell people that it is not as bad as they think, because life goes on when you are in it.

The Intricate Question of Home

Young people's relationship to the camp is often ambiguous. The camp may have been difficult, but it is also the place where these young people spent most of their lives and where their sensorial memory developed. For many, including people who left several years ago, it continues to be the location that feels the closest to home, in particular because their families are still there, and so are many of their friends. It is the place where they had the strongest sense of community, where they still have many landmarks and where most of the people who have a personal understanding of their experience live, as expressed by twenty-five-year-old Hajiro, who studies in Nairobi and lives in Eastleigh:

> I don't feel home here, even though I have friends, we don't share the same history. We don't share a lot. The kind of life they live is far from yours. When you are back in the camp, memories come back. My friends are there. We have the same history. Here, if you explain what you went through, people are in disbelief. Some don't even know that Dadaab refugee camp exists. They only know that Somalia has been in conflict for two decades, that there is terrorism. They think you must be psychologically affected, that you must be inferior. It is difficult to explain who you are and what you experienced. They say: "What do you mean missing a cup of tea? No clean water? No toilet? Are there places like that?" They don't understand. So you just talk about something else.

Although those who are able to do so visit their friends and family back in the camps, and might even work there, no one aspires to return to live there permanently. In fact, whenever possible, and often by working long hours and at the expense of their own comfort, they have helped their families to move to Nairobi. They may not miss the camp, but many who have resettled in the West yearn for the ease of being in Kenya. While they had limited rights there, having grown up in the country and been educated in the Kenyan system, Omar feels that they "became Somali *sijui*" (the term used for Kenyan Somalis that literally translates as "Somali-I-don't-know" and refers to the lack of command of the Somali language exhibited by those who grew up in Kenya). They speak Swahili and English fluently, know Kenya's cultural codes and, despite all the obstacles they faced in the camp, there was a freedom and flexibility in daily life there that they long for in the United States. For example, they could show up a few minutes late at work without being reprimanded and had time to be with friends and relax after their work day. They also had a reliable social network. Reflecting on the role of clans, twenty-eight-year-old Sagal, who now lives in Victoria, British Columbia, where Somalis are rare and thus, clans have a limited influence, points out that although they might have been used in a negative way, "clans also meant that you could ask someone for help, they are people you know, people help you because of those links."

Without denying their attachment to Kenya or even Somalia, others nurture no desire to return. For some, such as twenty-nine-year-old Samakab, who now resides in Canada, the camp and, by extension, their experience in Kenya have left lasting scars. He says that he has "internalized the encampment" and remains fearful of moving around and feels dislocated, even though he lives in a safe place. Those who left the camp to settle elsewhere in Kenya more commonly speak of their desire to make their home in Somalia than those who moved out of Africa. This may in part relate to their lack of legal status in Kenya, which maintains them in a relatively precarious position, but also to a greater physical and social proximity to Somalia. Hajiro, for example, aspires to return to her parents' country once she completes her master's degree in international relations and diplomacy. She says she wishes to participate in the bettering of Somalia, but also wants to stop being a refugee:

> I need to go back and contribute, give back to the community. I want to be part of the peace process and reconstruction. I want to tell them about my experiences, about how it feels to be out of your home country, one where you don't know the culture. At the end of the day, a refugee is always a refugee. Even in the U.K. or the U.S. Even if you have a citizenship, inside, you don't feel you are one of them. You are always a refugee, regardless of your level of education.

The question of belonging is complicated. Those whose families are still in the camp often say that when they think of home, they think of the camp. Yet, they also assume that if their families moved out, they would no longer relate to the camp in the same way. Their parents have often shared memories with them of where they came from. These have been nurtured and have created a strong attachment to a country they have never seen. But it remains difficult to call such an imaginary place home. Similarly, countries of adoption are often described in positive terms for the possibility they offer of living a "normal" life, but they hardly feel like home. "It feels terrible not to belong," laments Samakab. "I am not from here. Then, I speak Somali, but that doesn't make me Somali. Nothing links me to my heritage. We lost everything, not only our property, but even the pictures we had. Our whole life was buried." Somehow, he hopes that his children will end up putting down roots in Canada: "My daughter is learning Somali, English and French. I want her to feel part of this country. This is where she belongs. I don't want to uproot her. I want her to know she has a heritage, but we are not going back. I tell her about Somalia and Africa. I tell her about nomadism, poems, the beauty of our language."

Before moving to Canada, Samakab went back to Somalia to work, but not to his region of origin. He felt unwelcome, as "people were upset with those coming from other places because they were taking jobs." Had he landed in his region of origin, he believes things might have been different, which seems to be substantiated by the experience of those who did. Twenty-seven-year-old Absame, for example, moved to Afmadow, Somalia, in 2012, after growing up in Dadaab, studying in Nairobi and living in South Africa. Although he found the country devastated by the civil war and noticed people's strict way of dressing, he also felt at home: "I am in love with Somalia, with that feeling of belonging. Everybody calls me by my father's name, the son of Hassan. It is good." What is common to all is the expressed will to "help Somalia," either by going back there to work and contribute to the reconstruction of the country or by supporting projects there from abroad. Women, who were often already critical of the conditions of Somali women while they lived in the camp, frequently become more vocal about the issue. A recurring theme in their discourse relates to their desire to fight for the rights of Somali women.

Lines of Flight

Youth like Amin who were not resettled but returned to Somalia under their own steam often consider themselves in a better position than those who were. Unlike those who moved to the United States, Amin has secured a good job, has means to support his family and lives among other Somalis. His path actually epitomizes the fact that, although uninviting, the camp can, at times, be described as a land of opportunity. He says that he is not a Somali refugee, but a Kenyan Somali who grew up as a refugee in one of the Dadaab refugee camps, Hagadera, where he was registered as a refugee. He had arrived there in the early 1990s with his family, who, pretending to be refugees, moved to the camp out of poverty. There, they would at least have access to food. When his parents left the camp, he stayed behind with relatives who had come from Somalia so that he could continue his education. At the end of his time at secondary school, he realized his grades were not good enough to earn him one of the few available university scholarships. After his uncle living in the Somali capital agreed to support him, he moved to Somalia to study business administration at Mogadishu University. When he finished his degree, he went back to Kenya and to the camp, where he worked for an NGO as a refugee worker and was paid a small incentive. While living in Hagadera, he tried to get his Kenyan ID, but never managed to convince the officials that although he was registered as a refugee, he was in fact Kenyan. Given his limited prospects, he started looking for a job in Somalia. He found a respectable and well-paid position with a UN agency and underlines that it is because of the camp that he enjoys such good employment: "If I had started my education in Somalia, I would not be as good as I am today. I value the education I got in the camp. I look at myself as a product of Hagadera." But he also observes that not everybody managed so well and that some of his classmates left Dadaab to join al-Shabab or the Islamic Courts Union.[1]

It is true that those who are resettled tend to describe the process as taxing and unsettling, as recounted by Aziz at the start of this note. But while most—including those who went to Somalia or settled elsewhere in Kenya—say that the transition to life outside the camp is challenging, all specify that they do not regret the move. Many mention the struggle of having to learn to be financially independent. Arriving in Nairobi, Absame was initially afraid: "It was a big city. Staying in Dadaab was like being in jail and all of a sudden, you are in the sunlight. It was very scary. Even taking a *matatu* [minibus] was scary. You are suddenly on your own." In fact, everything requires major adjustment. When she came to Canada, Sagal found it hard to be away from her family while having to acclimatize to a very different lifestyle: "I had never slept in a room on my own, I had never spent so much time on my own. I could not sleep. I was so afraid. The lack of community life was so difficult. During the first year, I wanted to go back." Yet, both Absame and Sagal gradually reconciled themselves to their new lives and environment, and studied.

Assessing his situation, Warsame mentions that his early days in the United States were difficult, but talks of his potential success in a way that conjures up the American dream: "I am happy I came here. Here, dreams are valid, they can come true. I never thought I could own my own car. In Kakuma, I could have worked for thirty years and would never have been able to buy a car. Here, you can earn money, you can have two jobs … If you are hardworking, you can make it." When he was in Kakuma, Warsame insisted that he would study political science in the United States. A few months after he had arrived there, he called me to discuss whether he should be studying administration and management rather than political science, as he had been told that he would probably have better work prospects if did so. It made perfect sense to him to revise his plans, at least for the near future, as his priority was to support his mother and siblings back in Kenya. Such changes seem relatively common, as the young people I spoke with after they had left the camp had often adjusted their ambitions to their new reality.

As for clan loyalties, those who come from majority groups tend to claim that clan affiliation is no longer a defining characteristic outside the camp. Even those who returned to Somalia concur. However, those from minority groups or who settled in areas where they are in the minority (although they might belong to one of the main clan-families) often say otherwise. This is consistent with Bjork's observation that although clan remains part of people's daily life once in the West, it is not something that they easily admit, as clans seem "antithetical to modernity" (2007: 151). For example, Aden, who is Bajuni and thus from a minority group, comments on his return to Somalia, remarking that "hatred based on tribes is still there. When we come together, people still put their clan forward." Amin, who also moved to Somalia, sees things differently, but argues that this is not related to his belonging to a majority clan: "In Somalia, after 2006, the issue of killing because of clan stopped. It changed to a religious conflict. Someone will be killed for religious reasons. I came when the issue of clan was almost dying."

In a Better World

In short, just as youth in the camp described people who had stayed in Somalia as unlucky compared to them, those who have left the camp feel the same toward those who grew up in Somalia and also to those who are still in the camp. This is logical, considering that in the eyes of young people in Kakuma, the only way to make sense of the camp experience and benefit from it is to keep moving. Many of these young people enjoy living conditions that they deem better than those they had before, even if they often remain in economically unstable conditions. Most are now in a place where they can move and work freely, settle down legally and participate in the life of their community. A few have settled temporarily to work or study in particular locations and will most likely move again, but they have no intention of returning to the camp. They find the adaptation to a new setting demanding and miss the social network they had in the camp. Still, once out of the camp, they describe it as an even more forbidding place than they did when living there, although they continue to see it as the setting that allowed them to escape from Somalia's turmoil and become the person they are.

Notes

1. In 2009, Human Rights Watch reported that both al-Shabab and recruiters claiming to act on behalf of Somalia's Transnational Federal Government had been recruiting refugees in Dadaab (HRW 2009b). However, some such as Rawlence (Chatham House 2014: 3, see also Rawlence 2016) have argued that Dadaab's environment is not favorable to radicalization and have described Dadaab as an "engine for moderation." I have not heard such claims in Kakuma. Kakuma is not Dadaab; its social landscape is different from Dadaab's and it is located at the other end of Kenya, which makes it less accessible to recruiters.

Chapter 10

CONCLUSION

❧⊙•⊙❧

> I want to live in a palace, not a house, a home which is about
> three kilometers [wide]. Inside the palace, I want to have
> eighty-eight doors, excluding the main doors, which are the
> exit and the entry. More than nine hundred windows, two
> hundred rooms and two big meetings and resting conference
> rooms. I want the palace to be near the ocean, because that
> is where I will get some fresh air. And also, I want two
> swimming pools, two big gardens, and playing fields for any
> kind of sports. I want some trees for shade, at least ten big
> trees. Water and electricity should be permanent. And
> at last, I want the palace to be built with milk, not water.
> And at the entry door, on the upper side, my name should be
> written. At the exit door, the name of the country, Somalia.
> —Zahi, eighteen years old

I start this final chapter with Zahi's extravagant portrayal of his dream house
set in Somalia because it conveys the hopeful attitude of young Somali refugees in Kakuma and their buoyant way of mocking their situation. Of course,
Zahi knows he is unlikely to live in a palace. He is also doubtful whether he
will ever set foot in Somalia. However, like many of the young people I met,
he remains relatively light-hearted about his situation and is convinced that
although he has always lived in a refugee camp, this stage of his life will soon
be over. Still, his irony also conveys a sense of desperation and recognition of
the absurdity of being trapped in "indefinite stasis" (Griffiths 2014: 2001).

This might encapsulate this ethnography of Somali refugee youth who have spent most of their lives in Kakuma. I started this research with the aim of understanding how people who have grown up in camps experience their living environment and how growing up in such settings and in exile, with little or no memory of other places, structures their view of the present, the past and their country of origin, as well as of the future and its possibilities. I was guided by the belief that camps have been adopted as the expected long-term response to displacement because of the will to keep certain populations away from our borders, and wondered about the repercussions of restrictive policies in the daily lives of young refugees. I planned to resituate people's trajectories in a broader context extending beyond the humanitarian system. The conviction that refugees display agency in defining their lives and giving meaning to their own situation, even though there are clear limitations and constraints, was intrinsic to this project.

Although I have made many detours in discussing my findings, my observations can be abridged into a few broad statements: regardless of how long it has existed, the camp remains a space of containment, control and transition; young Somalis display agency despite limitations and survive (and sometimes thrive in) adversity, notably by interpreting their experience in a way that makes their present bearable; the refugee camp must be approached as a social world and not only as a non-place (Augé 1997 [1992]); disgruntlement grows when education is over and youth feel they should be establishing themselves as adults, but do not have the social and financial resources to do so. These remarks show the tension that permeates this study and that manifests in a myriad of ways. To some extent, the camp can be a productive and creative place, but that is only true if people eventually manage to leave, since the camp itself constitutes a site of control and confinement, and not of fulfillment and emancipation. Contradictions might also speak of the intricacy of grasping the experience of people growing up in a restrictive space that, while conceived as a rationally organized non-place, ineluctably becomes a messier social world where new practices develop and locality is produced (Appadurai 1996: 192).

I somewhat anticipated these conclusions. Yet, there are a number of important elements that I did not foresee, including the fact that young people rarely questioned being placed in a camp after displacement from their country of origin, or the existence of the camp itself. They see the camp as the place that has allowed them to survive and, in that respect, it can only be understood by considering gains and losses, constraints and opportunities, which is partly why I found it necessary to speak of tensions that pervade the camp experience. Similarly, the extent to which young people saw the camp as a fairly "normal" place when they were children surprised me as, seen from the outside, it appeared to be such an extraordinarily unacceptable place.

While I anticipated young people's strong will to leave Kakuma, I did not expect the focus on resettlement to be so overpowering. I knew it was central to people's experience, but had not properly grasped its impact on their lives and imagination. Finally, I had not truly appreciated the fact that containment policies not only explain the prevalence of camps as a response to displacement, but also have tangible effects on people's daily lives and social navigation by further restricting their movements.

To conclude, I wish to reflect once more on a few threads that crisscross the preceding pages: people's resilient social navigation; the spatiotemporal relationship between the past, the present and the future; and the need to grasp the inherent contradictions and tensions of being in the camp to capture refugees' experience there. I will also briefly discuss some of the limits of this study.

Social Navigation in a Refugee Camp

The camp is an inappropriate response to displacement that may fit the needs of donor countries and host countries by keeping populations deemed undesirable or dangerous (or both) at the margins, but certainly does not fit the needs of refugees or respect their rights. This observation runs through this book, as it is the backdrop against which young people's lives are formed and lived. Jansen (2011) argues that the camp might not be a worse environment than a poor and geographically isolated city in a poor country. Similarly, having limited access to higher education or salaried jobs, or struggling to establish oneself as an adult is not unique to young people growing up in camps; it is the reality of numerous children in contemporary Africa, as I have noted several times in earlier chapters. This suggests that we should avoid considering displacement as the explanation for all issues around refugee camps. At the same time, the camp is set up by the international community and host countries as a response to the arrival of refugees, which distinguishes it from an unplanned sprawling urban area. As Hyndman observes, "the discrepancy between a language of rights and the conditions of the camp is untenable" (1996: 285). Deliberately settling people for the long term in such settings entails becoming blind to their humanity and not seeing them as fellow humans. This brings us back to Arendt and her observations on refugees having fallen out of the human race merely by the fact of being noncitizens (1968 [1951]: 296–300).

The structural violence of the camp deeply affects people's daily reality and, to some extent, limits their expectations. Yet, people are not reduced to mere survival or turned into perfectly manageable bodies—hence the importance of looking both at the small scale and the broader context, so as to take into account the impact of encampment and restrictive policies. In the same vein, we see that global connectedness not only generates frustration, but can also open up new avenues and nurture hope. Somali youth navigate the camp and its (relatively sparse) opportunities, acting as social agents. Vigh's (2006: 13–15) notion of social navigation is useful in recognizing the complexity of people's experience by getting around the dichotomy between people as victims or agents, and in expressing people's agency, while acknowledging that constraints and policies affect their social navigation, and thus their present and future possibilities. Some are more successful navigators than others, which shows that the refugee population is heterogeneous, like any human collectivity. It is made up of individuals who might share parts of their history or memories, and a specific social, political or historical context, but who also possess their own characteristics, history and subjectivity. Thus, there is no ideal-type refugee or refugee navigation, regardless of common humanitarian and media representations that obliterate their individuality (Malkki 1995a: 511). Still, we can also find similarities in people's navigation. For example, as observed elsewhere, young men tend to fare better than their female counterparts, earning more scholarships and holding more jobs or leadership positions (Chatty 2007: 274–76). But this might be more related to socio-structural inequity, or to social forces that influence people's social navigation, than to the camp environment itself.

Ways of navigating, which could also be called coping mechanisms, are anchored in people's culture as well as in their personal and collective history. There are obvious similarities between the ways of navigating of Somali youth and those of the Palestinians and Sahrawis who grew up in camps (Chatty and Lewando Hundt 2005; Chatty, Fiddian-Qasmiyeh and Crivello 2010). As a way of transcending their condition, education, further migration and transnational networks are important to all of them (Chatty 2010a: 29). But while young Palestinians might turn to political activism "to make sense of their surroundings as well as expend their energy and release their sense of political and social frustration" (Chatty 2010b: 336), such mobilization is not manifest among the Somali youth in Kakuma. They appear to avoid being too vocal, perhaps given Kenya's manifest fatigue around playing host. In fact, although there are obvious similarities among the experiences of refugee youth growing up in camps in different settings, their experience is also particular, as it is structured by specific social, cultural, historical and political contexts, and individual characteristics. It is worth noting that particularities are observable not only between refugees of other origins, but also between refugees of the same origin growing up in a different context. For example, Somali youth growing up in Dadaab were not exposed to the same cultural diversity as were those in Kakuma. This would certainly make their experience somewhat different.

The Fluid Relationship between Past, Present and Future

The chronological sequencing of this book is meant to allow the reader to recognize the close connection and interaction between people's lived present, (imagined) past and envisioned future. While some themes might show up repeatedly (e.g., the continuing violence in Somalia and the focus on leaving the camp), such an approach also helps make sense of people's personal experience. The experience of the camp itself is often ambiguous and difficult to label, as it not only contains negative and positive aspects, but also remains complex, nuanced and filled with very human contradictions.

Young Somalis' narratives convey contradictory views of the camp. On the one hand, it is depicted as unlivable, hot, and fraught with danger and uncertainty. The contempt that the humanitarian system displays toward refugees is described with a great deal of resentment. On the other hand, the camp is portrayed as the place that has allowed refugees to survive and develop. Those conflicting views can, to some extent, be associated with people's temporal perspective. The way they recall and shape their family's past (and have vivid indirect recollections or "postmemories" (Hirsch 1998)) and the story of their arrival in Kakuma make the present tolerable. Talking of the past, youth repeatedly stress that their lives in Somalia would have been wasted and that their conditions in the camp have significantly improved over the years. Hence, they feel their present circumstances are better than they would have been in another context or a decade ago in the same location. The past as a resource for one's identification and identity (Baussant 2007) has not been undermined by exile, but the story of this past has been revisited. This somehow alters the reproduction of social life, a reproduction that "is always a matter of recurring 'loss' and 'recovery' of selective transmission and re-constructed history in changing circumstances" (Clifford 2007: 204). In the present, refugees live and "produce locality," as people are born, marry and have children in the camp (Appadurai 1996: 192). Narratives opening onto the future have a different orientation: they highlight Kakuma's difficulties and lack of possibilities, possibly because it is not a setting where Somali youth want to imagine their future. Their knowledge of the world and its possibilities fuels their discontentment and the impression that they must leave Kakuma to lead an acceptable life.

Young people's unsettledness in Kenya and their lack of physical connection with the Somali territory complicate their sense of identification. They feel they belong to both Kenya and Somalia, while also feeling alien to both places. Much as they may consider themselves at home in Kenya, they are also aware that they are unwelcome guests. Much as they may have a sense of being Somali, they also fear Somalia, do not know it and are not even sure they would be welcome there. This feeds into their sense of living in an eternal state of limbo. It might also explain some of the contradictions that young refugees express regarding their fantasy and socially expected desire to discover Somalia versus their great ambivalence toward the idea of "returning" to a foreign land.

The Camp as a Place of Tensions and Contradictions

Throughout this book, some seemingly contradictory observations emerge, more as tensions than binary oppositions, regarding the experience of the camp. These tensions are intrinsically connected, as they often originate from the refugees' response to environmental constraints. They also reflect the fact that refugees live beyond institutions and despite institutional limitations.

Although the camp seems cut off, its embeddedness with the rest of the country and the world is evident, which conjures up the compression of time and space evoked by Bauman (1998a: 121). People come and go, send money and news; the mass media bring the world into the camp every day; political decisions, sometimes made on the other side of the globe, deeply affect the fate and lives of refugees. Social, political and economic realities transcend locality, as refugees are well informed about people's living conditions in a variety of places, which plays a role in shaping their experience and reinforces resentment at being trapped in a camp; imagined possibilities are endless, but real life is full of restrictions.

This constant interaction also turns the camp into a space in motion. Kakuma becomes a long, difficult stop on a dreamed-of journey from Somalia to the West, ideally materialized by means of resettlement. Hopes of resettlement can create intense restlessness because of the unpredictability and lengthiness of the process, but also provide a real or imagined way out. This may help to nurture optimism and temper despair, at least for a period of time. Young people express little desire to live in Somalia, although several maintain that, in an ideal world, a person should reside in his or her country of origin. The camp is a stage of development and is manageable when considered as a part of a broader trajectory, an idea also nurtured by the Somali tradition of mobility. Still, the camp is also inexorably local and immobile, as refugees are theoretically constrained in a place that does not offer an acceptable life. Such immobility impels movement.

Immobility and mobility can also refer to the conflicting temporalities that overlap, interact and, at times, clash in Kakuma. The endless wait for a hypothetical departure turns the camp into a locale where time is suspended and unpredictable. But that same time speeds up remarkably when resettlement is announced. And while biological time passes, social time gives the impression of grinding to a halt once education is over and all avenues are blocked, making the transition to adulthood challenging. The temporary yet permanent nature of Kakuma also creates a temporal tension. The camp has been there for more than twenty years, a lapse of time that can hardly be described as ephemeral, but the idea of transiency surfaces in people's perceptions and from the limited sense of community between the various ethnic groups that cohabit in Kakuma. Although they have been coexisting in a generally convivial manner for a long time, they have not developed stronger bonds, in part because the camp was and continues to be a passage or, to some extent and in Augé's term (1997 [1992]), a "non-place," even when the passage is endless.

The camp can be described as a land of constraints, marked by its arbitrary power and the humanitarian system's will to contain and order populations. It can also be considered a restrictive land of transformation, as it gives access to education and hypothetical resettlement, and exposes residents to cultural diversity and to the wider world. To the victim label, refugees oppose the idea that being refugees has made them better and stronger. Most have not stopped believing in their capacities and ambitions, although they feel that the design of their future is partly beyond their reach. It is interesting to note that those who know they will not be resettled might feel that all hope of finding a decent exit is lost, while others simply refuse to assimilate the information. Yet for some, this rejection has an emancipating aspect, as they now assume responsibility for their future, although options are limited. Young people's experiences make them question cultural practices and social roles. Women assert themselves in a way they believe would have been impossible in Somalia, which brings to mind Malkki's observation that "the camp [hosting Burundian refugees in Tanzania] ended up being much more than a device of containment and enclosure; it grew into a locus of continual creative subversion and transformation" (1995b: 237). The camp becomes a place of emergence of a new social formation, a space of individual and collective social and political transformation, one that prompts further physical and symbolic movement. In such a setting, people may share their refugeeness, but they cannot be reduced to their refugeeness. In any case, in order to benefit from the knowledge and skills acquired in the camp, and to fulfill their responsibilities toward their parents, young Somalis must leave. Moreover, as moving out of the camp is collectively depicted as the expected path, inability to do so is most commonly experienced as failure.

Limitations and Further Considerations

As is the case for most ethnographies, my observations are based on social interactions with a relatively small group of people. I believe their experience is illustrative of that of a greater number of people in a similar situation, which can to some extent be verified in writings about other camps or other groups of refugees in Kakuma (e.g., Chatty (2010b) on Palestinian youth, Kamal (2010) on young Afghan refugees and Grabska (2010) on South Sudanese refugees in Kakuma). I am nonetheless certain that nuances and disparities can be noticed. In addition, there are realities and aspects of people's reality that must have escaped me, in part because there are many people I did not speak to and also because of the limitations of language and the incommunicable nature of parts of people's intimate experience that might, however, have a great impact on their lives. In that sense, this can only be a partial and imperfect translation of people's lived experience. Moreover, being among the lucky ones who can move freely across the globe—"tourists" in the terminology of Bauman (1998a: 88–92)—probably makes it difficult to truly grasp the reality of those who are stuck in one place.

I embarked on this research because I was uncomfortable with the humanitarian response to protracted displacement and hoped to clarify how practices and policies manifested themselves in the real life of a specific group of people. The experience of those I met in Kakuma reinforces my conviction that a refugee camp cannot be a solution to displacement, even when presented as a temporary measure. Given that camps have been the subject of severe criticism, including by the very same organizations that are involved in setting them up, it is difficult to understand why they are still being established by these same organizations and will, in all likelihood, continue to exist indefinitely. The inertia of humanitarian policies and organizations in this regard is disconcerting, and so is the patent inconsistency between theory and practice—however, the UNHCR's recent commitment to pursue alternatives to camps whenever possible is a welcome, and overdue, shift in the agency's formal approach. The 2014 *Policy on Alternatives to Camps* (2014b) will hopefully turn out to be more than aspirational and lead to tangible changes. I have repeatedly shown throughout this ethnography that refugees cannot be reduced to voiceless victims. This should be recognized in discussions on solutions to displacement, as people can and already do actively contribute to finding solutions for themselves, sometimes in very creative ways.

BIBLIOGRAPHY

Abdullahi, Ahmednasir M. 1993. "Protection of Refugees under International Law and Kenya's Treatment of Somali Refugees: Compliance or Contrary," unpublished manuscript. Nairobi: University of Nairobi.

Abduallhi, Mohamed Diriye. 2001. *Culture and Customs of Somalia.* Westport, CT: Greenwood Press.

Abdi, Awa M. 2004. "In Limbo: Dependency, Insecurity and Identity in Dadaab Camps," *Refuge: Canadian Periodical on Refugee Issues* 22(2): 2–31.

Africa News Service. 2002. "Ration Reductions Pose Threat of Malnutrition to Refugees," February 22.

Africa Watch and Physicians for Human Rights. 1992. *Somalia, No Mercy in Mogadishu: The Human Cost of the Conflict & the Struggle for Relief.* New York: Africa Watch and Physicians for Human Rights.

Agamben, Giorgio. 1998. *Homo Sacer Sovereign Power and Bare Life.* Stanford: Stanford University Press.

Agier, Michel. 2008. *Gérer les indésirables: des camps de réfugiés au gouvernement humanitaire.* Paris: Flammarion.

———— 2008 [2005]. *On the Margins of the World: The Refugee Experience Today.* Cambridge: Polity Press.

Agier, Michel, and Françoise Bouchet-Saulnier. 2003. "Espaces humanitaires, espaces d'exception," in Fabrice Weissman (ed.), À l'ombre des guerres justes: l'ordre cannibale et l'action humanitaire. Paris: Flammarion, pp. 303–18.

Ahluwalia, Pal. 2003. "The Wonder of the African Market: Post-colonial Inflections," *Pretexts, Literary and Cultural Studies* 12(2): 133–44.

Ahmed, Ismail I., and Reginald Herbold Green. 1999. "The Heritage of War and State Collapse in Somalia and Somaliland: Local-Level Effects, External Interventions and Reconstruction," *Third World Quarterly* 20(1): 113–27.

AI (Amnesty International). 2014. "Forced Returns to South and Central Somalia, Including to Al-Shabaab Areas: A Blatant Violation of International Law," AI.

Al-Rasheed, Madawi. 1994. "The Myth of Return: Iraqi Arab and Assyrian Refugees in London," *Journal of Refugee Studies* 7(2/3): 199–219.

Ambroso, Guido. 2002. *Pastoral Society and Transnational Refugees: Population Movements in Somaliland and Eastern Ethiopia 1988–2000.* Geneva: New Issues in Refugee Research, United Nations High Commissioner for Refugees.

Andrzejewski, B.W. 2011. "The Literary Culture of the Somali People," *Journal of African Cultural Studies* 23(1): 9–17.

AP (Associated Press). 2009. "Deadly Blast Hits Somali Graduation Ceremony," December 3.

Appadurai, Arjun. 1996. *Modernity at Large: Cultural Dimensions of Globalization.* Minneapolis: University of Minnesota Press.

Appiah, Kwame Anthony. 2006. "The Case for Contamination," *New York Times Magazine,* January 1.

Arendt, Hannah. 1968 [1951]. *The Origins of Totalitarianism.* Cleveland: Meridian Books.

——— 1969. "Reflections on Violence," *New York Review of Books,* February 27.

Armstrong, Kimberley. 2008. "'Seeing the Suffering' in Northern Uganda: The Impact of a Human Rights Approach to Humanitarianism," *Canadian Journal of African Studies* 42(1): 1–32.

Augé, Marc. 1987. "Qui est l'autre? Un itinéraire anthropologique," *L'Homme* 27(103): 7–26.

——— 1997 [1992]. *Non-places: Introduction to an Anthropology of Supermodernity.* London: Verso.

Banki, Susan. 2004. *Refugee Integration in the Intermediate Term: A Study of Nepal, Pakistan, and Kenya.* Geneva: Evaluation and Policy Unit, United Nations High Commissioner for Refugees.

Barthes, Roland. 1996. "Introduction à l'analyse structurale des récits," *Communications* 8(8): 1–27.

Basilien-Gainche, Marie-Laure. 2011. "Sécurite des frontières et/ou protection des droits," *Cités* 2(46): 47–68.

Bauman, Zygmunt. 1998a. *Globalization: The Human Consequences.* New York: Columbia University Press.

———. 1998b. "Assimilation into Exile: The Jew as a Polish Writer," in Susan Rubin Suleiman (ed.), *Exile and Creativity.* Durham, NC: Duke University Press, pp. 321–52.

Baussant, Michèle. 2007. "Penser les mémoires," *Ethnologie française* XXXVII(3): 389–94.

BBC (British Broadcasting Corporation). 2006. "Somalis under Siege in South Africa," October 20.

———. 2009. "Rainbow Nation's Outsiders Live in Fear," May 28.

———. 2011a. "South Africa: Somali-Owned Shops Attacked and Looted," May 26.

———. 2011b. "Somalia Famine: WFP Delays Airlift of Food to Mogadishu," July 26.

———. 2011c. "Ethiopian Troops 'Cross Border into Somalia,'" November 19.

———. 2013. "Westgate Attack: MPs to Call for Refugee Camps to Close," September 30.

Beckerleg, Susan. 2008. "Introduction," *Substance Use & Misuse* 43(6): 749–61.

Behnia, Behnam. 1996–97. "Distrust and Resettlement of Survivors of War and Torture," *International Journal of Mental Health* 25(4): 45–58.

Bender, Barbara. 2002. "Time and Landscape," *Current Anthropology* 43(S4): S103–S112.

Benwell, Matthew C., and Peter Hopkins. 2015. *Children, Young People and Critical Geopolitics.* Farnham: Ashgate.

Berger, John. 1980. *About Looking.* New York: Pantheon Books.

Besteman, Catherine. 1996a. "Violent Politics and the Politics of Violence: The Dissolution of the Somalia Nation-State," *American Ethnologist* 23(3): 579–96.

——— 1996b. "Representing Violence and 'Othering' Somalia," *Cultural Anthropology* 11(1): 120–33.

Bisharat, George E. 1997. "Exile to Compatriot: Transformations in the Social Identity of Palestinian Refugees in the West Bank," in Akhil Gupta and James Ferguson (eds), *Culture, Power, Place: Explorations in Critical Anthropology.* Durham, NC: Duke University Press, pp. 203–33.

Bjork, Stephanie R. 2007. "Modernity Meets Clan: Cultural Intimacy in the Somali Diaspora," in Abdi M. Kusow and Stephanie R. Bjork (eds), *From Mogadishu to Dixon: The Somali Diaspora in a Global Context.* Trenton: Red Sea Press, pp. 135–157.

Bloch, Maurice. 1995. "Mémoire autobiographique et mémoire historique du passé éloigné," *Enquête, anthropologie, histoire, sociologie* 2: 59–76.

Boelaert, Marleen, Fabienne Vautier, Tine Dusauchoit, Wim Van Damme and Monique Van Dormael. 1999. "The Relevance of Gendered Approaches to Refugee Health: A Case Study in Hagadera, Kenya," in Doreen M. Indra (ed.), *Engendering Forced Migration: Theory and Practice*. New York: Berghahn Books, pp. 165–76.

Bosire, Boniface. 2013. "Kenya: Concerns Rise about Suicides in Kenyan Refugee Camps," *Sabahi*, June 20.

Bourdieu, Pierre (ed.). 1993. *La misère du monde*. Paris: Seuil.

Bourgois, Philippe. 2003. "The Continuum of Violence in War and Peace: Post-Cold War Lessons from El Salvador," in Nancy Scheper-Hughes and Philippe Bourgois (eds), *Violence in War and Peace: An Anthology*. London: Basil Blackwell, pp. 425–34.

Bradbury, Mark, and Sally Healy. 2010. "Endless War: A Brief History of the Somali Conflict," In Mark Bradbury and Sally Healy (eds), *Whose Peace is it Anyway? Connecting Somali and International Peacemaking*. London: Accord, no. 21, Conciliation Resources, pp. 10–14.

Brouwer, Andrew, and Judith Kumin. 2003. "Interception and Asylum: When Migration Control and Human Rights Collide," *Refuge* 21(4): 6–24.

Buchanan-Smith, Margie, and Jeremy Lind. 2005. *Armed Violence and Poverty in Northern Kenya: A Case Study for the Armed Violence and Poverty Initiative*. Bradford, UK: Centre for International Cooperation and Security, University of Bradford.

Burton, Richard F. 1987 [1856]. *First Footsteps in East Africa or, an Exploration of Harar*. Mineola: Dover Publications.

Campbell, Elizabeth, Jeff Crisp and Esther Kiragu. 2011. *Navigating Nairobi: A Review of the Implementation of UNHCR's Urban Refugee Policy in Kenya's Capital City*. Geneva: Policy Development and Evaluation Service, United Nations High Commissioner for Refugees.

Canadian Forces. 1997. *Report of the Somalia Commission of Inquiry*. Ottawa: Department of National Defence and Canadian Forces.

Candau, Joël. 2005. *Anthropologie de la mémoire*. Paris: Armand Colin.

Carr, David. 1986. *Time, Narrative, and History*. Bloomington: Indiana University Press.

Carrier, Neil. 2012. "Khat: A Lingering Controversy," *Horn of Africa Journal* 2. Retrieved 2 January 2017 from http://afrikansarvi.fi/42-artikkeli/117-khat-a-lingering-controversy.

Cassanelli, Lee. 2001. "Rethinking History and Identity in the Somali Diaspora," in Muddle Suzanne Lilius (ed.), *Variations on the Theme of Somaliness: Proceedings of the EASS/SSIA International Congress of Somali Studies, Turku, Finland, Aug. 6–9, 1998*. Turku: Centre for Continuing Education Abo Akademi University, pp. 272–82.

Chatham House. 2014. *Somali Refugees in Kenya: The Case of the Dadaab Camp*. London: Royal Institute of International Affairs.

Chatty, Dawn. 2007. "Researching Refugee Youth in the Middle East: Reflections on the Importance of Comparative Research," *Journal of Refugee Studies* 20(2): 265–80.

——— (ed.) 2010a. *Deterritorialized Youth: Sahrawi and Aghan Refugees at the Margins of the Middle East*. New York: Berghahn Books.

——— 2010b. "Palestinian Refugee Youth: Agency and Aspiration," *Refugee Survey Quarterly* 28(2–3): 318–38.

Chatty, Dawn, Elena Fiddian-Qasmiyeh and Gina Crivello. 2010. "Identity with/out Territory: Sahrawi Refugee Youth in Transnational Space," in Dawn Chatty (ed.), *Deterritorialized Youth: Sahrawi and Aghan Refugees at the Margins of the Middle East*. New York: Berghahn Books, pp. 37–78.

Chatty, Dawn and Gillian Lewando Hundt. 2005. "Introduction: Children of Palestine Narrate Forced Migration," in Dawn Chatty and Gillian Lewando Hundt (eds), *Children of*

Palestine: Experiencing Forced Migration in the Middle East. New York: Berghahn Books, pp. 1–34.

Children Act. CAP. 141. 2010 [2007]. Parliament of Kenya.

Chimni, B.S. 1993. "The Meaning of Words and the Role of UNHCR in Voluntary Repatriation," *International Journal of Refugee Law* 5(3): 442–60.

——— 2000. "Globalization, Humanitarianism and the Erosion of Refugee Protection," *Journal of Refugee Studies* 13(3): 243–63.

——— 2002. "Aid, Relief, and Containment: The First Asylum Country and Beyond," *International Migration* 40(5): 75–94.

Chonghaile, Clar Ni. 2013. "Insecurity Rises in Dadaab as Kenya Reveals Plans to 'Round up' Urban Somali Refugees," *The Guardian,* January 25.

Clark-Kazak, Christina. 2009. "Representing Refugees in the Life Cycle: A Social Age Analysis of United Nations High Commissioner for Refugees Annual Reports and Appeals 1999–2008," *Journal of Refugee Studies* 22(3): 302–22.

——— 2011. *Recounting Migration: Political Narratives of Congolese Young People in Uganda.* Montreal: McGill-Queen's University Press.

Clifford, James. 2007. "Varieties of Indigenous Experience: Diasporas, Homelands, Sovereignties," in Marisol de la Cadena and Orin Starn (eds), *Indigenous Experience Today.* Oxford: Berg, pp. 197–224.

Colson, Elizabeth. 1999. "Gendering Those Uprooted by 'Development'," in Doreen M. Indra (ed.), *Engendering Forced Migration: Theory and Practice.* New York: Berghahn Books, pp. 29–39.

Connerton, Paul. 1989. *How Societies Remember.* Cambridge: Cambridge University Press.

Constitution of Kakuma Refugee Camp (final draft). 2011.

Convention and Protocol Relating to the Status of Refugees (with an introductory note by the United Nations High Commissioner for Refugees, 2010). 1951 and 1967.

Convention on the Rights of the Child. 1989.

Cooper, Elizabeth. 2005. "What Do We Know about Out-of-School Youths? How Participatory Action Research Can Work for Young Refugees in Camps," *Journal of Comparative Education* 35(4): 463–77.

Crisp, Jeff. 1999. *A State of Insecurity: The Political Economy of Violence in Refugee-Populated Areas of Kenya.* Geneva: New Issues in Refugee Research, United Nations High Commissioner for Refugees.

——— 2003. *No Solutions in Sight: The Problem of Protracted Refugee Situations in Africa.* Geneva: New Issues in Refugee Research, United Nations High Commissioner for Refugees.

Crisp, Jeff, and Karen Jacobsen. 1998. "Refugee Camps Reconsidered," *Forced Migration Review* 3: 27–31.

Daily Nation. 2011. "Al Shabaab Samosa Ban 'Linked to Symbol'," July 26.

Daniel, E. Valentine, and John C. Knudsen (eds). 1995. *Mistrusting Refugee.* Berkeley: University of California Press.

Davis, J. 1992. "The Anthropology of Suffering," *Journal of Refugee Studies* 5(2): 149–61.

De Waal, Alex. 1998. "US War Crimes in Somalia," *New Left Review* 230: 131–44.

——— 2007. "No Such Thing as Humanitarian Intervention," Blog, *Harvard International Review,* March 21. Retrieved 2 January 2017 from http://hir.harvard.edu/no-such-thing-as-humanitarian-intervention.

Doornbos, Martin, and John Markakis. 1994. "Society and State in Crisis: What Went Wrong in Somalia?" *Review of African Political Economy* 21(59): 82–88.

DRA (Department of Refugee Affairs of Kenya). n.d. "Verification of Camp Refugees," Retrieved 4 October 2013 from http://www.refugees.go.ke/index.php/verification-of-camp-refugees.

Dryden-Peterson, Sarah. 2011. *Refugee Education: A Global Review*. Toronto: Ontario Institute for Studies in Education, University of Toronto and United Nations High Commissioner for Refugees.

Dryden-Peterson, Sarah, Negin Dahya and Wenona Giles. 2013. "Education: A Challenge to Terror," *Huffington Post* (U.S. edition), September 30.

Dryden-Peterson, Sarah, and Wenona Giles. 2010. "Introduction: Higher Education for Refugees," *Refuge* 27(2): 3–9.

Dubernet, Cécile. 2006. "Quand l'espace humanitaire devient une zone de guerre: personnes déplacées et peurs sécuritaires," *Recueil Alexandries*, Collections Esquisses 4. Retrieved 2 January 2017 from http://www.reseau-terra.eu/article346.html.

Duffield, Mark R. 2007. *Development, Security and Unending War: Governing the World of Peoples*. Cambridge: Polity Press.

Dufour, Charlotte, Véronique de Geoffroy, Hugues Maury and François Grünewald. 2004. "Rights, Standards and Quality in a Complex Humanitarian Space: Is Sphere the Right Tool?" *Disasters* 28(2): 124–41.

EC (European Commission). 2001. Council Regulation (EC) No 539/2001 of 15 March 2001 Listing the Third Countries Whose Nationals Must Be in Possession of Visas When Crossing the External Borders and Those Whose Nationals are Exempt from That Requirement. Brussels: EC.

——— 2011. *Annual Report on Immigration and Asylum (2010)*. Brussels: EC.

Escobar, Arturo. 2001. "Culture Sits in Places: Reflections on Globalism and Subaltern Strategies of Localization," *Political Geography* 20(2): 139–74.

Essed, Philomena, Georg Frerks and Joke Schrijvers. 2004. "Introduction: Refugees, Agency and Social Transformation," in P. Essed, G. Frerks and J. Schrijvers (eds), *Refugees and the Transformation of Societies. Agency, Policies, Ethics and Politics*. New York: Berghahn Books, pp. 1–16.

European Court of Human Rights. February 23, 2012. *Hirsi Jamaa and others v. Italy*. Application No. 27765/09. Strasbourg.

Ewald, Wendy, coauthored by Alexandra Lightfoot. 2001. *I Wanna Take Me a Picture: Teaching Photography and Writing to Children*. Boston: Beacon Press, Lyndhurst Books and the Center for Documentary Studies.

Farah, Abdulkadir Osman, Mammo Muchie and Joakim Gundel (eds). 2007. *Somalia: Diaspora and State Reconstitution in the Horn of Africa*. London: Adonis & Abbey.

Farah, Nuruddin. 1998. "A Country in Exile," *World Literature Today* 72(4): 713–15.

——— 2000. *Yesterday, Tomorrow: Voices from the Somali Diaspora*. London: Cassell.

Farah, Randa Rafiq. 2009. "Refugee Camps in the Palestinian and Sahrawi National Liberation Movements: A Comparative Perspective," *Journal of Palestine Studies* 38(2): 76–93.

Farwell, Nancy. 2001. "'Onward through Strength': Coping and Psychological Support among Refugee Youth Returning to Eritrea from Sudan," *Journal of Refugee Studies* 14(1): 43–69.

Fassin, Didier. 2009. "Les économies morales revisitées," *Annales HSS* 6: 1237–66.

——— 2011. "The Trace: Violence, Truth, and the Politics of the Body," *Social Research* 78(2): 281–98.

Fassin, Didier, and Mariella Pandolfi. 2010. *Contemporary States of Emergency: The Politics of Military and Humanitarian Interventions*. New York: Zone Books.

Feller, Erika. 2006. "Asylum, Migration and Refugee Protection: Realities, Myths and the Promise of Things to Come," *International Journal of Refugee Law* 18(3–4): 509–36.

Finnström, Sverker. 2006. "Meaningful Rebels? Young Adult Perceptions on the Lord's Resistance Movement/Army in Uganda," in Catrine Christiansen, Mats Utas and Henrik E. Vigh (eds), *Navigating Youth, Generating Adulthood: Social Becoming in an African Context*. Uppsala: Nordiska Afrikainstitutet, pp. 203–27.

Fivush, Robyn. 2007. "Remembering and Reminiscing: How Individual Lives are Constructed in Family Narratives," *Memory Studies* 1(1): 45–54.

Foucault, Michel. 1995 [1975]. *Discipline and Punish: The Birth of the Prison.* New York: Vintage Books.

Fresia, Marion. 2007. "Les réfugies comme objet d'étude pour l'anthropologie: enjeux et perspectives," *Refugee Quarterly Survey* 26(3): 100–18.

Gibbs, David N. 2000. "Realpolitik and Humanitarian Intervention: The Case of Somalia," *International Politics* 37(1): 41–55.

Giddens, Anthony. 1996 [1991]. *The Consequences of Modernity.* Cambridge: Polity Press.

Gilroy, Paul. 2006a. "Multiculture in Times of War: An Inaugural Lecture Given at the London School of Economics," *Critical Quarterly* 48(4): 27–45.

——— 2006b. "Colonial Crimes and Convivial Cultures," Paper presented at the Conference Rethinking Nordic Colonialism, Greenland, April 21–May 14.

Glick Schiller, Nina, Tsypylma Darieva and Sandra Gruner-Domic. 2011. "Defining Cosmopolitan Sociability in a Transnational Age. An Introduction," *Ethnic and Racial Studies* 34(3): 399–418.

Goffman, Erving. 1975. *Stigmate.* Paris: Éditions de Minuit.

GoK (Government of Kenya). 2012. "Press Statement on the Relocation of Refugees," Nairobi: Department of Refugee Affairs, GoK.

Gomes, Nathalie. 2001. "Solidarité et réseaux dans l'exil. Les réfugiés somaliens clandestins au Kenya et en Éthiopie," in Luc Cambrezy and Veronique Lassailly-Jacob (eds), *Populations réfugiées: de l'exil au retour.* Paris: Éditions de l'IRD, pp. 301–19.

Goodman, Janice H. 2004. "Coping with Trauma and Hardship among Unaccompanied Refugee Youths from Sudan," *Qualitative Health Research* 14(9): 1177–96.

Grabska, Katarzyna. 2010. "Lost Boys, Invisible Girls: Stories of Sudanese Marriages across Borders," *Gender, Place and Culture* 17(4): 479–97.

——— 2011. "Constructing 'Modern Gendered Civilised' Women and Men: Gender-Mainstreaming in Refugee Camps," *Gender & Development* 19(1): 81–93.

Grayson, Catherine-Lune. 2007. "The Day I Will Be a Pilot, Somalia through Kids' Eyes," Short film. Retrieved 2 January 2017 from https://www.youtube.com/watch?v=kzQR89Dft–4.

——— 2009. *Once Upon a Time on a Sunny Continent: Pictures by Refugee and Displaced Teens from Somalia.* Nairobi: Danish Refugee Council.

Grayson, Catherine-Lune, Andre Epstein and Emily Coles. 2013. *Durable Solutions: Perspectives of Somali Refugees Living in Kenyan and Ethiopian Camps and Selected Communities of Return.* Nairobi: Danish Refugee Council and Norwegian Refugee Council.

Griffiths, Melanie B.E. 2014. "Out of Time: The Temporal Uncertainties of Refused Asylum Seekers and Immigration Detainees," *Journal of Ethnic and Migration Studies* 40(2): 1991–2009.

Gundel, Joakim. 2002. "The Migration-Development Nexus: Somalia Case Study," *International Migration* 40(5): 255–81.

Gundel, Joakim, and Ahmed A. Omar Dharbaxo. 2006. *The Predicament of the "Oday": The Role of Traditional Structures in Security, Rights, Law and Development in Somalia.* Nairobi: Danish Refugee Council and Novib-Oxfam.

Halbwachs, Maurice. 2002 [1925]. *Les cadres sociaux de la mémoire.* Paris: Félix Alcan. (electronic version prepared by Jean-Marie Tremblay).

Halcón, Linda L., Cheryl L. Robertson, Kay Savik, David R. Johnson, Marline A. Spring, James N. Butcher, Joseph J. Westermeyer and James M. Jaranson. 2004. "Trauma and Coping in Somali and Oromo Refugee Youth," *Journal of Adolescent Health* 35(1): 17–25.

Hammond, Laura. 2007. "Obliged to Give: Remittances and the Maintenance of Transnational Networks between Somalis at Home and Abroad," *Bildhaan* 10: 125–51.

Harindranath, H. 2007. "Refugee Experience, Subalternity, and the Politics of Representation," Paper presented at the Australian & New Zealand Communication Association Annual Conference, 2007: Communication, Civics, Industry, University of Melbourne, Victoria, July 5–6.

Harrell-Bond, Barbara E. 1986. *Imposing Aid: Emergency Assistance to Refugees*. Oxford: Oxford University Press.

———— 2000. *Are Refugee Camps Good for Children?* Geneva: New Issues in Refugee Research, United Nations High Commissioner for Refugees.

———— 2002. "Can Humanitarian Work with Refugees Be Humane?" *Human Rights Quarterly* 24(1): 51–85.

Hart, Jason. 2008. "Introduction," in Jason Hart (ed.), *Years of Conflict*. New York: Berghahn Books, pp. 1–20.

Hathaway, James C. 2005. *The Rights of Refugees under International Law*. Cambridge: Cambridge University Press.

Hautaniemi, Petri. 2007. "Diasporic Authenticity: Connecting Genes and Building Families through DNA-Testing in Somali Family Reunification in Finland," in Abdi M. Kusow and Stephanie R. Bjork (eds), *From Mogadishu to Dixon: The Somali Diaspora in a Global Context*. Trenton: Red Sea Press, pp. 119–33.

Hecht, Tobias. 1998. *At Home in the Street*. Cambridge: Cambridge University Press.

Hirsch, Marianne. 1998. "Past Lives: Postmemories in Exile," in Susan Rubin Suleiman (ed.), *Exile and Creativity*. Durham, NC: Duke University Press, pp. 418–46.

———— 2012. "Interview with Marianne Hirsch, Author of 'The Generation of Postmemory.'" *Columbia University Press Blog*. Retrieved 2 January 2017 from http://www.cupblog .org/?p=8066.

Honwana, Alcinda, and Filip De Boeck. 2005. *Makers and Breakers: Children and Youth in Postcolonial Africa*. Trenton, NJ: Africa World Press.

Hoodfar, Homa. 2008. "The Long Road Home: Adolescent Afghan Refugees in Iran Contemplate 'Return.'" in Jason Hart (ed.), *Years of Conflict*. New York: Berghahn Books, pp. 165–87.

Horst, Cindy. 2001. *Vital Links in Social Security: Somali Refugees in the Dadaab Camps, Kenya*. Geneva: New Issues in Refugee Research, United Nations High Commissioner for Refugees.

———— 2006a. *Transnational Nomads: How Somalis Cope with Refugee Life in the Dadaab Camps of Kenya*. New York: Berghahn Books.

———— 2006b. "Buufis Amongst Somalis in Dadaab: The Transnational and Historical Logics Behind Resettlement Dreams," *Journal of Refugee Studies* 19(2): 143–57.

———— 2006c. *Connected Lives: Somalis in Minneapolis, Family Responsibilities and the Migration Dreams of Relatives*. Geneva: New Issues in Refugee Research, United Nations High Commissioner for Refugees.

HRW (Human Rights Watch). 1992. *World Report 1991—Kenya*. New York: HRW.

———— 1993. *World Report 1992*. New York: HRW.

———— 1994. *Sudan: The Lost Boys: Child Soldiers and Unaccompanied Boys in Southern Sudan*. New York: HRW.

———— 2002. *Hidden in Plain View: Refugees Living without Protection in Nairobi and Kampala*. New York: HRW.

———— 2009a. *From Horror to Hopelessness: Kenya's Forgotten Somali Refugee Crisis*. New York: HRW.

———— 2009b. "Kenya: Stop Recruitment of Somalis in Refugee Camps: Deception Used to Enlist Refugees to Fight in Somalia," *News*. Nairobi: HRW.

———— 2009c. "Italie/Libye: Des migrants évoquent les retours forcés et les mauvais traitements: l'UE devrait faire pression sur l'Italie pour qu'elle mette fin aux retours forcés illégaux vers la Libye," *News*. Rome: HRW.

———— 2013a. *World Report 2013: Somalia.* New York: HRW.

———— 2013b. "Kenya: Don't Force 55,000 Refugees into Camps: Unlawful Transfer Plan to Begin January 21, Could Provoke Conflict," *News.* New York: HRW.

Human Rights Council. 2012. *Report of the Special Rapporteur on the Human Rights of Migrants, François Crépeau.* A/HRC/20/24.

Hyndman, Jennifer. 1996. "Geographies of Displacement: Gender, Culture and Power in UNHCR Refugee Camps, Kenya," Ph.D. dissertation. Vancouver: University of British Columbia.

———— 1998. "Managing Difference: Gender and Culture in Humanitarian Emergencies," *Gender, Place and Culture* 5(3): 241–60.

———— 2000. *Managing Displacement: Refugees and the Politics of Humanitarianism,* Borderlines. Minneapolis: University of Minnesota Press.

Hyndman, Jennifer, and Wenona Giles. 2011. "Waiting for What? The Feminization of Asylum in Protracted Situations," *Gender, Place & Culture: A Journal of Feminist Geography* 18(3): 361–79.

Hyndman, Jennifer, and Bo Viktor Nylund. 1998. "UNHCR and the Status of Prima Facie Refugees in Kenya," *International Journal of Refugee Law* 10(1–2): 21–48.

Hynes, Patricia. 2009. "Contemporary Compulsory Dispersal and the Absence of Space for the Restoration of Trust," *Journal of Refugee Studies* 22(1): 97–121.

ICMPD (International Centre for Migration Policy Development). 2007. *The East Africa Migration Routes Report.* Vienna: ICMPD.

IFRC (International Federation of Red Cross and Red Crescent Societies). 2007. *Annual Report 2006.* Geneva: IFRC.

IFRC/ICRC (International Federation of Red Cross and Red Crescent Societies and International Committee of the Red Cross). 1994. *Code of Conduct for the International Red Cross and Red Crescent Movement and Non-Governmental Organizations (NGOs) in Disaster Relief.* Geneva: IFRC and ICRC.

International Civil Service Commission. 2012. *Salary Scale for the Professional and Higher Categories: Annual Gross Salaries and Net Equivalents after Application of Staff Assessment.* New York: International Civil Service Commission.

———— 2013. *Hardship Classification: Consolidated List of Entitlement Circular.* New York: International Civil Service Commission.

International Covenant on Civil and Political Rights. 1966.

Inhetveen, Katharina. 2006. *"Because We are Refugees": Utilizing a Legal Label.* Geneva: New Issues in Refugee Research, United Nations High Commissioner for Refugees.

IRB (Immigration and Refugee Board). 1991. *The Horn of Africa: Somalis in Djibouti, Ethiopia and Kenya.* Research Directorate, IRB, Canada.

———— 1999. *Somalia: The "Benadir" Refugee Camp Including Location and Ethnic Backgrounds of Camp Dwellers.* Research IRB, Canada.

IRIN (Integrated Regional Information Networks). 1999a. "Kenya Orders Closure of 'Illegal' Refugee Camp," August 4. Retrieved 2 January 2017 from http://www.irinnews.org/news/1999/08/04/kenya-orders-closure-illegal-refugee-camp.

———— 1999b. "Kenya Relocates 690 Refugees to Kakuma Camp," August 10. Retrieved 2 January 2017 from http://www.irinnews.org/Report/8483/KENYA-Kenya-relocates-690-refugees-to-Kakuma-camp.

———— 2002. "Kenya-Somalia: UNHCR Preparing to Move Somali Bantus to Kakuma," May 9. Retrieved 2 January 2017 from http://www.irinnews.org/report/31830/kenya-somalia-unhcr-preparing-move-somali-bantus-kakuma.

Jacobsen, Karen. 2001. *The Forgotten Solution: Local Integration for Refugees in Developing Countries.* Geneva: New Issues in Refugee Research, United Nations High Commissioner for Refugees.

———— 2005. *The Economic Life of Refugees.* Bloomfield: Kumarian Press.

Jamal, Arafat. 2000. *Minimum Standards and Essential Needs in a Protracted Refugee Situation: A Review of the UNHCR Programme in Kakuma, Kenya.* Geneva: Evaluation and Policy Analysis Unit, United Nations High Commissioner for Refugees.

Jansen, Bram J. 2011. "The Accidental City: Violence, Economy and Humanitarianism in Kakuma Refugee Camp, Kenya," Ph.D. dissertation. Wageningen: Wageningen University.

Kagwanja, Peter, and Monica Juma. 2008. "Somali Refugees: Protracted Exile and Shifting Security Frontiers," in Gil Loescher, James Milner, Edward Newman and Gary Troeller (eds), *Protracted Refugee Situations.* New York: United Nations University Press, pp. 214–47.

Kamal, Sarah. 2010. "Afghan Refugee Youth in Iran and the Morality of Repatriation," in Dawn Chatty (ed.), *Deterritorialized Youth: Sahrawi and Aghan Refugees at the Margins of the Middle East.* New York: Berghahn Books, pp. 183–211.

KANEBU (*Kakuma News Bulletin*). 2004. "Mobile Telephones Start Operating in Kakuma Refugee Camp," April.

Kanere (*Kakuma News Reflector*). 2011. "Incentive Pay Raises and Terminations Targeting Incentive Staffs," August 21.

Kapteijns, Lidwien. 2009. "Discourse on Moral Womanhood in Somali Popular Songs, 1960–1990," *Journal of African History* 50(1): 101–22.

Kaufmann, Jean-Claude. 2006. *L'invention de soi: une théorie de l'identité.* Paris: Hachette.

Kemp, Charles, and Lance Rasbridge. 2004. *Refugee and Immigrant Health: A Handbook for Health Professionals.* Cambridge: Cambridge University Press.

Kenya National Bureau of Statistics. 2009. *Population and Housing Census.* Nairobi: Kenya National Bureau of Statistics.

Kenya National Commission on Human Rights. 2007. *An Identity Crisis? A Study on the Issuance of National Identity Cards in Kenya.* Nairobi: Kenya National Commission on Human Rights.

Kibreab, Gaim. 1999. "Revisiting the Debate on People, Place, Identity and Displacement," *Journal of Refugee Studies* 12(4): 384–410.

———— 2004. "Pulling the Wool over the Eyes of the Strangers: Refugee Deceit and Trickery in Institutionalized Settings," *Journal of Refugee Studies* 17(1): 1–26.

Kirkby, John, Ted Kliest, Georg Frerks, Wiert Flikkema and Phil O'Keefe. 1997. "Field Report: UNHCR's Cross Border Operation in Somalia: The Value of Quick Impact Projects for Refugee Resettlement," *Journal of Refugee Studies* 10(2): 182–98.

Kleist, Nauja. 2004. *Nomads, Sailors and Refugees: A Century of Somali Migration.* Sussex: Sussex Migration Working Paper, No. 23, Sussex Centre for Migration Research, University of Sussex.

Kusow, Abdi M. 2007. "From Mogadishu to Dixon: Conceptualising the Somali Diaspora," in Abdulkadir Osman Farah, Mammo Muchie and Joakim Gundel (eds), *Somalia: Diaspora and State Reconstitution in the Horn of Africa.* London: Adonis & Abbey, pp. 34–42.

Laitin, David D. 1977. *Politics, Language and Thought: The Somali Experience.* Chicago: University of Chicago Press.

Lammers, Ellen. 2007. "Researching Refugees: Preoccupations with Power and Questions of Giving," *Refugee Survey Quarterly* 26(3): 72–81.

Lewis, Ioan M. 1969 [1955]. *Peoples of the Horn of Africa.* Ethnographic Survey of Africa: North Eastern Africa, Part I. London: International African Institute.

———— 1993. "Literacy and Cultural Identity in the Horn of Africa: The Somali Case," in Brian V. Street (ed.), *Cross-cultural Approaches to Literacy.* Cambridge: Cambridge University Press, pp. 145–55.

———— 1994. *Blood and Bone: The Call of Kinship in Somali Society.* Lawrenceville, NJ: Red Sea Press.

———— 2002 [1965]. *A Modern History of the Somali*, 4th edn. Oxford: James Currey and Ohio University Press.

———— 2004. "Visible and Invisible Differences: The Somali Paradox," *Africa* 74(4): 489–515.

Lindley, Anna. 2007a. *Protracted Displacement and Remittances: The View from Eastleigh, Nairobi*. Geneva: New Issues in Refugee Research, United Nations High Commissioner for Refugees.

———— 2007b. *The Early Morning Phonecall: Remittances from a Refugee Diaspora Perspective*. Oxford: Centre on Migration, Policy and Society, University of Oxford.

———— 2010. "Leaving Mogadishu: Towards a Sociology of Conflict-Related Mobility," *Journal of Refugee Studies* 23(1): 2–22.

———— 2011a. *Unlocking Protracted Displacement: Somali Case Study*. Oxford: Working Paper Series, No. 79, Oxford Refugee Studies Centre, University of Oxford.

———— 2011b. "Between a Protracted and a Crisis Situation: Policy Responses to Somali Refugees in Kenya," *Refugee Survey Quarterly* 30(4): 14–49.

Lloyd, Cynthia B., Jere R. Behrman, Nelly P. Stromquist and Barney Cohen. 2006. "Introduction," in Cynthia B. Lloyd, Jere R. Behrman, Nelly P. Stromquist and Barney Cohen (eds), *The Changing Transitions to Adulthood in Developing Countries: Selected Studies*. Washington, DC: National Academies Press, pp. 15–31.

Loescher, Gil, James Milner, Edward Newman and Gary Troeller. 2008. "Introduction," in Gil Loescher, James Milner, Edward Newman and Gary Troeller (eds), *Protracted Refugee Situations*. New York: United Nations University Press, pp. 20–42.

Loizos, Peter. 1981. *The Heart Grown Bitter: A Chronicle of Cypriot War Refugees*. Cambridge: Cambridge University Press.

Long, Katy. 2010. *No Entry! A Review of UNHCR's Response to Border Closures in Situations of Mass Refugee Influx*. Geneva: New Issues in Refugee Research, United Nations High Commissioner for Refugees.

———— 2014. "Chapter 37: Rethinking 'Durable' Solutions," in Elena Fiddian-Qasmiyeh, Gil Loescher, Katy Long and Nando Sigona (eds), *The Oxford Handbook of Refugees and Forced Migration Studies*. Oxford: Oxford University Press, pp. 475–86.

Luling, Virginia. 1997. "Come Back Somalia? Questioning a Collapsed State," *Third World Quarterly* 18(2): 287–302.

Lustig, Stuart L., Maryam Kia-Keating, Wanda Grant Knight, Paul Geltman, Heidi Ellis, David Kinzie, Terence Keane and Glenn N. Saxe. 2004. "Review of Child and Adolescent Refugee Mental Health," *Journal of the American Academy of Child and Adolescent Psychiatry* 43(1): 24–36.

Malkki, Liisa. 1992. "National Geographic: The Rooting of Peoples and the Territorialization of National Identity among Scholars and Refugees," *Cultural Anthropology* 7(1): 24–44.

———— 1995a. "Refugees and Exile: From 'Refugee Studies' to the National Order of Things," *Annual Review Anthropology* 24(1): 495–523.

———— 1995b. *Purity and Exile: Violence, Memory, and National Cosmology among Hutu Refugees in Tanzania*. Chicago: University of Chicago Press.

———— 1996. "Speechless Emissaries: Refugees, Humanitarianism, and Dehistoricization," *Cultural Anthropology* 11(3): 377–404.

Maltou, Patrick. 1999. "Upsetting the Cart: Forced Migration and Gender Issues, the African Experience," in Doreen M. Indra (ed.), *Engendering Forced Migration: Theory and Practice*. New York: Berghahn Books, pp. 128–45.

Marchal, Roland. 2002. *A Survey of Mogadishu's Economy*. Nairobi: European Commission/Somali Unit.

Markus, Hazel, and Paula Nurius. 1986. "Possible Selves," *American Psychologist* 41(9): 954–69.

McMillan, David W., and David M. Chavis George. 1986. "Sense of Community: A Definition and Theory," *Journal of Community Psychology* 14(1): 1–23.

Meintel, Deidre. 1990. "Récits d'exil et mémoire sociale des réfugiés," in François Laplantine, Joseph Lévy, Jean-Baptiste Martin and Alexis Nouss (eds), *Récit et connaissances*. Lyon: Presses Universitaires, pp. 55–74.

———— 1993. "Introduction: Nouvelles approches constructivistes à l'étude de l'ethnicité," *Culture* XIII(2): 10–15.

———— 2008. "Identités ethniques plurielles et reconnaissance connective en Amérique du Nord," in Jean-Paul Payet and Alain Battegay (eds), *La Reconnaissance à l'épreuve*. Villeneuve d'Ascq: Septentrion, collection Sciences sociales, pp. 311–19.

Menkhaus, Ken. 2005. *Kenya-Somalia Border Conflict Analysis*. Nairobi: USAID/REDSO.

———— 2008. *Current Political and Socio-economic Dynamics in Somalia*. Nairobi: UNICEF Somalia.

———— 2009. "Somalia: 'They Created a Desert and Called it Peace(building).'" *Review of African Political Economy* 36(120): 223–33.

———— 2010. "Stabilisation and Humanitarian Access in a Collapsed State: The Somali Case," *Disasters* 34(S3): 320–41.

Michira, Moses. 2011. "Low Income Earners to Pay Less Tax in New Plan," *Business Daily*, November 14.

Miller, Kenneth E., Hallie Kushner, Jill McCall, Zoë Martell and Madhur Kulkarni. 2008. "Growing up in Exile: Psychosocial Challenges Facing Refugee Youth in the United States," in Jason Hart (ed.), *Years of Conflict*. New York: Berghahn Books, pp. 58–86.

Milner, James. 2009. *Refugees, the State and the Politics of Asylum in Africa*. New York: Palgrave Macmillan.

Mink, Louis O. 1970. "History and Fiction as Modes of Comprehension," *New Literary History* 1(3): 541–58.

Möllering, Guido. 2001. "The Nature of Trust: From Georg Simmel to a Theory of Expectation, Interpretation and Suspension," *Sociology* 35(2): 403–20.

Montclos (Pérouse de), Marc-Antoine. 1999a. *Exodus and Reconstruction of Identities: Somali "Minority Refugees" in Mombasa*. Paris: Aid Watch.

———— 1999b. "Les reconstructions identitaires de l'exode: les réfugiés somaliens à Mombasa (Kenya)," *Autrepart* 11: 27–46.

———— 2008. "Humanitarian Aid, War, Exodus, and Reconstruction of Identities: A Case Study of Somali 'Minority Refugees' in Kenya," *Nationalism and Ethnic Politics* 14(2): 289–321.

Montclos (Pérouse de), Marc-Antoine and Peter Mwangi Kagwanja. 2000. "Refugee Camps or Cities? The Socio-economic Dynamics of the Dadaab and Kakuma Camps in Northern Kenya," *Journal of Refugee Studies* 13(2): 205–22.

Moret, Joëlle, Simone Baglioni and Denise Efionayi-Mäder. 2006. *The Path of Somali Refugees into Exile: A Comparative Analysis of Secondary Movements and Policy Responses*. Neuchâtel: Swiss Forum for Migration and Population Studies.

MPC (Migration Policy Centre). 2013. *Migration Profile: Libya*. Florence: MPC.

Murray, Laura K., Judith A. Cohen, B. Heidi Ellis and Anthony Mannarino. 2008. "Cognitive Behavioral Therapy for Symptoms of Trauma and Traumatic Grief in Refugee Youth," *Child and Adolescent Psychiatric Clinics of North America* 17(3): 585–604.

Ni Raghallaigh, Muireann. 2014. "The Causes of Mistrust amongst Asylum Seekers and Refugees: Insights from Research with Unaccompanied Asylum-Seeking Minors Living in the Republic of Ireland," *Journal of Refugee Studies* 27(1): 82–100.

Nurmi, Jari-Erik. 1991. "How Do Adolescents See Their Future? A Review of the Development of Future Orientation and Planning," *Developmental Review* 11(1): 1–59.

Nyers, Peter. 2006. *Rethinking Refugees: Beyond States of Emergency.* New York: Routledge.

OAU (Organization of African Unity). 1969. *Convention Governing the Specific Aspects of Refugee Problems in Africa.*

Obura, Anna P., in association with David W. Khatete and Zipporah Rimbui. 2002. *Peace Education Programme in Dadaab and Kakuma, Kenya: Evaluation Summary.* Geneva: United Nations High Commissioner for Refugees.

Odengo, Rose. 2011. "Inside Kenya's Death Camps," *Daily Kenya Living Supplement, Daily Nation,* Nairobi, June 29, 2–3.

OHCHR. 2006. *Frequently Asked Questions on a Human Rights-Based Approach to Development Cooperation.* New York: Office of the United Nations High Commissioner for Human Rights.

Oka, Rahul. 2011. "Unlikely Cities in the Desert: The Informal Economy as Causal Agent for Permanent 'Urban' Sustainability in Kakuma Refugee Camp, Kenya," *Urban Anthropology* 40(3–4): 223–62.

Omar, Yusuf Sheikh. 2008. "Somali Youth in Diaspora: A Comparative Study of Gender Perceptions of Further Studies and Future Career (Case Study: Somali Youth Melbourne, Australia)," *Bildhaan* 8: 52–95.

Ong, Aihwa. 2006. "Mutations in Citizenship," *Theory, Culture and Society* 23(2–3): 499–504.

Ongeri, Boniface, and Victor Obure. 2004. "Fading Images: How Province is Fighting One-Eyed Bandit's Legacy," *The Standard,* December 9.

Oriol, Michel. 1985. "L'ordre des identités," *Revue européenne des migrations internationales* 1(2): 171–85.

Otha, Itaru. 2005. "Coexisting with Cultural 'Others': Social Relationships between the Turkana and the Refugees at Kakuma, Northwest Kenya," in Kazunobu Ikeya and Elliot Fratkin (eds), *Pastoralists and Their Neighbors in Asia and Africa.* Osaka: National Museum of Ethnology, pp. 227–39.

Paardekooper, B. 1999. "The Psychological Impact of War and the Refugee Situation on South Sudanese Children in Refugee Camps in Northern Uganda: An Exploratory Study," *Journal of Child Psychology and Psychiatry* 40(4): 529–36.

Palriwala, Rajni. 2005. "Fieldwork in a Post-colonial Anthropology. Experience and the Comparative," *Social Anthropology* 13(2): 151–70.

Parliament of Kenya. 1995. *Kenya National Assembly Official Record.* Nairobi: Parliament of Kenya.

——— 1996. *Kenya National Assembly Official Record.* Nairobi: Parliament of Kenya.

Pavanello, Sara, Samir Elhawary and Sara Pantuliano. 2010. *Hidden and Exposed: Urban Refugees in Nairobi, Kenya.* London: Humanitarian Policy Group.

Pennings, E.J.M., A. Opperhuizen and J.G.C. van Amsterdam. 2008. "Risk Assessment of Khat Use in the Netherlands: A Review Based on Adverse Health Effects, Prevalence, Criminal Involvement and Public Order," *Regulatory Toxicology and Pharmacology* 52(3): 199–207.

Polman, Linda. 2010 [2008]. *The Crisis Caravan: What's Wrong with Humanitarian Aid?* New York: Metropolitan Books.

The Prohibition of Female Genital Mutilation Bill. 2010. Nairobi: Parliament of Kenya.

Prunier, Gérard. 1997. "Segmentarité et violence dans l'espace somali, 1840–1992," *Cahiers d'études africaines* 37(146): 379–401.

Raffaelli, Marcela, and Silvia H. Koller. 2005. "Future Expectations of Brazilian Street Youth," *Journal of Adolescence* 28(2): 249–62.

Rahman, A., and A. Hafeez. 2003. "Suicidal Feelings Run High among Mothers in Refugee Camps: A Cross-sectional Survey," *Acta Psychiatrica Scandinavica* 108(5): 392–93.

Rajaram, Prem Kumar. 2002. "Humanitarianism and Representations of the Refugee," *Journal of Refugee Studies* 15(3): 247–64.

Rawlence, Ben. 2016. *City of Thorns: Nine Lives in the World's Largest Refugee Camp.* Toronto: Penguin Random House Canada.

Razack, Sherene H. 2004. *Dark Threats and White Knights: The Somalia Affair, Peacekeeping and the New Imperialism.* Toronto: University of Toronto Press.

——— 2008. *Casting Out: The Eviction of Muslims from Western Law and Politics.* Toronto: University of Toronto Press.

RCK (Refugee Consortium of Kenya). 2012. *Asylum under Threat: Assessing the Protection of Somali Refugees in Dadaab Refugee Camps and Along the Migration Corridor.* Nairobi: RCK.

The Refugee Act. 2006. Nairobi: Parliament of Kenya.

Reini, James. 2013. "Kenya Tensions Spark Somali Refugee Flight," *Al Jazeera,* February 8.

Ricoeur, Paul. 1991. "Narrative Identity," in Daniel Wood (ed.), *On Paul Ricoeur: Narrative and Interpretation.* London: Routledge, pp. 188–99.

Rousseau, Cécile, Tahar M. Said, Marie-Josée Gagné and Gilles Bibeau. 1998. "Between Myth and Madness: The Premigration Dream of Leaving among Young Somali Refugees," *Culture, Medicine and Psychiatry* 22(4): 385–411.

Salmela-Aro, Katariina. 2010. "Personal Goals and Well-Being: How Do Young People Navigate Their Lives?" *New Directions for Child and Adolescent Development* 130: 13–26.

Salmela-Aro, Katariina, Kaisa Aunola and Jari-Erik Nurmi. 2007. "Personal Goals during Emerging Adulthood: A 10-Year Follow up," *Journal of Adolescent Research* 22(6): 690–715.

Said, Edward. 1994 [1984]. "Reflections on Exile," in Marc Robinson (ed.), *Altogether Elsewhere: Writers on Exile.* London: Faber & Faber, pp. 137–49.

Samatar, Abdi Ismail. 1992. "Destruction of State and Society in Somalia: Beyond the Tribal Convention," *Journal of Modern African Studies* 30(4): 625–41.

——— 1997. "Leadership and Ethnicity in the Making of African State Models: Botswana versus Somalia," *Third World Quarterly* 18(4): 687–708.

Samatar, Abdi, and A.I. Samatar. 1987. "The Material Roots of the Suspended African State: Arguments from Somalia," *Journal of Modern African Studies* 25(4): 669–90.

Samatar, Ahmed I. 1985. "Underdevelopment in Somalia: Dictatorship without Hegemony," *Africa Today* 32(3): 23–40.

Sassen, Saskia. 1999. *Guests and Aliens.* New York: New Press.

Saunders, Mark, and Adrian Thornhill. 2004. "Trust and Mistrust in Organizations: An Exploration Using an Organizational Justice Framework," *European Journal of Work and Organizational Psychology* 13(4): 493–515.

Seginer, Rachel. 2008. "Future Orientation in Times of Threat and Challenge: How Resilient Adolescents Construct Their Future," *International Journal of Behavioral Development* 32(4): 272–82.

SG (Secretary General). 2003. *Secretary General's Bulletin: Special Measures for Protection from Sexual Exploitation and Sexual Abuse.* New York: United Nations Secretariat.

Sheikh, Hassan, and Sally Healy. 2009. *Somalia's Missing Million: The Somali Diaspora and its Role in Development.* United Nations Development Programme.

Simmel, Georg. 1950. *The Sociology of Georg Simmel.* New York: Free Press.

Sommers, Marc. 2001. *Youth: Care & Protection of Children in Emergencies: A Field Guide.* Save the Children.

Stevenson, Jacqueline, and John Willott. 2007. "The Aspiration and Access to Higher Education of Teenage Refugees in the UK," *Compare: A Journal of Comparative and International Education* 37(5): 671–87.

Stoddard, Sarah A., Susan J. Henly, Renee E. Sieving and John Bolland. 2011. "Social Connections, Trajectories of Hopelessness, and Serious Violence in Impoverished Urban Youth," *Journal of Youth and Adolescence* 40(3): 278–95.

Straziuso, Jason. 2013. "World Food Program Feeds 3M after Typhoon: Aid in Kenya Camps Cut," *Associated Press*, November 22.

Swann, Jr., William B. 1987. "Identity Negotiation: Where Two Roads Meet," *Journal of Personality and Social Psychology* 53(6): 1038–51.

Taboada-Leonetti, Isabelle. 1989. "Cohabitation pluri-ethnique dans la ville: stratégies d'insertion locale et phénomènes identitaires," *Revue européenne des migrations internationales* 5(2): 51–70.

Tefferi, Hirut. 2008. "Reconstructing Adolescence after Displacement: Experience from Eastern Africa," in Jason Hart (ed.), *Years of Conflict*. New York: Berghahn Books, pp. 23–37.

Throop, Jason C. 2003 "Articulating Experience," *Anthropological Theory* 3(2): 219–41.

Tomlinson, John. 1999. "The Possibility of Cosmopolitanism," in *Globalization and Culture*. Chicago: University of Chicago Press, pp. 181–205.

Turner, Aaron. 2000. "Embodied Ethnography. Doing culture," *Social Anthropology* 8(1): 51–60.

UN General Assembly. 2001. *Investigation into Allegations of Refugee Smuggling at the Nairobi Branch Office of the Office of the United Nations High Commissioner for Refugees*. Report of the Secretary General on the activities of the Office of Internal Oversight Services, A/56/733.

UNFPA (United Nations Population Fund). 2012. "Settling the Status of the Population in Somalia," United Nations Population Fund. Retrieved 2 January 2017 from http://countryoffice .unfpa.org/somalia/2012/11/30/5895/settling_the_status_of_the_population_in_somalia.

UNHCR (United Nations High Commissioner for Refugees). n.d. *Mombasa Camps Profile (Marafa, Utange, Hatimi)*. UNHCR.

——— 1994. *Review of UNHCR's Kenya-Somalia Cross-border Operation*. Geneva: Evaluation Reports, UNHCR.

——— 1995. *The State of the World's Refugees 1995: In Search of Solutions*. Oxford: UNHCR and Oxford University Press.

——— 1998. "Re: Request for Verification of Status of Refugees in Kenya," UNHCR.

——— 2003. *Handbook for Registration (Provisional Release)*. Geneva: UNHCR.

——— 2004. *Protracted Refugee Situations*. Geneva: Executive Committee of the High Commissioner's Programme, UNHCR.

——— 2005. *Population as at December 2005*. Kakuma: UNHCR.

——— 2007a. *2006 Global Trends: Refugees, Asylum-Seekers, Returnees, Internally Displaced and Stateless Persons*. Geneva: UNHCR.

——— 2007b. *Population as at December 2007*. Kakuma: UNHCR.

——— 2007c. *Handbook for Emergencies*. Geneva: UNHCR.

——— 2008. *Population as at December 2008*. Kakuma: UNHCR.

——— 2009a. *Population as at 31 December 2009*. Kakuma: UNHCR.

——— 2009b. "UNHCR Relocates First Somali Refugees from Dadaab to Kakuma," *Briefing Notes*, August 18. Geneva: UNHCR.

——— 2010. *Eligibility Guidelines for Assessing the International Protection Needs of Asylum-Seekers from Somalia*. Geneva: UNHCR.

——— 2011a. *Population Statistics Jan–Dec 2011*. Kakuma: UNHCR.

——— 2011b. *Global Report*. Geneva: UNHCR.

——— 2011c. "World Refugee Day: UNHCR Report Finds 80 Per Cent of World's Refugees in Developing Countries," UNHCR. Retrieved 2 January 2017 from https://secure.flickr .com/photos/unhcr/5852749832/in/photostream.

——— 2011d. *60 Years and Still Counting: UNHCR Global Trends 2010*. Geneva: UNHCR.

——— 2012a. *Situation Report: Somali Border Regions/Gedo, Lower and Middle Juba.* Nairobi: UNHCR.

——— 2012b. *Kakuma Camp Population Statistics, 16 Oct. 2012.* Kakuma: UNHCR.

——— 2012c. *Population Statistics Jan–Dec 2012.* Kakuma: UNHCR.

——— 2013a. *Kakuma Camp Population Statistics, 14 April 2013.* Kakuma: UNHCR.

——— 2013b. *Somalia Fact Sheet.* Geneva: UNHCR.

——— 2014a. *Global Trends: UNHCR Global Trends 2013.* Geneva: UNHCR.

——— 2014b. *Policy on Alternatives to Camps.* Geneva: UNHCR.

——— 2016a. *World at War: Forced Displacement in 2015.* Geneva: UNHCR.

——— 2016b. *UNHCR Position on Returns to Southern and Central Somalia (Update I).* Geneva: UNHCR.

UNHCRa. *Statistical Online Population Database.* Geneva: UNHCR. Retrieved 2 January 2017 from http://popstats.unhcr.org/en/overview.

UNHCRb. *Refugee in the Horn of Africa: Information Sharing Portal.* Geneva: UNHCR. Retrieved 2 January 2017 from http://data.unhcr.org/horn-of-africa/regional.php.

UNHCR Excom. 1981. *Conclusions No. 22 (XXXII) Protection of Asylum-Seekers in Situations of Large-Scale Influx.* Geneva: UNHCR.

UNHCR and SC-UK (Save the Children-UK). 2002. *Note for Implementing and Operational Partners by UNHCR and Save the Children-UK on Sexual Violence & Exploitation.* UNHCR and Save the Children-UK.

UNHCR, UNICEF and Education Partners. 2012. *Joint Assessment of the Education Sector in Kakuma Refugee Camp.* Kakuma: UNHCR.

United Nations Human Settlements Programme. 2006. *The State of the World's Cities Report 2006/2007.* London: Earthscan.

UNOCHA (United Nations Office for the Coordination of Humanitarian Affairs). 2002. *Somalia: A Study on Minorities in Somalia.* New York: UNOCHA.

——— 2012. *Mid-year Review of the Consolidated Appeal for Somalia 2012.* Nairobi: UNOCHA.

USCR (U.S. Committee for Refugees and Immigrants). 2001. *World Refugee Survey 2001—Kenya.* Washington: USCR.

——— 2004. *World Refugee Survey 2004—Kenya.* Washington, DC: USCR.

Utas, Mats. 2005. "Victimcy, Girlfriending, Soldiering: Tactic Agency in a Young Woman's Social Navigation of the Liberian War Zone," *Anthropological Quarterly* 78(2): 403–30.

Van Damme, Wim. 1999. "Do Refugees Belong in Camps? Experiences from Goma and Guinea," *The Lancet* 346(8971): 360–62.

Verdirame, Guglielmo, and Barbara E. Harrell-Bond. 2005. *Rights in Exile: Janus-Faced Humanitarianism.* New York: Berghahn Books.

Verdirame, Gugliemo. 1998. *Refugees in Kenya: Between a Rock and a Hard Place.* Oxford: Refugee Studies Programme, University of Oxford.

Verhoeven, Harry. 2009. "The Self-fulfilling Prophecy of Failed States: Somalia, State Collapse and the Global War on Terror," *Journal of Eastern African Studies* 3(3): 405–25.

Vigh, Henrik. 2006. *Navigating Terrains of War: Youth and Soldiering in Guinea-Bissau.* New York: Berghahn Books.

——— 2008. "Crisis and Chronicity: Anthropological Perspectives on Continuous Conflict and Decline," *Ethnos* 73(1): 5–24.

Voutira, Eftihia, and Harrell-Bond, Barbara E. 1995. "In Search of the Locus of Trust: The Social World of the Refugee Camp," in E. Valentine Daniel and John C. Knudsen (eds), *Mistrusting Refugee.* Berkeley: University of California Press, pp. 207–24.

Wafula, Paul. 2013. "How Foreigners Give Hefty Bribes to Acquire Kenya's IDs," *The Standard,* September 7.

224 • Children of the Camp

Waldron, Sidney, and Naima A. Hasci. 1994. *Somali Refugees in the Horn of Africa: State of the Art Literature Review.* Oxford: Studies on Emergencies and Disaster Relief, Refugee Studies Programme, University of Oxford.

Walkup, Mark. 1997. "Policy Dysfunction in Humanitarian Organizations: The Role of Coping Strategies, Institutions, and Organizational Culture," *Journal of Refugee Studies* 10(1): 37–60.

Warfa, Nasir, Axel Klein, Kamaldeep Bhui, Gerard Leavey, Tom Craig and Stephen Alfred Stansfeld. 2007. "Khat Use and Mental Illness: A Critical Review," *Social Science & Medicine* 65(2): 309–18.

Warsame, Ali A. 2001. "How a Strong Government Backed an African Language: The Lessons of Somalia," *International Review of Education* 47(3–4): 341–60.

Whittaker, Hannah. 2008. "Pursuing Pastoralists: The Stigma of the *Shifta* during the '*Shifta* War' in Kenya, 1963–68," *Eras,* 10. Retrieved 2 January 2017 from http://arts.monash.edu.au/publications/eras/edition–10/whittaker-article.pdf.

Wise, Amanda. 2007. "Multiculturalism from Below: Transversal Crossings and Working Class Cosmopolitans," Paper presented at COMPAS Annual Conference (extended version), Oxford, July 5–6.

World Health Organization. "Sexual and Reproductive Health: Female Genital Mutilation and Other Harmful Practices," Retrieved 2 January 2017 from http://www.who.int/reproductivehealth/topics/fgm/prevalence/en.

Yamamoto, Donald Y. 2011. "The Untapped Power of the Somali Diaspora," *Blog. U.S. Department of State.* Retrieved 2 January 2017 from http://blogs.state.gov/stories/2011/08/26/untapped-power-somali-diaspora.

Yowell, Constance M. 2002. "Dreams of the Future: The Pursuit of Education and Career Possible Selves among Ninth Grade Latino Youth," *Applied Developmental Science* 6(2): 62–72.

Zetter, Roger. 1991. "Labelling Refugees: Forming and Transforming a Bureaucratic Identity," *Journal of Refugee Studies* 4(1): 39–62.

——— 2007. "More Labels, Fewer Refugees: Making and Remaking the Refugee Label in an Era of Globalisation," *Journal of Refugee Studies* 20(2): 172–92.

Zimmerman, Susan. 2009. "Irregular Secondary Movements to Europe: Seeking Asylum Beyond Refuge, and the Links between These Stages," *Journal of Refugee Studies* 22(1): 74–96.

Zucker, Lynne G. 1985. *Production of Trust: Institutional Sources of Economic Structure, 1840 to 1920.* Los Angeles: Working Paper Series, Department of Sociology, University of California.

Appendix

A SHORT OVERVIEW OF KEY INFORMANTS

During my research, I conducted over a hundred interviews and all of them contributed in one way or another to shaping my perception. For this reason, the following overview of key informants can only be partial. It focuses on individuals who are repeatedly quoted in this ethnography and draws attention to some significant relationships between people. Except as noted, the individuals listed below are Somalis from Somalia.

Outspoken *Khadra,* twenty, lived with her two parents and siblings in the old Somali neighborhood of Kakuma I. She arrived in Kenya in 1992 from Kismayo, Somalia, when she was a few months old. Her family moved to Kakuma in 1997. Prior to that, she lived in two coastal camps, Utange and Swale Nguru. She has completed her secondary education and worked for an NGO. She was resettled to the United States on her own while I was in the camp.

Khadra introduced me to *Xaawo,* twenty-one. She has lived with her uncle and grandmother in the old Somali neighborhood of Kakuma since 1995, as her parents died in Somalia. She arrived in Kenya from Kismayo as a baby and first stayed in Marafa camp on the Kenyan coast. She claims to be among the Somalis who have been in the camp the longest. Her family has been rejected for resettlement, which brings a lot of distress to her life. She has completed secondary school and is unemployed.

The Nuur family: *Zaynab,* eighteen, *Awo,* twenty-one, *Aziz,* twenty-three, and *Fartuun,* twenty-six, are siblings who arrived in Kakuma with their parents and two older brothers in 1998. Their family left Baidoa, Somalia, in 1995. The family was relatively wealthy and stayed in Nairobi until they had exhausted their resources. It is an exceptional family, in that all the children have completed their secondary education and most have held prestigious positions with NGOs. All the children still lived with their parents in a relatively mixed neighborhood of Kakuma II. I first met Zaynab and gradually came to know the rest of the family. The whole family was resettled in the United

States after I left the camp, except for Awo, who went to study in Canada with a scholarship.

Ayan, eighteen, and *Deeqa,* twenty-one, are two friends who both arrived in Kenya in 1992 and in Kakuma in 1997, after living in Hatimy camp, also on the Kenyan coast. I met with them through Aziz, as they were enrolled in a filmmaking class he was instructing. Both have completed their primary schooling. Deeqa did not go to secondary school, while Ayan started but dropped out to help her mother at home. Ayan's father works in Nairobi to support the family in the camp.

Khadra also introduced me to *Faarax,* twenty-one, who arrived in Kenya from Kismayo in 1992 and first lived in Jomvu camp, along with many other Somali Bajuni. His family was transferred to Kakuma in 1998 and settled in the Bajuni area, in Kakuma II, but later moved to the old Somali neighborhood of Kakuma I. He lived with his mother and younger siblings, who were still in school. Their father had been resettled to the United States with his other wife several years earlier. Faarax had completed secondary school and worked for an NGO, until he decided to leave for Nairobi. The whole family was resettled to the United States after I had left Kakuma.

Mahdi, twenty-one, arrived in Kakuma from Mogadishu, Somalia, in 1992 when he was a few months old. Known as a peacemaker among his peers, he has been in Kakuma for the longest period among the Somalis whom I met. He lived in the old Somali neighborhood of Kakuma I with his mother, siblings and stepfather. He has completed primary school, but did not study further. He desperately searched for a job, but could not find one. He was enrolled in the journalism class that I gave. He left for Nairobi with Faarax while I was in the camp and is still there.

The Ahmed family: I met with *Nuradin,* twenty-one, *Warsame,* twenty-three, and *Luula,* eighteen, in different contexts and only realized they were siblings later. Nuradin was in the journalism class, an aid worker introduced me to Warsame, and Luula attended my photography class. Their family arrived in Kenya in 1991 from Mogadishu and first lived in three of the coastal camps. They were transferred to Kakuma in 1997. Nuradin looked after the small family shop in the Somali market. Warsame was the chairman of one of the Somali youth groups and worked as a youth mobilizer. He had completed his secondary education and was enrolled in a long distance university course. Luula was in high school and was one of my photography students. They lived with their mother and younger siblings. Warsame and Nuradin were resettled to Ohio, United States, after I left the camp. Their mother and other siblings are still in Kenya, but moved to Nairobi with the financial support of the two brothers.

I met Mahdi and Nuradin through the journalism class that I gave. They turned out to be Faraax's close childhood friends.

Faarax introduced me to *Dayib,* thirty-three, the elected leader of his neighborhood who briefly stayed in Dadaab and Nairobi before arriving in Kakuma in 2003. Dayib introduced me to several adults and elderly people who had been in the camp for long periods of time. He works for an NGO.

Faarax also introduced me to *Idris,* forty, who has been displaced for most of his life. He is a Somali from the Ogaden in Ethiopia. He was five years old when, in 1978, his parents fled the Ogaden to Hargeisa, in northwestern Somalia (Somaliland). He grew up in a refugee camp there. In 1988, when he was fifteen, the Somali government attacked the city and people fled en masse. In the process, he was separated from his parents. He went to Mogadishu and never saw his parents again. When the situation deteriorated in Mogadishu, he hit the road once more. In 1991, he crossed the Kenyan border and arrived in Liboi. He was transferred to Dadaab, but was sent to a boarding school in Garissa. When he finished his secondary education, he was transferred to one of the coastal camps. When that camp closed in 1997, he moved to Kakuma. He works for an NGO.

Warsame introduced me to *Osman,* fifty-two, a Somali lawyer from Mogadishu who first lived in Dadaab and moved to Kakuma I in 2010. He studied law in Somalia and later in Switzerland and Italy. When the regime collapsed in Somalia, he fled to Ethiopia, where he worked as a judge. He moved to Kenya as he was told that he could be resettled. This did not materialize and he ended up in the camp, with his wife and six children. He has no paid work.

Abdikadir, thirty-one, arrived on the Kenyan coast from Kismayo in 1993 and first lived in Jomvu camp. He moved to Kakuma with his parents in 1998 and lived in the Bajuni neighborhood of Kakuma II. He has finished his secondary school education and is enrolled in a long-distance-learning university program. He is married and has young children. He worked for an NGO. He was resettled to the United States in 2013.

Zahara, twenty-three, came to Kenya with her older sister in 1993. Their parents had died. The sisters lived in Jomvu camp until 1997, when they were transferred to Kakuma. They did not stay in Kakuma, as they found the conditions too difficult. They settled in Mombasa, where Zahara's sister died. At that point, Zahara decided to return to Somalia where her grandmother still lived, but she soon left again. She stayed with a family on the Kenyan coast for a few years while she completed her secondary schooling. Then, jobless and without resources, she moved to Kakuma. She works for an NGO.

Abdullahi, twenty-four, arrived in Kenya from Buale in 1991 and first lived in Dadaab. He was transferred to Kakuma in 2002, as part of the resettlement of Somali Bantus to the United States. His family was rejected from the process and thus ended up staying in Kakuma. He lives with his elderly mother, siblings and wife in the Bantu neighborhood of Kakuma IV. He resigned from his job with an NGO while I was in Kakuma.

Abdullahi introduced me to *Yasin,* twenty-eight, who also lives in the Bantu area, although he is not Bantu. Yasin arrived in Kenya from Sako in 1991 and stayed in Dadaab. He "resettled" himself to Kakuma in 2010, after completing high school, as he believed that business opportunities were better there. He is self-employed.

Mulki, twenty-one, grew up in Dadaab. She was transferred to Kakuma in 2010 because she was deemed to be unsafe in Dadaab, as the family of her former husband (who had left for Somalia with their three children) was threatening her. She completed her primary schooling, but could not continue her studies as she was married. She does not have a job.

INDEX

Afghanistan, refugees from, 1, 17, 106, 186, 188, 208
Abdullahi, Ahmednasir M., 30
Afgoye, 43
agency, 3, 6–7, 17, 81, 116, 130, 165, 167, 175, 187–88
Agier, Michel, 51, 107
Al-Rasheed, Madawi, 185
Al-Shabab, 26–27, 36, 39, 42–43, 135, 187, 198, 202–4
AMISOM, 26
Appadurai, Arjun
    on imagination, 116
    on production of locality, 7, 202, 205
Arendt, Hannah, 2, 7, 166, 203
    on bare life, 165–66
Armstrong, Kimberley, 175
Ashraf, minority group, 53
asymmetry between researcher and the researched, 10, 15
Augé, Marc, non-place, 207

Baidoa, 36–37, 55, 63, 225
Bajuni, minority group, 34, 52, 57, 96, 102–4, 121, 199, 226–27
Bantu, minority group, 34, 52–53, 65, 96, 98, 104–6, 157, 227–28
Barawa
    camp, 29, 41, 49, 52
    minority group, 34, 53, 104–5
Barre, Siyad, 16, 24–25, 28, 31, 36, 39, 41
Bauman, Zygmunt, 89, 117, 134, 206, 208
Behnia, Behnam, 143
Benadir
    camp, 28, 33
    minority group, 34, 52, 105

Bender, Barbara, 55
Bisharat, George E., 174
Bjork, Stephanie R., 199
Bloch, Maurice, 39
Bouchet-Saulnier, Françoise, 107
Bourdieu, Pierre, 15
Bourgois, Philippe, 51, 59
    everyday violence, 59–61

camp economy, 62–67, 136, 151
    Ethiopian market, 62–64
    incentive workers, 63, 81–87, 135, 147, 169, 171
    remittances, 132–33
    Somali market, 52, 63–64, 66, 86, 106, 226
camp leadership
    camp leaders, 15, 53, 59, 97–99, 103, 140, 144–45
    community leaders, 11, 99
    youth leaders, 11, 111
Camp, Constitution of the, 97, 144
Canada, 67, 76, 115, 119, 131, 135, 139, 186, 188, 194–98
Carr, David, 37
charity, aid as, 146, 166–68, 170, 177
Chatty, Dawn, 17, 75, 176, 186, 188
clan
    dynamics, 25, 29, 31, 34–35, 51, 54, 59, 62, 103, 105–7, 112, 155, 194, 196, 199
    families, 50, 68, 103–6, 118, 130
    majority, 59, 98, 104–6, 118, 155, 199
    (see also Darod, Hawiye)
coastal camps. See Mombasa camps
coexistence, 24, 94–100

Colson, Elizabeth, 112
coming of age, 18–19, 73, 87–89, 103, 180,
    202–3, 207
community, sense of, 49–51, 55–69, 97–98,
    107, 142, 154–55, 195, 207
confinement. *See* containment
containment, of refugee, 2–7, 16, 19,
    128–29, 202–3, 207
Convention Relating to the Status of
    Refugees, 5, 33, 166
conviviality. *See* Gilroy
Crisp, Jeff, 57
Crivello, Gina, 186
Cross-Border Operation, 32, 42
cultural change, 19, 94, 100–3, 105–13,
    166
cultural diversity, 94–100, 112–13, 135,
    204, 207
cultural identity, 17, 19, 94, 100–13
cultural transmission, 15, 100–6, 112

Dadaab (camp), 1–3, 13, 27, 30, 32, 34–35,
    45, 50, 52–55, 57, 67, 85, 87, 111,
    119, 123, 125–26, 132, 135, 157,
    194–95, 197–98, 204
Darod, majority clan, 34, 52, 58–59, 64–65,
    103–6
De Boeck, Filip, 8
Department of Refugee Affairs, 9, 54, 123,
    145
diaspora, 67, 89, 118, 123
diversity, *See* cultural diversity
Don Bosco, 64, 80, 124

Eastleigh, 35, 54, 124, 195
education, 8, 16, 50, 63, 72–86, 169, 173,
    180, 183, 198, 202–4, 206–7
    access to, 3, 18, 34, 38, 42, 54–55,
    122–24, 126, 128, 130, 177, 194–95
    aspirations, 17–18, 186–90
    girls and, 76–77, 109–12
    postsecondary, 72, 75, 78–80, 82, 121,
    135
    secondary, 72, 76–78
    World University Service of Canada
    (WUSC), 76, 78–79, 121, 156–57,
    194
employment. *See* camp economy

encampment, 32, 58, 72, 123, 204
Essed, Philomena, 103, 112
Ethiopia, 25–26, 119
    army, 27
    refugees, 12–13 , 34, 53, 57–58, 78, 87,
    94, 97–99, 111, 131, 144, 148, 172

Fiddian-Qasmiyeh, Elena, 186
FilmAid, 9–10, 12, 61, 80, 82, 86, 108, 167
Finnström, Sverker, 75
Fivush, Robyn, 37
Frerks, Georg, 103, 112
future aspirations, 45, 180–91

gender, roles and dynamics, 19, 61, 87, 99,
    103, 108–13, 167, 176–77, 185, 188,
    197
General Service Unit, 31, 58
George, David M. Chavis, 51, 68
Giddens, Anthony, 141–42, 154, 159
Gilroy, Paul, conviviality, 94–95, 100, 112
Goffman, Erving, 174

Harrell-Bond, Barbara E., 71–72, 140–42,
    154, 159
Hatimy camp. *See* Barawa camp
Hawiye, majority clan, 35, 53, 58–59, 65,
    103–5
healthcare. *See* medical care
Hecht, Tobias, 10
Hirsch, Marianne, postmemory, 37, 46, 205
Holocaust, 37, 40
Honwana, Alcinda, 8
Hoodfar, Homa, 106, 187
Horst, Cindy, 12, 131–32
    on *buufis*, 119, 130
    on transnational nomads, 118
host community, coexistence with refugees,
    35, 57–58, 69, 95, 100, 136, 140–41
humanitarian governance, 6, 12, 72, 101,
    107, 140–54, 158–59, 167–68
humanitarian system, 17–18, 73, 140, 143,
    148–54, 158, 170, 174–75, 202, 205,
    207
Hyndman, Jennifer, 2, 5, 50, 203

incentive workers. *See* camp economy
indefinite stasis, 184, 192, 201

www.ingramcontent.com/pod-product-compliance
Lightning Source LLC
Chambersburg PA
CBHW070921030426
42336CB00014BA/2481